The Widow's Quest

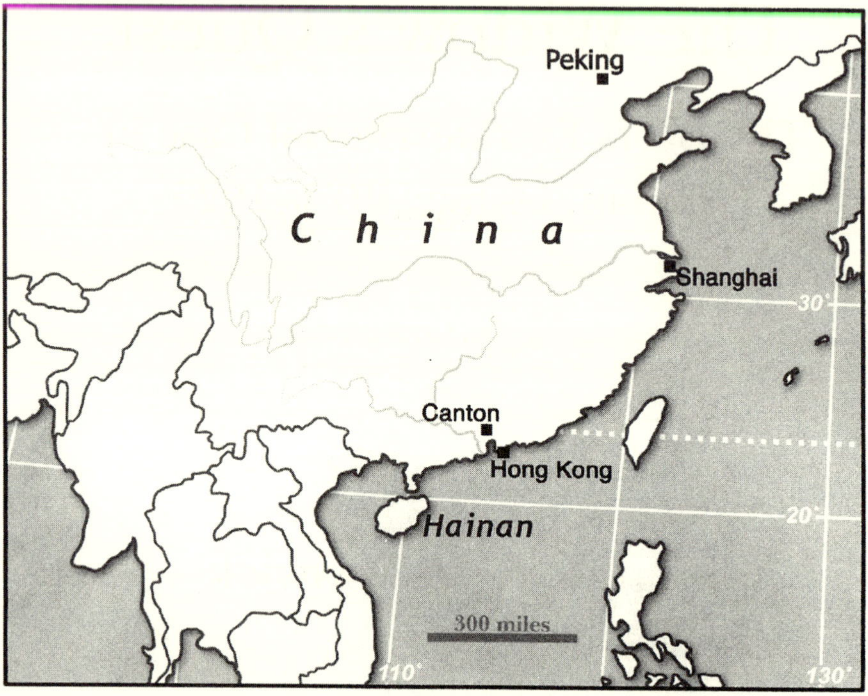

Hainan Island in Relation to Major Chinese Cities
Map by Mark Harrower

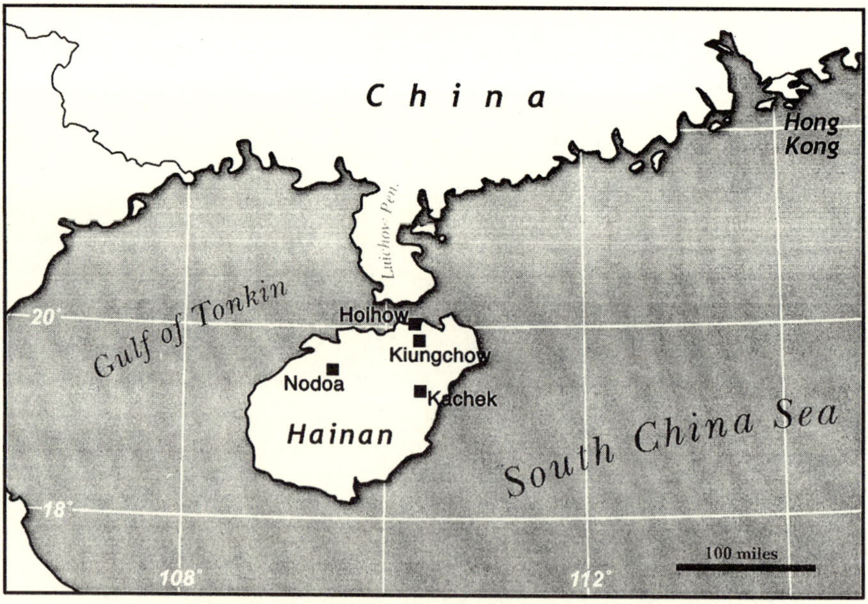

American Presbyterian Mission Locations on Hainan (1885–1942)
Map by Mark Harrower

The Widow's Quest

The Byers Extraterritorial Case in Hainan, China, 1924–1925

Kathleen L. Lodwick

Lehigh
University
Press

Bethlehem
Lehigh University Press
London: Associated University Presses

Associated University Presses
2010 Eastpark Blvd.
Cranbury, NJ 08512

Associated University Presses
16 Barter Street
London WC1A 2AH, England

Associated University Presses
P.O. Box 338, Port Credit
Mississauga, Ontario
Canada L5G 4L8

The paper used in this publication meets the requirements of the American National Standard for Permanence of Paper for Printed Library Materials Z39.48-1984.

Cataloging-in-Publication Data
is on file with the Library of Congress.

PRINTED IN THE UNITED STATES OF AMERICA

Dedication

To both my Kathryn Elizabeths—my mother for her love, unfailing support, and encouragement over the years and my daughter who came to me from Phnom Penh, Cambodia, while I was working on this monograph, adding great joy to my life.

Contents

Acknowledgments 9
Author's Note 11
Brief Chronology of Some Events in China 15
List of People and Church Bodies Involved 17
List of Abbreviations 25

1. The Murder and the Milieu 29
2. The Immediate Aftermath of the Murder 56
3. The Extraterritoriality Case 78
4. The Indemnity is Collected 106
5. The BFM and Support for the Byers Family 137
6. Conclusion 168

Notes 175
References Cited 192
Index 196

Acknowledgments

NO ONE EVER WRITES A BOOK ALONE AND I AM INDEBTED TO MANY people who have helped with this one. First, to Daniel Bays, now at Calvin College, whose University of Kansas/Luce Foundation Project on the History of Christianity in China provided me with a grant to visit Hainan and to participate in a colloquium on Chinese Christianity. At that session it was Suzanne Wilson Barnett of the University of Puget Sound who first suggested that the Byers case might be interesting material for a monograph, and for her comments I am indebted.

At Penn State I am indebted to many people particularly Robert Secor, Vice Provost, and Eugene Slaski, recently retired as the Lehigh Valley Academic Officer, for their help and encouragement. Also at Lehigh Valley I am indebted to my colleague, Barbara Cantalupo, for her encouragement and words of advice and to Ronald Garber for his computer help, always cheerfully given. Thanks, too, to Mark Harrower of Penn State's Department of Geography who drew the maps.

Special thanks are due to Philip Metzger and Judith Mayer at Lehigh University Press and Christine Retz at Associated University Presses for their help in getting the manuscript into publishing form.

Douglas J. Machle, Department of Classics, University of Washington, provided information on the Lienchow Incident in Kwangtung in 1905 which killed his grandfather's first wife Mrs. Edward C. Machle, and her daughter, Amy, and other Presbyterian missionaries of that station. All references to that case included here are the results of his research and generosity in providing the materials to me. Over the years he has also graciously shared information on the Hainan mission which he has come across in relation to his study of the Canton mission.

Father Robert Carbonneau, C.P., assisted me with information on the extraterritoriality case involving the Passionist fathers and their converts and the Roman Catholic position on indemnities, and has over the years always been willing to share what he knows of the archives on these cases.

Phil Billingsley and Xu Youwei who were researching extraterritoriality cases as I was working on this monograph willingly assisted me in many ways, particularly with the names of those involved in such cases in China, even though some remain which we cannot fully identify.

I have had help from numerous staff people at the U.S. Library of Congress and at the National Archives, in Britain at the Public Record Office at Kew, and at the Presbyterian Historical Society, Philadelphia, where the former archivist, Kristin Gleeson, and the current archivist, Nancy Taylor, are due a special thanks, and from several Chinese colleagues who attempted to find archival sources in their country.

A special thanks goes to all the Hainan missionaries and their children and grandchildren who have encouraged my research on the mission over the years. The Byers sons Robert, David, and Laurence provided encouragement and help, but none lived to see this project completed. Robert clarified several points including how old he was when his father was murdered. David remembered his family's voyage back to America and his mother's friendship with Mrs. Mabel Roys. Laurence read early parts of the manuscript and was very enthusiastic about my work.

The Rev. Daniel Ray also provided insight into the kidnaping of his father, which is mentioned here along with his mother's relationship to the Hainan mission. Others of the Hainan mission family who have helped are the Rev. Robert and Evelynn Thomas, who first introduced me to the Hainan family; Mrs. Evelyn French, who served in Hainan with her husband; and the missionaries' descendants: Ruth Tappan Bauer; Samuel Braden; Arthur French and Kathy French Whyte; Marie Melrose and Sylvia Melrose Ryan; Geneva Steiner Liebsney; Peggy Gilman Checkur; Dorothy Barnes and Mary Techner, nieces of Margaret Moninger; Carolyn McCandliss; and Ronald Seaton; and their respective spouses and children.

My dedicated friends and colleagues who read various versions of the manuscript and offered suggestions are Judith Liu, University of San Diego, and Christine W. Kulikowski, sometimes of Rutgers University. And a special thanks is due my mother who read every version of every chapter without complaint.

Author's Note

At a time when the American government spends decades seeking the remains of military personnel killed in Vietnam and spares no expense to recover spies caught at work in foreign countries or to rescue a single military pilot shot down in a hostile action against a country with which the United States is legally at peace, it may be difficult to understand the total lack of concern on the part of American officials in both China and the United States about the murder of the Rev. George D. Byers, an American civilian, working in a peaceful occupation in China, where, like it or not, Americans had treaty provisions to protect their citizens. With extreme difficulty American diplomats, upon hearing of the Byers murder, worked themselves up into a great "ho, hum." China was of little concern to American diplomats in the 1920s and of even less to the American public. In the Byers case it took the Department of State three months and two days to inform Byers's brother in California of his death! Further evidence that the Byers case was never of major concern to the United States government comes from the consul general at Canton who, when informing the American minister at Peking of Byers's death, complained that handling such cases interfered with the work of his office.

Titles

Although it is the fashion today not to use titles, particularly those that indicate one's gender, I have chosen to do so in this work simply because there are a great many people involved and since the issue of support of Mrs. Byers and her family by the Presbyterian Board of Foreign Missions (BFM) was gender-linked it is important that the reader be able to immediately identify the gender of each person involved in the case. I have further used the designation "the Rev." for the members of the clergy to help the reader distinguish them from the diplomats, as the top American diplomat in China in these years held the title "minister." Further, although some of the clergy were also referred to as "Dr." in the official correspondence, I have limited that usage here to those of the medical community, which also figures in this story.

Sources

The primary sources for this work are from the National Archives and the Library of Congress; the archives of the Presbyterian Church (USA) in Philadelphia, particularly the papers of Margaret Moninger, long-time member of the Hainan mission; and the papers of Robert E. Speer, long-time secretary of the BFM which are at the archives of Princeton Theological Seminary, Princeton, New Jersey. I have been unable to locate any Chinese sources that would provide another dimension to the story despite the generous help of several scholars in China who searched various Chinese archives of this period, and the staff of the Library of Congress China Section. Given the chaotic political situation in Hainan at the time of the Byers murder, it is likely no Chinese records have survived. Also, although the British consul on Hainan was involved in the case the only British records concerning the matter survive in the United States Archives. Interestingly, the Public Record Office, Kew, London, has many hundreds of pages from various British consuls in Hoihow on issues involving the American missionaries, but not one page concerning the Byers murder is among them.

Romanization

I have used the Wade-Giles romanization system because it was the system in use at the time of my story. Various romanizations appear in the documents and the missionaries' papers, but I have tried to maintain consistent use of Wade-Giles. For prominent officials, such as Sun Yat-sen and V. K. Wellington Koo, I have used the spellings they used and for other individuals I have used the form appearing in the Department of State papers. For the Hainan place names, I have followed the spellings of the Hainan missionaries. Developed years after this story took place, the pinyin system of romanization is more commonly used today. The pinyin equivalents for the major

Hainan place names are: Hoihow (Haikou); Kiungchow (Chiungshan); Kachek (Jiaji); Nodoa (Nada).

Money

Various currencies were in use in China in the 1920s and they provide an endless source of frustration to those who must deal with them. The Mexican [Mex.] silver dollar which arrived in Asia by way of the galleon trade from Acapulco was a much-desired coin in China because of its high purity and many prices were stated in it. When Chinese used the term "dollar" they generally meant a Mexican silver dollar. The use of the term "gold" by missionaries in China generally meant U.S. dollars, as it does in the context of this work. (Gold could also have meant a Haikwan customs unit, but that was not often used by missionaries.) Although exchange rates fluctuated daily Mexican dollars were generally worth about half a gold dollar. In this book the "$" is used to denote U.S. dollars, unless some other currency is specifically indicated.

Brief Chronology of Some Events in China

1809	Protestant missionary work begins
1839–1842	Opium War
1856	Arrow Incident
1858	United States–China Treaty of Tientsin signed, contained provision regarding missionaries
1858–1860	Warfare between China and Western countries
1885	Presbyterian mission established on Hainan Island
1898–1900	Boxer Uprising kills many missionaries and Chinese Christians in north China
1911	Republican revolution overthrows the Ch'ing dynasty
1911–1927	Rival factions vie for political control of Chinese state; banditry is rife in the countryside
1919	May Fourth Movement followed by growing Chinese nationalism in the 1920s
1927	Nationalist government establishes capital at Nanking

List of People and Church Bodies Involved

Individuals Involved in the Case

Because of the large number of people involved in this story, a list of them, along with their affiliations is provided here: (Those in italics were most involved in the case.)

The Byers Family

Rev. George, Presbyterian missionary, Kachek, Hainan, the victim
Mrs. Clara Laura Primm, the widow
Robert, son, age 11 at the time of the murder
Margaret, daughter, age 8 at the time of the murder
David, son, age 6 at the time of the murder
Laurence, son, age 3 at the time of the murder
Georgia, daughter, born September 1924
James, brother of George

Friends of the Byers Family

Rev. William S. Abernathy, minister, Calvary Baptist Church, Washington, D.C.
John B. Brown, superintendent, Indian School, Phoenix, Ariz.
Mr. Case, president, Federal Reserve Bank, New York, N.Y.
Mrs. Lydia Lord Davis, Oberlin, Ohio
Miss Kirby, sister of Mrs. McKelvey, La Mesa, Calif.
Wallace H. Lee, president, Albany College, Albany, Ore.
Mr. Marston, merchant, San Diego, Calif.
Rev. and Mrs. McKelvey, clergyman and wife, La Mesa, Calif.
William D. Murray, attorney at law, New York, N.Y.
Mrs. Ina Rittenhouse, San Diego, Calif.

Presbyterian Missionaries in China

IN HAINAN (1924–1925)

Kachek Station (includes Chinese Christians)
Nathaniel Bercovitz, M.D. and Mrs. Bercovitz
Dr. Chu

Rev. and Mrs. Samuel Ensign
Mr. Lin
Miss Caroline McCreery, a nurse
Miss Margaret Moninger, a teacher and mission secretary
Miss Katherine Schaeffer, a teacher

Kiungchow/Hoihow Station
Rev. and Mrs. Ura Brogden
Rev. Wilbur Campbell and Mrs. Campbell
Miss Mae Chapin, a teacher
H. M. McCandliss, M.D. and Mrs. McCandliss
Miss Grace MacDonald, mission business manager
Stuart Seaton, M.D. and Mrs. Seaton
Miss Alice Skinner, a teacher
Rev. and Mrs. John Steiner
Rev. William Stinson
Rev. David S. Tappan and Mrs. Tappan

Nodoa Station
Mrs. John (Margaret) Melrose
Rev. and Mrs. Paul Melrose
Clarence Salsbury, M.D. and Mrs. Salsbury
Miss Mary Taylor, a teacher

On Furlough in the United States
Rev. William Leverett
Rev. and Mrs. David Thomas

Previous Members of the Hainan Mission
Rev. and Mrs. Frank P. Gilman
Carl C. Jeremiassen
Mrs. J. Franklin (Lillian Marks) Kelly
Rev. John Melrose
Mrs. Rex (Janet Gilman) Ray

Members of the Hainan Mission after 1925
Rev. and Mrs. Arthur French
Rev. Ngou

At Other Locations in China

CANTON

Rev. B. C. Henry
John G. Kerr, M.D. and Mrs. Kerr, parents of Mrs. H. M. (Olivia) McCandliss

SHANGHAI

Rev. J. Walter Lowrie, member, Presbyterian China Council (PCC)
Rev. Charles Patton, member, PCC

Presbyterians In the United States

BOARD OF FOREIGN MISSIONS (BFM), NEW YORK

Rev. Arthur J. Brown, secretary
Russell Carter
Miss Ruth Elliott
Rev. Charles R. Erdman
Rev. J. C. R. Ewing
Miss Hodge
Miss Jean Mackenzie
Mrs. Charles K. (Mabel L.) Roys, executive secretary, Foreign Department
Miss Schultz
Rev. George T. Scott, executive secretary, Foreign Department
Miss Lucy Leeper, later Mrs. Lucy Leeper Shaw
Rev. Robert E. Speer, secretary
James M. Speers
W. Reginald Wheeler

BOARD OF MINISTERIAL RELIEF, NEW YORK

Rev. Orville Reed

WOMEN'S MISSIONARY SOCIETY, PRESBYTERY OF LOS ANGELES, CALIF.

Mrs. R. W. Cleland

MISSIONARIES AND CHINESE OF OTHER DENOMINATIONS

In China

KWANGSI

Rev. Rex Ray, Southern Baptist Mission, husband of Janet Gilman

PEKING

Dr. [William W.?] Peter

SHANGHAI

Rev. E. C. Lobenstine, secretary, National Christian Council (NCC)
Rev. Frank Rawlinson, editor, *The Chinese Recorder (CR)*
Rev. J. Hudson Taylor, founder China Inland Mission (CIM)
C. T. Wang, YMCA

Government Officials

AMERICAN

In the United States

PRESIDENT

Calvin Coolidge

SENATOR

Selden P. Spencer, [Missouri]

REPRESENTATIVES

Ernest R. Ackerman, [5th District, N. J.]
Willis C. Hawley, [1st District, Ore.]
Carl Hayden, [At Large, Ariz.]
Phil D. Swing, [11th District, Calif.]

Diplomats

AMERICAN

In the United States

Joseph Grew, Acting (and Under) Secretary of State
Charles Evans Hughes, Secretary of State
Frank Kellogg, Secretary of State
F. P. Lockhart, Acting Chief Division of Far Eastern Affairs
John Van Antwerp MacMurray, Assistant Secretary of State
J. Butler Wright

IN CHINA

Canton

C. B. Chamberlain, Vice Consul
Maxwell M. Hamilton, Vice Consul
Douglas Jenkins, Consul

Peking
Edward Bell
Ferdinand Mayer
Jacob Gould Schurman, Minister

Shanghai
Edwin S. Cunningham, Consul General
Milton D. Purdy, Judge, United States Court for China

Swatow
C. J. Spiker, Consul

BRITISH IN CHINA

Hoihow
H. H. Bristow, Consul

On the mainland
Sir Rutherford Alcock

United States Navy In China
Ensign Beard
Mr. Byrd
Lt. W. C. Calhoun
Captain Davis
Mr. Fletcher
Captain Smith
Admiral Thomas Washington

Chinese Officials
On the mainland
General Ch'en Chiung-ming
V. K. Wellington Koo
Sun Yat-sen

ON HAINAN
General Ch'en Feng-ch'i
General Ch'en Tan-shu, Chief of Staff
Ch'en Yun-liang, Lieutenant of Lin Shu-piao
General Feng Ming-kai, Rehabilitation Commissioner
Colonel Ho Chia-yu, officer in charge at Kachek

General Teng Pen-yin, military administrator of Hainan
Colonel Teng Po-ch'i, nephew of Teng Pen-yin
Wang Ta-feng, District Magistrate

The Suspects
Ch'en Chi-yu
Huang Chung-hua
Huang Hui-wen
Li Tse-hsiung
Li Tse-ying
Lin Shu-piao, bandit chief
Su Chung-t'ai

The Witness
Li Tse-hsiang

Victims in Previous Extraterritorial Cases
IN CHINA

Eleanor Chesnut, M.D., Presbyterian missionary, Lienchow, Kwangtung
Charles Coltman, American businessman
Hicks
Mrs. Edward C. Machle, Presbyterian missionary, Lienchow, Kwangtung, and daughter Amy
O'Brien
Rev. John R. and Mrs. Rebecca G. Peale, Presbyterian missionaries, Lienchow, Kwangtung
William A. Reimert, Reformed missionary, Acting Principal, Lakeside College, Yochow, Hunan

IN PERSIA
Major Imbrie

Church Bodies Involved in the Case

Board of Foreign Missions (BFM)—an administrative division of the Presbyterian Church (USA) located in New York, it recruited, employed, assigned, and supported missionaries worldwide. As an official agency of the church it dealt with the United States government when necessary.

Presbyterian China Council (PCC)—a body composed of two or more representatives of each of the church's missions located in China, it met twice yearly in Shanghai and decided priorities for staffing and funding before sending such requests to the BFM. It also dealt officially with government agencies in China on issues of concern to the China missions.

Hainan Mission—one of the Presbyterian missions in China. Its administrative board consisted of representatives of each of the mission's stations, at Kiungchow/Hoihow, Kachek, and Nodoa.

National Christian Council (NCC)—an ecumenical, Protestant body concerned with the Chinese Church and all types of Christian activities, it was composed of institutions and individuals, a majority of whom were Chinese. It was organized in 1922 but grew out of the earlier all-China mission conferences and the World Missionary Conference of Edinburgh of 1910. Closely attuned to the nationalist changes of the country in the 1920s and vocal about how Westerners should react to those changes, its role in the Byers case was only advisory.

List of Abbreviations

ABCFM	American Board of Commissioners for Foreign Missions
BFM	Board of Foreign Missions, Presbyterian Church (USA)
CIM	China Inland Mission
CIMCS	Chinese Imperial Maritime Customs Service
MP	Moninger Papers, Presbyterian Archives, Philadelphia
NA	National Archives
NCC	National Christian Council (China)
PCC	Presbyterian China Council
SP	Speer Papers, Archives, Princeton Theological Seminary

The Widow's Quest

1
The Murder and the Milieu

DEAD. THE REV. GEORGE BYERS WAS DEAD. DEAD IN FRONT OF HIS HOME, in the arms of his wife Clara, in the presence of his eldest son Robert, just three days past his eleventh birthday. Dead far from his homeland, in the town of Kachek in the remote interior of Hainan Island, off the south coast of China, on the night of 24 June 1924.[1] Dead at the hands of Chinese kidnappers, intent upon holding the missionary for $20,000 Mexican [Mex.] ransom.

Dead. There would be no ransom now; the culprits knew that as they fled into the night. They knew, too, the deed they had done would bring retribution from Chinese officials, who certainly would be pressured by foreigners to find and punish those responsible for the death of the American missionary. Just as certainly, the culprits knew that retribution would be taken against innocent people if they were successful in keeping their identities hidden.

They had not planned a murder; they were kidnappers. They had taken a calculated risk—for high stakes, $20,000 [Mex.] if they were successful—a huge amount of money. They had been sure the Presbyterian missionaries would pay to ransom one of their own. They knew, too, that the political instability of Hainan had allowed some corrupt officials to gain prominence in the island's administration, and that was in their favor. They had gambled that they would be able to elude capture, even if they had to pay off some of those corrupt officials with part of the ransom. They knew the missionaries had money, they were all so much richer than the Chinese; all foreigners had money. So, the kidnappers had proceeded. The night was carefully planned—only one missionary family would be at the Kachek mission compound. Getting that information had been easy; anyone in Kachek who had watched or asked would have learned that the other missionaries had departed for the coast as they did every year after their schools closed for the summer holidays. Anyone in Kachek who had observed the comings and goings at the mission compound knew, too, that the Rev. Byers made evening rounds at the hospital across the road from his home. He did that every night.

It should have been easy; there were three of them and only one missionary. The kidnappers lay in wait. The Rev. Byers came. The kidnappers sprang into action, slipped a noose around their victim's neck, and then disaster—the Rev. Byers struggled violently to get free, and shouted for his wife to help him. No one dreamed he would try to fight three. But fight he did, and in the melee, the gun, pressed tight against the missionary's abdomen, went off. In an instant, the planned kidnapping became murder. Then Mrs. Byers and Robert appeared, something else the kidnappers had not planned on. The culprits fled into the darkness of the Chinese countryside, never stopping to retrieve their ransom note. They had not expected this—a dead foreigner and no ransom.

As they fled, they undoubtedly wondered why the Rev. Byers had resisted. Indeed, the unanswerable question of the event was why the missionary had struggled against three attackers. Was it to defend his honor or to protect his wife and children in their nearby home?

Since the Rev. Byers had already lived eighteen years in Hainan at the time of his murder, one questions why he struggled so hard to avoid being kidnapped. He certainly knew the dangers of living in the interior of Hainan where bandits were rife and the government exercised little control. He and his colleagues had been very worried in the previous few months about the increasing lawlessness evident around them, and had even taken the step of asking the British diplomat on the island, who took care of their concerns, to request that the Chinese military increase patrols in the area around Kachek.[2]

The missionaries all knew Chinese who had been kidnapped and then ransomed. Even the Rev. Byers's last letters to supporters at home had mentioned kidnappings. He certainly also knew that death was not the usual end for those kidnapped in China; kidnappers wanted money, just money. Since the Rev. Byers had written letters about the kidnapping of Chinese, one must ask if it were a cultural misunderstanding that caused him to resist kidnapping so strenuously. The ultimate cultural misunderstanding is, of course, the one that results in death.

Clearly, he knew lawless Chinese kidnapped both Chinese and foreigners, but he seemed to have had no understanding of why disreputable men might want to kidnap him. Was his death the result of his unwillingness to bend his Western principles to adapt to Chinese realities? It is impossible to know exactly what went through the Rev. Byers's mind in the last moments of his life, but his colleagues in the mission knew he believed in the lessons of Western culture—stand up for yourself; defend yourself; do not let bullies frighten you.

The Rev. Byers also knew only too well that, in all the years he had been in China, few Chinese had heeded his preaching about Christianity. Was it a question of pride with him that if they would not accept his religion then he would not bend to accommodate himself to anything Chinese—particularly not to brigands intent on kidnapping him for ransom? Certainly, his colleagues in the days after his death thought he had been foolish to resist, since resistance had cost him his life.[3]

The Rev. Byers did not die a martyr's death as there is no evidence to suggest the kidnappers had any personal animosity toward him, nor is there evidence to suggest the act was anti-Christian. His widow acknowledged both facts in the weeks immediately after his death.[4] He had simply been a foreigner and an easy target.

Foreigners had been frequent targets for brigands in China in the years prior to the Rev. Byers's death when the absence of civil order had made it difficult to maintain peace. The Lincheng Incident, in which a whole train was seized by bandits who carried off hundreds of Chinese and some thirty foreigners to hold for ransom, had occurred in north China the previous year. That episode had begun a series of attacks on trains on the China mainland, to the extent that foreigners began to fear riding them. Throughout rural China dozens of missionaries and many of their Chinese converts, as well as others, had been kidnapped for ransom or had had their property destroyed during these years.[5]

The China Weekly Review of February 1924, published a list of "Killings, Kidnappings and Outrages" that had happened since the Lincheng Incident the previous May as part of an article on the subject. Those killed were an Italian priest, two British missionaries, two Japanese officers, an American missionary, a Belgian priest, a British ship's captain, and a Chinese student returned from America. More than thirty others had been kidnapped and held for ransom.[6]

The conditions for the Byers kidnapping had been nearly perfect. As the Rev. Byers, his pregnant wife, and their young children were the only foreigners on the mission compound, the kidnappers likely assumed Mrs. Byers would be unable to mount a quick rescue force, thus giving them time to get far away with their prize. Time was essential to their success, but things had changed completely with their prey dead. Byers's foiled kidnapping caused many unforeseen repercussions for his family, his mission, his country, and the Chinese he had sought to convert, as well as for Chinese officials and the people of the Kachek area from whom compensation was extracted. Several Chinese, totally innocent of this crime, were put to death by officials anxiously trying to convince the foreigners they were doing something about Byers's murder. All mission work in the interior of Hainan ceased for a year as both the Kachek and the Nodoa stations were evacuated. Diplomats spent weeks, months, finally half a year, trying to figure out which Chinese held power in Hainan and which officials could be held responsible for the murder. And Mrs. Byers, soon to give birth to her fifth child, quickly found herself trapped in the conundrum of American society, and particularly its political and religious bureaucracies, which offered little help to a widow with young children.

The Presbyterian Board of Foreign Missions (BFM), located in New York, was the official administrative arm of the Presbyterian Church (USA), which appointed and supported its denomination's missionaries throughout the world, but its members felt it had no responsibility to support Mrs. Byers and her family, once they were no longer on the mission field. The BFM's members took their position because their contributors gave money for the support of foreign missions, not for the maintenance of those widowed and orphaned on the field. Yet the BFM also insisted Mrs. Byers could not claim an indemnity from the American government as a missionary, since that action could jeopardize future mission work in China, but she could make such a claim as a private citizen! Thoroughly baffled by such a position on the part of the BFM which had sent her husband to China and had supported her family for years, Mrs. Byers countered that they would not have been in China as private citizens, but were there solely at the BFM's request and with their support.

With five children, the oldest only eleven, Mrs. Byers had few options. Her own parents were dead as were her husband's. Her only siblings were two half-brothers, both married, and neither likely to want to have six more people to support. Of course, as a college graduate she might have sought employment in the business world, but that would clearly have involved hiring someone to look after her children, as she readily acknowledged. Her best option seemed to be to convince the BFM to assist her family and in this she was particularly fortunate to have Mrs. Charles K. (Mabel L.) Roys, an executive secretary of the Foreign Dept. of the BFM whom she had never met, as an ally.

American Diplomats Become Involved

Under the treaties between China and the Western nations, most of them dating from the nineteenth century, foreigners were permitted to station diplomatic representatives in the designated treaty ports, of which Hoihow was one. But the United States had no commercial interests in Hainan and, aside from the Presbyterian missionaries, the only other Americans who ever lived on the island were in the employ of the Chinese Imperial Maritime Customs Service (CIMCS), so the Americans had never had a diplomatic representative at Hoihow. As a courtesy to the Americans, and with full diplomatic agreement, the British consul, resident at Hoihow, acted on behalf of the Americans on those occasions when they needed to deal with Chinese officials on routine matters. But as murder was not routine the Byers case needed to be handled directly by Americans, so the British consul notified the American diplomats at Canton of Byers's death and summoned them to the island to handle the matter.[7] With Byers's death all mission work in the interior of Hainan ceased as H.B.M. Consul H. H. Bristow ordered the missionaries at Nodoa to abandon that station and join their colleagues residing at the port of Hoihow and the adjacent capital city of Kiungchow until the matter was resolved.[8] The Kachek station was, of course, unstaffed with the departure of Mrs. Byers and her children, who briefly joined their colleagues at Kiungchow/Hoihow and then departed for America. The future of any mission work on the island was complicated by the question of the collection of an indemnity, and the Hainan missionaries themselves were divided over the issue. The right of the American government to collect an indemnity from the Chinese government for the death of one of its citizens at the hands of Chinese was guaranteed by treaty provisions, yet in practice funds for indemnities were usually extracted from the people of the areas where the crimes occurred, with the central government being appealed to only if local efforts failed. Thus some of the Hainan missionaries thought the local Chinese officials would extract money for an indemnity from the innocent people of the

Kachek region and thus hinder the work of the mission, while others believed the local collection of the indemnity was necessary to prevent further attacks on them.

The United States government always collected the indemnities due them in China, as a matter of principle and to preserve the right to do so. Thus U.S. Vice Consul C. B. Chamberlain, who had arrived on the island from Canton, as a matter of course asked Mrs. Byers to submit her claim and when she responded she set the process in motion. Her action was to be the source of great controversy in the months ahead as she increased her initial request of $30,000 to $50,000, just before she left China. Also, as she was about to depart for home she wrote to the BFM objecting to the Hainan mission's executive committee having voted to support a request for $20,000 to be raised locally, arguing that the amount was too low and that the committee took their action in the absence of any member of the Kachek station. (The Hainan mission's executive committee was composed of missionaries from all three of the mission's locations and was responsible for official communications with both the Presbyterian China Council (PCC) in Shanghai and the BFM in New York. It also handled financial matters and filed various reports required both by their church and by ecumenical groups working in China.)

After the news of the Hainan executive committee's action reached the PCC in Shanghai, that body insisted the Hainan mission had no authority to seek an indemnity without the PCC's approval. Then the BFM in New York disavowed Mrs. Byers's request for an indemnity if she undertook it as a missionary, but acceded her right to request compensation as a private American citizen! But the American government, in its own plodding way, was going to collect some amount of indemnity despite what any or all of the Presbyterians might desire. Everyone did agree that the murderers needed to be apprehended, although that was to prove even more difficult than resolving the money issue, and was never accomplished.

Yet the Byers case was a quintessential extraterritoriality incident because it involved a murder, bandits, a widow with five children, Chinese officials, foreign diplomats, gunboats, and an indemnity. The events that transpired after the Rev. Byers was killed are the story of gunboat diplomacy in China at a time when foreigners held special privileges there under the extraterritoriality provisions of their treaties. But in the Byers case the first gunboat ran low on coal and departed Hainan waters quickly and the diplomat the gunboat had transported to the island to settle the case was only twenty-three years old! This was gunboat diplomacy writ small.

It was slightly more than six months after the murder of Byers before any serious action was taken. Then a bigger gunboat, carrying a more senior diplomat, this one twenty-eight years old, reached Hainan. In a move that typified many actions in the case, when the ship's captain was ordered to fire the customary seven-gun consul's salute to announce the diplomat's arrival, he complied, but the consul later reported the salute had had no effect, since Hoihow's notoriously poor port facilities placed anchorage so far offshore that no one on land could hear the guns! Young as he was, this vice consul, in the words of one of the Hainan missionaries, stuck to the Chinese army officer in charge of Hainan "like a burr to a cow's tail."[9] He did, however, succeed in collecting an indemnity—a better resolution to the case than many might have anticipated in the political chaos of the island and the indifference of the American government to missionary concerns.

The Legal Issues

The indemnity that was sought in the Byers case raised numerous issues. Monetary compensation for the loss of property or life by Westerners in China during the nineteenth and early twentieth centuries was regulated by treaties that had been negotiated between the Ch'ing dynasty and the Western nations. Imposed on the Chinese government after its defeat in the Opium Wars, the unequal treaties spelled out that foreign nationals were not subject to Chinese laws and if they committed crimes were to be tried under the laws of their own countries. Indeed, this is the usual understanding of the term "extraterritoriality" under which all Westerners in China lived. However, the unequal treaties also specified that the Chinese government was responsible for the safety and security of the lives and property of nationals of the signatory countries wherever they were in China, and if losses were incurred the foreign nations might collect indemnities.

As most of the foreigners in China had settled along the coast or along waterways it became fairly common for them to ask their diplomats to dispatch naval vessels to the scene whenever they believed the Chinese were not properly protecting foreign rights and interests.[10] Such intimidation usually worked. In 1868 when the Rev. J.

Hudson Taylor, founder of the China Inland Mission (CIM), tried to open a station at Yangchow, near the junction of the Yangtze River and the Grand Canal, and was attacked by a mob, Sir Rutherford Alcock sent four gunboats up the river to protect the missionary.[11] Although such tactics generally produced the results the foreigners sought, particularly if, as in the Byers case, the gunboat carried a consular official who was to investigate the matter, the missionary community realized such actions were a double-edged sword. Although the foreigners' views might eventually prevail, the use of gunboats had the effect of arousing xenophobia among the Chinese who witnessed or learned of such actions. (Taylor would be one of the first missionaries to disavow such actions and cautioned those of his mission against any involvement with Chinese or foreign government officials.)

The unequal treaties had been signed in the mid-nineteenth century following the Opium War (1839–1842), Arrow Incident (1856), and the 1858–1860 hostilities. For Americans the first mention of extraterritorial rights appeared in the Treaty of Tientsin signed in 1858. In this treaty the United States claimed the right to hunt down pirates who attacked American vessels in the seas adjacent to China. The right of Americans to own property in China was conceded in Article XII of that treaty while Article XI "guaranteed the protection of foreign lives and property, by prompt punishment of robbers and rioters." Because the United States–China treaties contained the most-favored nation clause, any more favorable conditions negotiated by other countries also applied to the United States even though that clause had "never been extended to cover extraterritorial rights."[12]

Because of these treaty provisions, and similar ones in other countries' treaties, in the nineteenth century the Chinese government sought to confine Westerners to the treaty ports, but that was unacceptable to the foreigners, specifically because the Christian missionaries wanted access to all parts of China so that they might spread their message. Indeed, although there is ample evidence that Western diplomats considered their primary work to be in support of business, missionary concerns, however bothersome, could not be ignored due to the influence of the Christian churches at home and the need of the early treaty negotiators to rely on missionaries as translators and interpreters since no American diplomats assigned to China knew the language. Thus missionary concerns entered the list of topics discussed in treaty negotiations. Chinese officials engaged in these negotiations knew full well it would be extremely difficult to guarantee the safety of foreigners in the interior of China. Since it was the missionaries who were most interested in living in the countryside, most problems with these treaty clauses involved them. Further complicating the issue, some missionaries, admittedly a small group, tried to extend their extraterritorial rights to their Chinese converts, arguing they were persecuted because of their Christianity and thus should be protected by Western nations.[13]

Guaranteeing the safety of foreign lives and property throughout China became extremely difficult in the aftermath of the 1911 republican revolution which overthrew the Ch'ing dynasty. Despite several attempts to establish a strong central government which could maintain peace and security, the republican cause collapsed in 1917. In the absence of central governmental authority, warlords gained control of much of the country, and virtually every area suffered at the hands of bandits.

During these years rural China, in particular, suffered as bandits, both the traditional kind and a new variation from the ranks of the country's military, created mayhem. As Phil Billingsley has pointed out, China in the 1920s was a bandit nation with two major types of bandits—"occasionals" who resorted to mayhem to avoid starvation or to satisfy some short-term need for cash, and "professionals" who for their own reasons established gangs and had "well-defined hideouts beyond the reach of the law."[14] With the collapse of the central government, those local government officials who continued in their jobs, when not in collusion with the brigands, generally lacked the resources to suppress the lawlessness and guarantee security to the people of their areas.[15]

Additionally, some foreigners thought they had suffered a loss of prestige as a result of World War I which saw the repatriation of many Westerners from China as well as the influx of large numbers of indigent Russians particularly at Shanghai. Many missionaries were acutely aware that the superiority they had attributed to Christian nations had been negated by the war.[16]

These conditions put foreigners, particularly missionaries living in remote parts of the country, into an unusually precarious situation. To a much greater extent than their urban colleagues on the coast, the missionaries in remote towns or in the countryside daily had to negotiate the chaos of Chinese life in the absence of any government able to maintain social stability—or even a rudiment of order.[17]

All missionaries were aware of the privileges they enjoyed under extraterritoriality, and they exercised those rights most specifically in their preaching and in the land they owned and used for mission homes, schools, and hospitals. But missionaries also knew that extraterritorial rights could pose problems. They did not want the Chinese, whom they were trying to convert, to think they could achieve their goal only by enforcing their treaty rights. It was a complicated balancing act, but it generally worked until disaster struck. One of these disasters was the murder of the Rev. Byers.

The missionaries, undoubtedly, would have preferred to work in a world free from political interference, but such a world never existed, and those who journeyed abroad carrying the message of their gospel had to contend with civil governments, laws, treaties, and authorities. These relationships between missionaries and government officials existed on many levels and could be extremely complicated.

Negotiating these relationships could be tricky and, in most cases, individual problems were resolved based on expediency rather than by absolutes. Thus, in 1912 the *Chinese Recorder* (*CR*), an ecumenical Protestant periodical published at Shanghai, editorialized that missionaries needed to heed the advice of the civil authorities, that is, their consular officials, even when they disagreed with that advice since their consular officials acted in the interests of all their citizens and with a view to the total situation in China. The editor wrote that when there was a difference of opinion the missionaries needed to "remember the injunction to obey those who have the rule over us."[18] Indeed, as one churchman would later write all missionaries, beginning with Paul, had had to negotiate governmental regulations, and in some cases restrictions, on their work.[19]

The foreign missionary's first contact with government regulations usually came when one sought to obtain a passport from one's own country. There was always the possibility that the government might decline to issue a passport. The receiving country also had to agree to allow the missionary to enter, but in the nineteenth and early twentieth centuries in China this permission was guaranteed by treaty. When taking up residence in China, Americans were required to register with consular officials, a procedure still recommended in all countries. This registration alerted the consular officials to the presence of their nationals, who might need their services or protection in a wide variety of circumstances.

Although American missionaries in China duly registered themselves, consular personnel thought of missionaries, when they thought of them at all, as nuisances who took time away from their commercial work.[20] The Rev. Byers had duly registered the residence of himself, his wife, and children in the town of Kachek with the nearest American consular office, located in Canton, a five-day journey from their home. Their presence was also made known to the British consul in Kiungchow who acted on behalf of the Americans on the island when necessary.

Although missionaries in China in the nineteenth and early twentieth centuries could appeal to their consular officials to seek compensation for lost lives and/or property, in practical terms this was very difficult for those in the hinterlands. From both of Hainan's interior mission stations it was a two-day journey to Kiungchow/Hoihow and another two-and-a-half-day trip to Canton via Hong Kong, not including any wait for a coastal steamer at Hoihow or a riverboat at Hong Kong. As a result, the missionaries at Kachek and Nodoa, like their colleagues in other remote locations, generally handled minor extraterritorial violations themselves—tracking down thieves who had stolen from them and recovering their property, for instance.

For the China mission community as a whole, the greatest demand for indemnities had come as a result of the Boxer Uprising of 1898–1900 in which scores of missionaries, and many Chinese, had lost their lives and property. When the foreign nations realized the Boxer indemnity they had extracted from China was too large for the losses incurred, they began to remit it in the form of scholarships for Chinese who wanted to study in Western countries.

In the years after the decision was made to remit part of the Boxer indemnity, some mission boards in the United States decided to reevaluate their positions on indemnities. Although the collection of indemnities was governed by international treaties it posed a special problem for the missionaries. Some missions had given up seeking indemnity for the loss of life even before the Boxer Uprising, claiming that missionary lives lost were the "blood of martyrs," which had strengthened the Christian Church through the centuries. Yet, while a home church board or sending agency might renounce its right to claim an indemnity, most did so only for themselves, allowing that surviving relatives were free to seek such compensation on their own.

Whatever position mission officials might adopt, the United States government always collected an indemnity for the loss of an American life or property as a matter of principle as was spelled out in its treaties with China. During the discussions of the Byers case, officials of the BFM stated they had not claimed any indemnity in the Lienchow case in 1905, but the United States government had both claimed and collected an indemnity for the relatives of those killed in that incident.[21] The honest, hard-working Chinese who had not committed the crime but from whom the money to pay the indemnity was extracted undoubtedly cared nothing for the niceties of such arguments.

When the Rev. Byers was murdered the British consular official on Hainan and the American consular officials in Canton had to decide how to proceed with the case, but they were certain from the beginning that an indemnity would be collected. When the first American consular representative arrived on Hainan, he matter-of-factly asked Mrs. Byers to submit her claim. Pregnant and in shock over the loss of her husband, Mrs. Byers submitted the requested claim, apparently giving little, if any, thought to the controversy she was starting by doing so. The whole question of an indemnity posed serious moral issues for the Presbyterian missionaries on Hainan and elsewhere in China, and for the BFM, as each wrestled with the "blood of martyrs" argument and the necessity for providing for Mrs. Byers and her children.

Indeed, the indemnity argument was a difficult one for all Christian missionaries. At the moment the Rev. Byers was murdered, many members of the Protestant mission community in China, centered at Shanghai, were engaged in discussions with the more educated of their Chinese converts, and with other influential Chinese elites, over the entire issue of extraterritoriality. Chinese nationalism which had manifested itself so forcefully in the May Fourth Movement begun in 1919 had brought into question the unequal treaties and extraterritoriality in particular. The fallen Ch'ing dynasty which had negotiated those treaties was now viewed as a relic of the past, rather than the government of China only a few years earlier. Young, well-educated Chinese nationalists, many of them the products of mission schools, yearned to have their country accepted on the basis of equality with the nations of the West.

Missionaries were particularly sensitive to the idea that their teachings would have had no followers, save for the treaties which permitted them to propagate their beliefs to the Chinese. In December 1918 the *Far Eastern Review* had published an article, "The Principle and Practice of Extraterritoriality in China," by Charles Denby, who had been the chief American diplomat in China from 1885 to

1898, in which he wrote that the missionaries in China had "entirely outgrown" extraterritoriality as they had numerous mission stations throughout the country, but few consuls, which meant that should a missionary seek to sue under treaty provisions he could do so only by traveling great distances.[22] As a result of these changed conditions in China many mission groups urged the United States government to revise the treaties and eliminate extraterritorial privileges.

During 1923, the year prior to Byers's death, the subject of extraterritoriality was much discussed in the mission community. At the mountain resort established by missionaries at Kuling, Kiangsi, where many took their summer vacations, about one hundred people attended a meeting to

> discuss the desirability of sending a statement to the Governments represented by those present, requesting that no military protection be afforded them and that no ransoms, indemnities or punitive expeditions be allowed should they be captured by bandits.

The leaders of the meeting had previously prepared this statement:

> Without attempting to enter into the general question of extraterritorial rights but having regard to the fact that we are here as messengers of the Gospel of Peace and that our task is to establish peace by leading men and women one by one into that new life in Christ which takes away the occasion of all wars, we express our earnest desires that no form of military pressure may be exerted to protect us or our property, that in the event of our capture by lawless persons or our death at their hands no money may be paid for our release, no punitive expedition be sent out and no indemnity exacted. We take this stand believing that the way to maintain righteousness and peace is through suffering wrong without retaliation, and through bringing the Spirit of personal good will to bear on all persons under all circumstances. So we understand the teaching and example of Christ Jesus our Lord and it is to the extension of His Kingdom that our lives are dedicated.[23]

In October 1923 a *CR* editorial noted that the resolution had not passed, but that many were in favor of a statement that omitted reference to military protection of persons and property. Citing the recently expressed idea that Christianity had failed because it had followed not led the governments of the world, the editor suggested that the missionaries needed to rethink their position on extraterritoriality.[24] One must, of course, argue that whatever resolutions missionaries might adopt, their governments were going to enforce their treaty rights, which included the collection of indemnities, simply to preserve the right to do so.

Under the editorship of Frank Rawlinson, the *CR* often expressed the liberal side of mission opinion. In 1923 in the aftermath of the Lincheng Incident, although it was not specifically mentioned, the *CR* took an editorial stand on its front page against extraterritorial privileges. While carefully stating that he wished to dictate to no one, the editor argued that depending on extraterritorial privileges gave credence to Bertrand Russell's charge that "Christian idealism and Western imperialism go together and depend on one another." The editor continued that the missionaries could never "expect the Chinese church to venture forth boldly trusting in God alone, if their Western brothers try to straddle two planks—one extraterritorial privileges and the other trust in God." Acknowledging that extraterritorial privileges constituted a Gordian knot, the editor stated, "The only arms the Western Christian should depend on are the arms of God."[25]

Published responses to the *CR*'s editorials demonstrated the range of opinions on the topic. One letter by the Rev. T. Z. Koo of the YMCA wondered if the missionaries would "play it safe" and endorse the foreign business groups who were calling for intervention by their governments. If they did, he wrote, it would confirm their critics' charge that "the missionaries preach the doctrine of universal love from their front door while in their back yards they have a battleship ready to enforce the preaching." Koo was pleased the issue was being discussed because as a patriotic Chinese who was also Christian, he acknowledged that missionaries in the interior were in constant danger of bandit attacks and asked if they should not withdraw or stay at their own risk.[26]

The other side of the issue was argued by the Rev. Paul L. Corbin of the American Board of Commissioners for Foreign Missions (ABCFM) in Taiku, Shansi, who stated it was extremely rare at that time for missionaries to try to extend extraterritoriality privileges to their converts, noting that he did not even pursue cases of persecution in the Chinese courts unless there was "extreme violence." Yet he questioned the missionaries putting themselves and their families totally under the jurisdiction of Chinese courts, noting that in the "model province" of Shansi there was "no class of lawyers trained to plead for one" in the courts. While acknowledging that one might "'take joyfully the spoiling' of our personal effects [as] some members of the missionary fraternity have done," he questioned what the responsibility of the missionary was to those in the home countries who had sent their "'sacrificial gifts.'" He reported that Chinese friends who had been questioned about the issue had replied, "'The time is not yet ripe.'" Another writer, the Rev. E. E. Aiken of Taiyuan, Shansi, detailed the torture that those accused of crimes in the "model province" of Shansi were subjected to and stated he did not want to be "in danger of this sort of thing."[27]

Thomas Barclay of the British and Foreign Bible Society at Tainan, Taiwan, wrote that missionaries could think about giving up their foreign protection guaranteed under the extraterritoriality provisions of the treaties, but they would still need to depend on local authorities to provide protection from "bandits and other evil-doers," just as the Chinese did. He mentioned that since the Taiwan missionaries had given up their extraterritorial rights, they had enjoyed "perfect security of life and property" under the Japanese police and military forces.[28] (Japan had taken possession of Taiwan after their 1895 war with China so the missionaries there lost extraterritorial rights when they were eliminated in the renegotiation of Japan's treaties with the Western countries.)

A Shantung missionary, the Rev. R. B. Whitaker, ABCFM, wrote that bandits were constantly around their compounds and hospitals and were numerous in the areas where he did winter itineration. He suggested the only way to avoid "difficulty and suffering" was to return home, but added that Christ never promised his disciples immunity from such problems. Whitaker thought the approach of the missionaries to extraterritoriality was all wrong. He thought they should emphasize their Christian privileges.

> It may be my *right* as an American citizen to demand protection from my consul, but it is my *privilege* as a child of God and as one who would follow the example of Christ my Master to give up that right for the sake of a better way in keeping with the gospel I preach. It is my *right* to claim better legal and military protection than is possible for my Chinese friends and associates; it is my *privilege* to give it up that I may work with them, and if need be, suffer with them, as a part of a common brotherhood.

He continued that Jesus would not have sought extraterritorial rights, so it was wrong for his followers to seek them.[29]

Bishop John Hind of the Church Missionary Society in Fukien suggested that extraterritoriality hindered Christian work in China, but he thought it was impossible for an individual to give up a right his government had secured unless the person sought Chinese citizenship. Hind suggested that the National Christian Council (NCC) needed to poll every missionary in China to ascertain what the dominant opinion was and then transmit the information to the Western governments.[30]

A CIM missionary from Kweichow, D. W. Crofts, related the situation of some German missionaries who had been cheated in an attempt to purchase land and who, having lost extraterritorial privileges due to their country's defeat in the war, were unable to settle the matter which had dragged on for more than three years, even though he believed the Chinese judge was quite willing to help the German women.[31]

Professor T. C. Chao, a prominent Christian, wrote an editorial which appeared in the *Chinese Christian Advocate* on 10 October 1923, and which was reprinted in the *CR* in April 1924. Quoting statements from missionaries who insisted Chinese Christians wanted the foreigners' extraterritorial privileges extended to them, Chao noted if these were true, then "shame on us." He continued that missionaries had told him of one case in which they did not seek an indemnity and "people laugh[ed] at us" because of it. Another missionary reported that the Chinese Christians liked the protection foreign gunboats offered. Chao thought these were hindrances to the Gospel of Peace and the Kingdom of God. He believed such actions caused a "loss to the honor and dignity of the nation and creat[ed] suspicion of our countrymen. This means that we do not love China and therefore are not true citizens of the Republic of China." He urged his fellow Christians not to seek foreign protection when in danger and not to accept indemnities for the loss of lives or property through the help of the missionaries. Only God, he concluded, could protect Chinese Christians from harm.[32]

Another Chinese Christian argued it was not time for the ending of extraterritoriality because once it became "known among the lawless element that missionaries are protectionless . . . they would be molested far more than now—there would be more trouble in China than ever." Someone identified only as a Methodist preacher in Peking thought extraterritoriality should be ended and the missionaries be protected by the Chinese government. D. E. Hoste argued it was best for missionaries and Chinese Christians to act as though extraterritoriality did not exist.[33]

A person identified only as "K" at Shanghai in a letter to the editor termed China a "no-man's land" due to the "widespread and complicated civil war." The writer thought "the nominal Government in order to secure foreign recognition accepts responsibility which it has little expectation of being able to discharge." Continuing, the writer questioned whether the missionaries

> should willingly prolong this embarrassment or whether it would not be more just to frankly recognize the unfairness of asking protection or indemnities from a people in such a situation. Even the Chinese Christians in many places, are feeling that the presence of the foreign missionaries, even of doctors, is an expensive luxury.

Adding that indemnities were "usually extracted *locally*," the writer questioned if foreigners should be living in areas of China where the government had little control. He thought growing families should not need to risk "capture, death or future poverty" and thus should withdraw. The solution suggested was that only those missionaries who were "willing to dispense with indemnity for loss of life or property suffered, and who are ready to urge their own national Government not to take upon itself to embarrass the Chinese people militarily on their behalf" should remain to do the work.[34]

Still others questioned if China were not being held to a higher standard than other governments, when the foreigners demanded the Chinese government protect them. If foreigners were killed in China, were their governments making demands that would not have been made "in a country of higher standards of civilized administration"?[35]

The Rev. G. G. Warren of the English Wesleyan Mission in Hunan preferred the term "extrality" to the uncouth tongue-twisting "extraterritoriality" in the article he wrote for the *CR.* Extrality concerned only "law and legal administration" and was "intended to make the country on which it is imposed as one which has not attained to the standard of jurisprudence which the country imposing it has established," he stated. He thought it would be wrong to abolish it at present, as it did no wrong to any Chinese or their government, and retaining it would be "the best lever there is at present working to raise the Chinese people to our level; its abandonment is more likely than any other movement to confirm the Chinese on their present level." He believed the system was good because "the Chinese people do not enjoy the liberty and justice which we who come from the lands which send missionaries to China enjoy." He cited the many Chinese who had been "arrested, fined, and even executed, not for any crime, but merely because they have said what they thought." From visiting prisons he believed that the republican government then had more innocent people imprisoned than the Ch'ing dynasty had ever had and therefore extrality should not be abolished.[36]

The *CR* continued to editorialize on the subject. The editor wrote that while there was a great diversity of opinion on the subject of extraterritorial rights among Chinese Christians and missionaries, it was becoming clear that those rights were more of a liability than an asset. Arguing that the Christian movement in China was too foreignized, and that it seemed to be an "adjunct to political expansion," Rawlinson wrote that the problem needed to be "solved and not shelved," even if, as yet, no one had a solution. He suggested that as there was "no Christian committee in China to whom can be entrusted the study of this dilemma" it needed to be studied in private, quietly so that some "really helpful step forward" might be suggested before change was forced on them.[37]

Another writer in the *CR* stated that within the mission community those with the longest years of service tended to favor continuation of extraterritorial rights and those with the fewest years of service favored abolition, while those in between were more likely to argue both sides of the question. Additionally, it was thought that evangelistic missionaries, that is, those who traveled about the countryside and had contact with all classes of Chinese, were more in favor of continuing extraterritorial rights, while those in educational work, whose contacts were mostly with more-educated Chinese, favor abolition, while the medical workers were less vocal on the subject.[38]

Tyler Dennett wrote in *The Christian Century* in 1923: "I do not believe that [extraterritoriality] has ever been anything but an embarrassment and injury to mission work," adding if the missionaries were to make a "voluntary relinquishment" of it "not one of them would suffer physical harm."[39]

It was not only liberal Protestants concerned with modern nation-building who opposed missionaries claiming indemnities for the deaths of their brethren. The "blood of martyrs" argument prevailed within conservative Christian groups as well. The Roman Catholic Church, which in the nineteenth century often sought excessive compensation for lives and property losses, had by 1927 decided to refuse compensation for the loss of their missionaries' lives.

But, of course, Roman Catholic missionaries had no surviving spouses nor children in need of support. Further, Roman Catholic policy was dictated by the Vatican which had diplomatic relations with Nationalist China, and although this might have resulted in disputes with the secular governments of the countries that sent Roman Catholic missionaries to China, the latter deferred to the Vatican on this issue.[40]

Some conservative Protestant groups also took this position, notably the CIM, which even before the Boxer Uprising had decided to refuse all compensation for injury and loss of life and to accept nothing for property lost.[41] Yet one might argue that as a faith mission, that is, one that relied on prayer not a well-financed board in the home country to pay their missionaries' salaries, the CIM had no other option.

The many diverse arguments over extraterritoriality and indemnities raged on in the pages of the *CR* long after the indemnity had been collected in the Byers case. Interestingly, the Byers indemnity, although reported in the *CR*, was never mentioned in any of the subsequent articles.

The civil unrest in China continued and plagued missionaries in various parts of the country, particularly in 1927 when during the Northern Expedition the Nationalist forces moved from Canton to consolidate their hold on the whole of China. At that time most missionaries from the interior stations fled, many at consular direction, to the coastal cities and the protection of their diplomats and gunboats. It should be noted that treaty revision did not occur in the 1920s, and extraterritoriality remained the law under which foreigners lived in China until 1943 when it was abolished by revision of the treaties. Of course, in that year there were few Westerners living in China due to the war with Japan.

Mrs. Byers likely knew of the "prompt punishment of robbers and rioters" clause in the American Treaty of Tientsin of 1858, as others in the Hainan mission did, for she constantly insisted the United States government needed to take action to clean the bandits out of Hainan, adding that she knew the local Chinese would appreciate the end to the brigandage. The American consular officials certainly knew of this clause in the 1858 treaty, but they also realized that the political conditions in Hainan in the mid-1920s meant that enforcing it was going to be difficult, if not impossible. When local officials in Hainan arrested and executed people for the Byers murder, the missionaries living on the island knew those individuals were not guilty of the crime.

While the BFM was equivocating on providing support for the Byers family and insisting Mrs. Byers could accept the indemnity only as a private citizen, the United States government informed her it had collected the money. Confused and not wanting to jeopardize support from the BFM, she cabled the Department of State declining the indemnity, only to learn the BFM wanted her to accept it since it would reduce their obligation to her. Yet when the BFM decided to acquiesce in the "blood of martyrs" argument and not seek an indemnity for the loss of a missionary's life, it reserved the right to seek compensation for property lost, placing themselves in the position of seeming to value property more than human life. The account of Byers's murder and its aftermath can be understood only in the context of Chinese and American governmental rules, regulations, and treaty rights, particularly extraterritorial rights; the relationships between the BFM and its missionaries and between the missionaries and the BFM on one side and the United States government on the other; and within the social and civil chaos which was so widespread in China in the 1920s. In sum, it was a difficult balancing act that all engaged in.

The Hainan Mission

The Presbyterian mission on Hainan, southernmost of all mission locations in China, was far from China's centers of opinion. Removed as they were from their colleagues on the mainland, the Hainan missionaries nonetheless lived under the same rights of extraterritoriality as did those in the more cosmopolitan areas. The Presbyterians had, of course, exercised those rights when they purchased land to established their mission stations, where missionaries lived, at the interior towns of Kachek and Nodoa and at both Kiungchow and Hoihow. The mission also had a number of outlying chapels and schools which were staffed by Chinese assistants. The Hainan mission had begun in 1885 as an outstation of the one in Canton, but achieved separate status in 1893.

The idea for a mission on the island had come from Carl C. Jeremiassen, a Dane in the employ of the CIMCS, who had studied medicine for several months with John G. Kerr, M.D., of the Presbyterian mission at Canton. Jeremiassen knew Hainan had no Protestant mis-

Hainan Mission, Kachek, February 1923. *Hainan NewsLetter*, 1923. *Standing from left:* Rev. William Leverett (?), Miss Grace Macdonald, Rev. David Thomas, Miss Mae Chapin, Dr. Frank Whelply(?), Miss Mary Taylor, Rev. William Stinson, Miss Margaret Moninger, Rev. Paul Melrose, Mrs. Esther Melrose, Rev. John D. Ferguson(?) (Union Church, Manila, Philippines, visitor), Mrs. Meta Thomas, Dr. Clarence Salsbury, Mrs. Cora Salsbury, Dr. Nathaniel Bercovitz, Mrs. Elva Bercovitz, Rev. Wilbur Campbell, Rev. David Tappan, Rev. John Steiner, Rev. George Byers. *Seated from left:* Mrs. Florence Whelply(?), and Arlene(?), Mrs. Luella Tappan and David, Mrs. Margaret Melrose and Jean, Mrs. Mary R. Doolittle(?) (field secretary, Women's Mission Board of the Northwest, Presbyterian Church [USA], visitor), Miss Katherine Schaeffer(?), Mrs. Inetta Campbell(?) and Jean Thomas(?), Mrs. Madeleine Steiner and Betty, Mrs. Clara Byers and Larry. *On ground from left:* John Bercovitz, David and Daniel Thomas, Jack and Hugh Melrose, Geneva Steiner, Margaret Byers, Chalmers Salsbury, Robert Byers, Miss Caroline McCreery and Betty Bercovitz, Nathaniel Bercovitz, David Byers.

Rev. George D. Byers
Presbyterian Historical Society, Philadelphia

sion and the Presbyterians at Canton were interested in claiming the location for their church since under the comity agreements which most of the Protestant missions in China had signed they did not compete for converts, but rather divided up China's territory for the purpose of propagating Christianity. (A small Roman Catholic mission had been on the island since the seventeenth century and at the time of this story it was staffed by French priests of the Missions Étrangères.)

Jeremiassen and the Rev. B. C. Henry of the Canton mission traveled about the island in the early 1880s surveying the possibilities for mission work and decided the island was a suitable place. They believed the aborigines of the island, whom they called Miao,[42] would be more amenable to Christian conversion than were the Han Chinese of the mainland who missionaries had discovered were very reluctant to embrace Christianity. It was to be close to the Miao territory that the first station of the Hainan mission was established at Nodoa in 1885. Property was acquired in Kiungchow the following year and coastal land in Hoihow was purchased in 1894 from a German coolie contractor who closed his business. The Kachek station was established in 1901.

The first missionaries to live on the island were the Rev. and Mrs. Frank P. Gilman and H. M. McCandliss, M.D., who arrived in 1886. Dr. McCandliss soon married Olivia Kerr, daughter of Dr. and Mrs. Kerr of the Canton mission. The Hainan missionaries were joined by other colleagues in the 1890s, notably the Rev. and Mrs. John Melrose, Miss Katherine L. Schaeffer, and the Rev. and Mrs. Wilbur Campbell. As the personnel increased in number, the missionaries established hospitals and schools at their stations, which served the Han and Hakka populations of the island. But the missionaries did not abandon their earlier goal of converting the aboriginal peoples and took turns several times a year journeying into the island's mountainous interior to visit the Miao people as well as the Loi tribes.

The Rev. Byers, a native of Nova Scotia but a naturalized American citizen, graduate of Albany College in Oregon and the San Anselmo Theological Seminary in California, joined the mission along with the Rev. David S. Tappan in 1906. Byers, assigned to evangelize the Miao, was stationed at Kachek. Six years after he arrived on Hainan he married Clara Laura Primm, a graduate of the University of Chicago, who was working as a secretary to the director of the YMCA in Shanghai when she met her husband-to-be.[43]

Mrs. Clara Laura Primm Byers
Presbyterian Historical Society, Philadelphia

Mrs. Charles K. (Mabel L.) Roys
Presbyterian Historical Society, Philadelphia

The Different Views of the Case

The details of the Byers case as seen from the perspectives of the American and British consuls and other foreign service personnel and the missionaries and church officials in China and America, and Mrs. Byers, residing in California, provide an interesting story of the extraterritoriality issues that ensued in the aftermath of the murder. This is the story of how the American government reacted to the death of one of its citizens in a foreign country and how the Americans interested in the case were able to get their government to take the action they desired. It is also the story of a single mother, newly widowed, struggling to provide for her family in a society that would have preferred not to admit such families existed. It is the story, too, of the ultimate triumph of Mrs. Byers's staunch ally Mrs. Roys, the sole female member of the BFM, which in the end agreed to support the family as long as they needed help. Thus this is an account, not about the Byers murder, but about its aftermath and how Mrs. Byers finally resolved the complicated affairs into which she was plunged with the death of her husband.

Central to this story are Mrs. Byers, and her ally Mrs. Roys, who kept the issue before the church and the United States government for many long months. When Michael Hunt wrote in the early 1980s that the role of women in mission activity needed further study, and "we are far from having a clear sense of the global ramifications of United States mission interests," he might have added, we have even less understanding of how those missionary women, and specifically those widowed by violence, influenced American foreign policy.[44] Extraterritoriality rights and the question of indemnities were a conundrum difficult to extricate oneself from as the Byers case clearly illustrates, but both the widow and her ally insisted these issues be addressed.

A great many individuals were involved in this case, but this monograph deals primarily with Mrs. Byers and her actions, and particularly her relationship with Mrs. Roys, as they struggle to find a way for Mrs. Byers to support herself and her children. It is likely neither of these women would have allowed herself to be called a feminist, but the fact remains that just four years after women in the United States received the right to vote, these two determined women were astute enough about how the American political system worked to convince the government, and the Presbyterian Church, to take the actions they desired. Mrs. Byers did this through her never-ending letter-writing to anyone who might be remotely interested in her family's plight, asking them to write their respective congressional representatives on her behalf. Mrs. Roys's contribution was her insistence that the BFM not leave the Byers family destitute. It is also a story of how women can influence American foreign policy, in this case toward China.[45] This is Mrs. Byers's story and how she successfully extricated herself from the extraterritoriality/indemnity conundrum.

2

The Immediate Aftermath of the Murder

"It is my painful duty to report the murder yesterday of an American missionary, Rev. G. D. Byers, at Kachek."[1] With those words H.B.M. Consul H. H. Bristow, resident at Kiungchow, Hainan island, informed U.S. Consul Douglas Jenkins at Canton that bandits had killed the Presbyterian missionary at his interior station on the night of 24 June 1924, setting off an extraterritoriality incident which was to last nearly a year. It involved Byers's widow Clara; Bristow; the American consul and two vice consuls in Canton; the American minister and other diplomats in Peking; the American consuls in Shanghai and Swatow; the American navy; two American secretaries of state; the French consuls at Pakhoi and Hoihow; the Chinese minister of foreign affairs; the Presbyterian Board of Foreign Missions (BFM) in New York; the members of the Presbyterian mission on Hainan; the Presbyterian China Council (PCC) and the larger Protestant-wide National Christian Council (NCC) of China, both located in Shanghai; friends of the Byers family; four American congressmen and a senator; and various Chinese officials from Kachek to Peking. Sometimes they worked together but frequently they worked at cross purposes, particularly on the issues of whether any action was being taken to arrest the murderers and whether an indemnity should be sought. Months of foot-dragging on the part of the American and the Chinese governments saw the British official on Hainan take the most direct action in the matter, at one point writing to the American consul in Canton, in the event that the American government were still interested in the case, he might like to know that the chief witness, who had named the culprits, had been executed by the Chinese military![2]

The Extraterritoriality Issue

Unfortunately for those who wanted the Byers matter resolved, the murder occurred just at the time the American government was trying to decide what to do about treaty revisions with China and particularly whether it should abrogate the extraterritoriality provisions of those treaties. The Washington Conference of 1922 had set limits on naval vessels, but more important for the Chinese it had left the question of treaty revisions undecided and as a result "Chinese opinion was more vehemently anti-imperialist than ever before."[3] The extraterritoriality treaty provisions gave all foreigners special privileges in China—putting them outside the reach of Chinese law, allowing indemnities to be collected for lost lives and property, and permitting the propagation of Christianity. The lack of action in the Byers case can be related to the American government's concern about these treaty provisions, and to the fact that, in 1924, China was not a country that attracted much attention from the United States. One can argue, as Warren I. Cohen has, that the American government had no China policy and responded to changes in China in these years with "indifference at best and occasional hostility."[4] Indeed, Cohen has stated that from 1922 to 1925 "essential control" of United States–China policy was in the hands of Jacob Gould Schurman, American minister to China, resident in Peking, and John Van Antwerp MacMurray, assistant secretary of state, in Washington.[5] Another scholar has asserted that "the very hallmark of MacMurray's China policy was unquestionably the need to backup diplomacy with force," as MacMurray had demonstrated when he strongly supported Minister Schurman when the latter was involved in an extraterritoriality incident in 1922.[6]

Liberals among the Christian missionaries, such as the Rev. Frank Rawlinson, editor of the *Chinese Recorder (CR)*,[7] and the members of the NCC had long favored the abrogation of the extraterritorial clauses in the Sino-foreign treaties. They argued their work did not need the protection of foreign governments and, indeed, the treaty protection afforded Christianity made it more difficult for them to appeal to young, nationalistic Chinese. Indeed, for several years missionaries throughout China had been forced to deal with the new nationalism which was extremely anti-Christian.[8] The last problem the missionary community and the American diplomats wanted in 1924 was an extraterritorial case involving the murder of a missionary. But Byers had been murdered and the American government had to do something about it.

Because Byers was killed in the interior of remote Hainan, far from the nearest American consulate in Canton, it was somewhat easier for the American government to ignore the case than it would have been had it occurred near, say, Shanghai or Peking. When the matter was finally resolved, the solution satisfied no one completely, but given the political uncertainties of China in the 1920s it was deemed the best that could be done.

Although Bristow's first letter to Jenkins about the murder had been a very formal one, primarily giving only the news of Byers's death and the likely responsible parties, Bristow sent a far different message to Jenkins the following day, urging him to "come personally, preferably in a warship" which he thought "would create a good impression." Bristow thought the American consul should conduct a "joint inquiry" with the Chinese officials in charge of Kachek, adding "there is a strong feeling here that if severe measures are not taken in the present case foreign lives will no longer be safe in Hainan." He concluded, "if you offered American military assistance to put down the brigands I think it would stimulate Chinese activity."[9]

In early July, an American gunboat arrived off Hainan bearing a young vice consul, C. B. Chamberlain, who had been sent to investigate the murder. The gunboat quickly became a matter of discussion and concern among the Christian community on the China mainland, which certainly did not want the Chinese to think they could only propagate their religion at the point of a gun and would seek recourse to the extraterritorial treaty rights whenever necessary. Yet these matters were of concern more to those foreigners living in Shanghai, center of all Christian mission activity in China, than to those missionaries on Hainan.

Unstable Conditions on Hainan

Over the years the Hainan mission had been a relatively safe one for the missionaries, although some of them had been victims of thievery and piracy, including the Byers family who were robbed by bandits in 1919 on the way from Kachek to the annual mission meeting in Nodoa. The family was not with their carriers when about $600 worth of their possessions were taken, including one of each pair of daughter Margaret's shoes, newly arrived from the United States, and Mrs. Byers's wedding dress. When soldiers caught up with the thieves one of them was wearing the dress, minus the lace which he apparently did not like.[10] Yet, in their confrontations with thieves, few of the missionaries had ever been injured, and none seriously.

Hainan, like much of China, was unstable politically in the 1920s. The Ch'ing dynasty, which had ruled China since 1644, had been toppled by the 1911 revolution led by Sun Yat-sen and the years that followed were marked by political chaos. Sun, who had lived many years abroad, established himself in Canton, but lacked any real power base or an army strong enough to establish republican control over the country. Yuan Shih-k'ai, who earlier had served the Ch'ing dynasty, headed a rival government in Peking and then in 1916 established a short-lived dynasty which ended with his death six months later. Control of the Peking government then fell into the hands of powerful northern military leaders. In the absence of real centralized power, various factions composed of local elites, remnants of the Ch'ing armies, bandits, warlords, and gangsters gained control of most of the countryside. During these years of political chaos, many areas suffered lawlessness and Hainan was no exception. Brigandage became more common and by the 1920s the local populace frequently suffered the consequences of the actions of the various armies, supporting both the Canton government and the one in Peking, which sought to control the island.[11]

Protected by the extraterritoriality guaranteed in their treaties, the missionaries assumed that the disputes were Chinese affairs and of no particular concern to them. Indeed, one might say that the Hainan missionaries behaved in a most incautious manner given the instability of the political situation on the island. For example, in December 1923, Miss Margaret Moninger, who was treasurer of the Kachek station, wrote to her family in America that the Rev. Byers and Nathaniel Bercovitz, M.D., had moved two thousand Mexican silver dollars from the station safe to the hospital safe which was across a public road. She reported that in the process they discovered that $1000 [Mex.] weighed sixty-two pounds. She also wrote that she frequently carried $200 or $300 [Mex.] home from the market and often had several hundred dollars in her road baskets when traveling to Kachek from Hoihow.[12] In fact, it was common for missionaries everywhere in China to carry cash in their road baskets and to keep large amounts of Mexican silver dollars at their compounds. Such practices were generally known among the Chinese as the missionaries in Hainan, and elsewhere, frequently acted as informal bankers particularly for Chinese Christians. Given the chaos of China in the 1920s, the missionaries were thus easy targets for disreputable men in need of ready cash. Perhaps it was no coincidence that the Byers murder happened just six months after the missionaries moved the $2000 [Mex.] Miss Moninger had mentioned—on the first occasion when only one mission family was left on the compound.

In the last letters the Rev. Byers wrote he reported that the political conditions in Hainan were quite bad and had been for the past year. To this supporting church, he explained,

> many of our members have suffered . . . some have lost their lives and others have been captured and held for ransom. About two months ago the home of one of our well-to-do members was broken into and the head of the family carried off. He has just obtained his release by paying $800 [Mex.].

To his colleague, Miss Katherine L. Schaeffer, who was home on furlough, Byers wrote that in the Christian village of Tintai, thirty miles south of Kachek, "soldiers raided one of the robber camps in the moonlight. The robbers ran away and the soldiers released twenty-one prisoners being held for ransom. One was an old woman nearly eighty years of age."[13] Indeed, the year before the Byers murder a number of Chinese Christians in Kachek had been kidnapped and held for ransom and the missionaries had sent a report of these incidents to the *CR* in Shanghai, which published them.[14]

Mrs. Byers was also well aware of the unsettled conditions of the countryside, and acknowledged, in a letter to the BFM after her husband's death, that the Americans took no precautions despite the unrest.

> Banditry [had] been going on around Kachek for a long time. Some of the men [were] ex-soldiers, some [were] local farmers turned thieves. In many villages not a person dare[d] sleep in their home for fear of kidnaping. At dusk they [took] their children and mats and [went] to the hedges to sleep. Often it is their next-door neighbor whom they fear. Many of them . . . brought their deeds and valuables to us for safekeeping. The common saying was "They will not attack the foreigners." We had gone about as freely as in America and had never known fear. The officials had been so busy gambling and opium smoking that they had made practically no effort to improve conditions. On them lies much of the blame.

She also noted that just two days before her husband was killed she had said to him, "I somehow am prepared to hear at any time that you have been taken for ransom. I wonder when our turn will come."[15]

The violence, of which the Byerses were well aware, now struck their family. Although the other missionaries were shocked at the brutality of the murder, within days of the Rev. Byers's death some of his colleagues took the view that he had been foolish to resist. Earlier, the missionaries had discussed among themselves the possibility of being kidnapped, and several later recalled that the Rev. Byers had stated he would never allow himself to be taken for ransom. His colleagues attributed this to his being a "stubborn Scotsman."

No written record remains to suggest why the missionaries had had a discussion about what to do if one of them were kidnapped, but it might have resulted from the kidnapping on the Chinese mainland of the Rev. Rex Ray of the Southern Baptist Mission on 28 May. The Hainan missionaries would have learned of Ray's kidnapping from reports in Hong Kong newspapers, which regularly arrived at Hoihow within days of their publication as coastal steamers called at the port almost daily. In an incredible coincidence, the Rev. Ray was married to Janet Gilman, daughter of the Rev. and Mrs. Frank P. Gilman, pioneers of the Hainan mission. Miss Gilman had served as a missionary in Hainan for two years before her marriage. Her husband was kidnapped along with three other foreigners and twenty Chinese men from the river steamer *Roanoke.* Two of the missionaries were released almost immediately so that they could transmit the kidnappers' demand for $200,000 [Mex.] ransom. Ray, who was held three weeks, escaped when he was left on a mountaintop with the single guard and that man simply walked away.[16]

Just after the Byers murder the Rev. David S. Tappan, Byers's closest friend in the Hainan mission, spent the Fourth of July alone in Kachek where he was packing the Byers family's belongings. On that day he wrote a lengthy memoir of his friend noting,

> The Chinese all said it would have been wiser not to have resisted, but to have gone with the bandits and made officials ransom him. Perhaps it would, but it is hard for Scot[s]man to surrender even with the rope around his neck and four [*sic*] armed bandits dragging him over the ground.

(Despite the fact that the Hainan missionaries maintained a formality among themselves by addressing one another by titles and surnames, the Revs. Tappan and Byers, who had traveled to China together in the same cabin and spent three years at the same station learning the language, called one another by their given names.)[17]

The Attack

The Hainan mission was the smallest of the Presbyterian missions in China having only a few people at each of its stations. In the early summer, at the close of the school term, it was customary for the missionaries to leave their stations for vacations away from the island, which were deemed necessary by the mission's medical committee. Because it was thought unwise to leave the stations without a foreigner in residence, one person or family always remained behind. Thus it was on that June night only the Rev. Byers, his pregnant wife Clara, and their four children—Robert, eleven; Margaret, eight; David, six; and Laurence, three—were at the Kachek compound. Their colleagues, Miss Moninger, a teacher, and Miss Caroline McCreery, the station's nurse, had departed for Hoihow where they were preparing to embark for Hong Kong. Despite Mrs. Byers's pregnancy, Dr. Bercovitz and his family were also in Hong Kong on vacation. In addition to Miss Schaeffer, the Rev. and Mrs. David H. Thomas and their children, also assigned to Kachek, were in the United States on furlough.[18]

On his way home from religious services at the mission hospital that Tuesday evening, the Rev. Byers was waylaid by three men who wanted to kidnap him. According to the official statement sworn to by Mrs. Byers, she heard the family's dog bark and a "cry of alarm." Recognizing her husband's voice, she and her son Robert

> grabbed the lamp and ran down stairs and were suddenly confronted with three men, who were dragging my husband thru [*sic*] a small ravine below the house, by means of a rope slipped through a bamboo pole tied around his neck. He was already bleeding terribly and unable to stand. The men came to a dead halt when they saw us.

Robert cut the rope from around his father's neck and started to run to the hospital only to have one man grab him. Robert managed to "wriggle loose. All three then raised their guns and fired directly at us, one shot spattering Robert with sand as he ran, one shot overturned the lamp. The men then ran away leaving the rope. Mr. Byers died in a few minutes before we got him into the house." Byers had been shot twice, once in the left thigh and once in the abdomen.[19]

Mrs. Byers would later remember that she heard no shot. "Probably when [Mr. Byers] put up a fight and resisted, [the culprits] pressed their guns against his body and fired."[20] That Byers put up a terrific struggle was evident to those who viewed the scene later. They reported "the ground was all torn up in the direction of a well that is off a little to one side of the path leading from the front door of the house—showing where Mr. Byers had dug his heels into the ground in an effort to resist the bandits."[21]

Dr. Chu, who was in charge of the mission hospital in the absence of Dr. Bercovitz, had left Kachek that afternoon for a long-planned trip to Peking. So Robert, whom many Chinese would later extol as having been very brave, ran for help, locating the hospital's medical assistant Mr. Lin in the nearby market.[22] The Rev. Byers was dead when the assistant arrived, but, assessing the wounds, he told Mrs. Byers that nothing could have saved her husband. She reported, "most of the Chinese fled in terror when they heard the news." Although the Byers's servants had just returned from the service the Rev. Byers had conducted, Mrs. Byers had great difficulty getting them to come out of the house to help her and "when they did venture forth they hid behind trees and it was a long time before I could get anyone to help carry him into the house." She wanted to get a message to Dr. Chu, who she knew was spending the night twenty miles away at the town of Uidiok, on his way to the port, and so "offered the auto company $100 [Mex.] if they would take the message with an armed escort that night. They refused, saying there was not enough money in America to send them out in the *dark*."[23]

News of the murder spread quickly in the town and Chinese soldiers with a captain appeared at the compound some time later and offered to use their recently-installed telephone linking Kachek to Kiungchow to inform the foreigners on the coast of Byers's death. When the captain departed to make the telephone call, he left, at Mrs. Byers's request, six soldiers to guard the family and the compound. Instead of patrolling the mission grounds, as she asked, the six men informed her "they could watch better from the upstairs veranda." About midnight when Mrs. Byers finally felt she could retire for the night, she found the soldiers "three asleep in my bedroom cross wise of the bed, one asleep on the cot, one in the hammock outside and one in the steamer chair." An hour later, in response to loud knocking and pounding, Mrs. Byers attempted to rouse the soldiers to investigate the noise, but succeeded only in disturbing them enough so that two more joined the three already in her bed. The soldiers departed at daybreak. Four other soldiers spent the day in the mission school. All were Cantonese speakers so Mrs. Byers could communicate with them only through an interpreter.[24]

All the missionaries then at Kiungchow and Hoihow had gathered on the evening of the 24th to celebrate Miss Alice Skinner's birthday. Miss Moninger, who was staying at the home of Dr. and Mrs. H. M. McCandliss, later joined the Rev. Wilbur Campbell in writing to the PCC and the BFM about how they learned of the murder. According to their report at 11 p.m. the doctor had received a Chinese letter detailing the telephone call from Kachek at 9 p.m., telling of the murder. The letter was "roughly translated . . . as follows: 'Four ruffians entered the compound to bind and carry off Mr. Byers. He refused to go so was shot in the abdomen and killed. Tell the others. Please come at once to Kachek to make arrangements for burial. (Signed) Mrs. Byers.'" (Upon receiving this letter in late July the BFM officials in New York immediately published this account and concluded, quite correctly, "this is not a general anti-foreign uprising nor an attack on the station. It seems to be a frustrated attempt to secure ransom.")[25]

Upon learning of the murder, several of the male missionaries at Hoihow went to the British consul's home and then to the military governor's office, and at dawn the Revs. Tappan and John Steiner left on the two-day trip to Kachek to assist Mrs. Byers and her children in traveling to the port.[26]

At Kachek the morning following the murder Mrs. Byers was summoned to the telephone at the military headquarters where, she later reported, she found "the captain of the soldiers smoking opium on his bed in front of the telephone." She was told a message had come some hours earlier to the effect that the Revs. Tappan and Steiner were en route to Kachek. Mrs. Byers would later learn that the missionaries at Hoihow had not tried to telephone the night before having been told "the Chinese officials would be asleep and it would not be worthwhile to try."[27] The Byers's Chinese servants were afraid "an attempt would be made to steal Mr. Byers's body for ransom and they wanted the whole garrison brought in" to protect the compound. Mrs. Byers had placed her husband's body in another of the houses on the compound because of the small children in her home. Seven soldiers were sent to patrol the compound the second night; but when they refused to do so and retired to sleep in the school, the Chinese servants "were in the state of panic."[28]

While awaiting the arrival of her colleagues to assist her, Mrs. Byers received the condolences of her many friends in Kachek. She would later write that "one of the hardest things the two days we were in Kachek alone was receiving the many women who came sobbing, to throw themselves at my feet. It seemed that they were the ones to be comforted by me."[29]

The Diplomats Become Involved

At the time of the murder the cable between Hoihow and Hong Kong was not working so Miss Moninger, as secretary of the Hainan mission, wrote a letter to the mission's bank, the Hongkong and Shanghai Bank in Hong Kong, asking them to cable New York and Shanghai with the news.[30] Thus word of the death reached the outside world.

When Bristow sent his initial communication to Jenkins, he suggested two possible culprits—the outlaw Ch'en Chi-yu, who the missionaries insisted was on excellent terms with them since they had offered asylum to his wives when they were in danger; and the brigand Lin Shu-piao,[31] who was responsible for the deaths of several Christians and who had been punished for burning a mission school. In his letter Bristow also noted that Ch'en Tan-shu, the local chief of staff, "was up the greater part of the night arranging for escort and communication with the Military Officials at Kachek, who have behaved exceedingly well."[32] Bristow would later learn from Mrs. Byers that his report on the conduct of the military officials was a grave exaggeration.

Bristow also reported that he had spoken to Mrs. Byers and that the attack was "entirely unforeseen" and that the "officials can only be held responsible for the general disturbed state of the country and not for negligence in this particular case." The British official noted he had written to the commissioner for foreign affairs on 21 February 1924, at the request of Dr. Bercovitz, asking that "military forces . . . use greater vigilance in guarding against brigands who enter [Kachek] freely."[33]

Determining exactly who was responsible for the murder of the

Rev. Byers was to prove exceedingly difficult as Bristow's letter suggested. Bristow related that the Chinese authorities tried to attribute the murder to the outlaw Ch'en Chi-yu.

> The story goes that Ch'en sent to the mission for a doctor to attend him for a wound which was bleeding dangerously, and the only available doctor, a Chinese, refused to go for fear that he might not be permitted to return. . . . He is said to have fled to Hoihow to avoid being kidnaped, leaving Mr. Byers to stave off the demands for medical assistance. The story goes on to say that the four men were outlaws of Ch'en's band, who entered Mr. Byers [*sic*] compound to request him to accompany them to treat their wounded chief, and that, on Mr. Byers refusing, they shot him in desperation.[34]

The consul's report of the story concerning Ch'en Chi-yu correctly noted that he and the missionaries were on good terms. But the Consul apparently did not know that the story was faulty in that the Chinese doctor, whom he reported had fled to Hoihow, had in fact left Kachek several hours before the murder on a planned trip to Peking. The story was further flawed in that the Rev. Byers, although he had no formal medical training, most likely would have agreed to assist Ch'en had he been "bleeding dangerously." Bristow continued that the story favored by the mission attributed the outrage to the brigand named Lin Shu-piao, who, in addition to burning the school and killing several Christians, was reported to have

> threatened to carry off Miss Schaeffer of the mission, in order to hold her for ransom. This lady has hastened to her departure from Kachek on that account. It is supposed that the idea was then conceived to carry off Mr. Byers for the same purpose, and that he was killed while resisting capture.

Bristow continued his letter to Jenkins noting, "I give these stories for what they are worth. In neither does there appear sufficient motive for murder."[35]

Mrs. Byers would later write that although Lin Shu-piao had terrorized

> the Chinese community for two or three years, kidnaping children, etc. He was known to some of our mission personally, had even had tea with Miss Schaeffer shortly before she went home on furlough. Ransom apparently was the only reason for the outrage. Knowing we were all alone,

> and having had no resistance from the Chinese and no interference from the officials they had gotten bold [enough] to attack the foreigner himself.[36]

The validity of the missionaries' assumptions as to who was responsible for the murder was demonstrated when the Rev. Steiner found a note at the Kachek compound from Lin Shu-piao demanding a $20,000 [Mex.] ransom and promising to burn the mission if the demand were not met. Reporting this to the American diplomats in Canton, Bristow wrote, "I venture to express the hope that you will take strong measures to ensure prompt action against the brigands of Hainan. Your personal presence in Kachek would be the greatest incentive to activity on the part of Chinese authorities."[37]

While Bristow was urging the American consul to action, the body of Byers was being accompanied to Hoihow by his family and the Rev. Steiner. They arrived on 29 June and funeral services were held that afternoon, attended by the chief military officer's deputy, the district magistrate, Chinese Christians, and most of the foreigners in the port.[38]

The News Reaches America

On 30 June, the BFM in New York learned of Byers's death by the cable Miss Moninger had requested the Hongkong and Shanghai Bank dispatch on behalf of the missionaries. It read, "Byers murdered Kachek Family Moninger McCreery Bercovitz safe." Although the BFM staff had no way of knowing the location of Miss Moninger, Miss McCreery, and the Bercovitz family, they correctly interpreted the few words of the cable, and guessed that the Byers family was with him in Kachek when the murder occurred. The BFM also noted that the Associated Press reported the murder of Byers on 24 June and the departure of Vice Consul Chamberlain on the USS *Sacramento* for Hainan.[39]

In Washington on the morning of 30 June, the Department of State received a cable from the American Minister Schurman informing them that Byers had been murdered. The cable continued, "suggest that American consular officer and gunboat be sent to make joint investigation with Chinese authorities. USS *Sacramento* leaving Hong Kong Tuesday morning with Vice Consul C. B. Chamberlain for Hoihow." Late that same afternoon the Department of

State received the first official communication from the BFM, a telegram stating simply, "Cablegram reports George D. Byers killed by bandits Kachek Hainan China. Please keep us advised." The following day Secretary of State Charles Evans Hughes responded to the BFM confirming the death of Byers and informing them of the departure of the USS *Sacramento* for Hoihow.[40]

Jenkins at Canton informed Minister Schurman in Peking that Chamberlain was to "make a careful investigation of the affair and at the same time impress upon the Chinese authorities the seriousness of the crime and necessity of speedy action on their part to effect the arrest and punishment of the individuals guilty of the outrage." He continued that both Chamberlain and the commander of the USS *Sacramento,* a man named Fletcher, understood force was not to be used unless they had specific instructions from the department approving it. Jenkins also wrote: "I do not consider it would be advisable to land the marines . . . even if [Chinese] authorities should invite such cooperation." Instead, Chamberlain was to impress upon the Chinese the responsibility they had to arrest and punish the outlaws. Jenkins left the question of an indemnity to the department. It was in this letter that the first hint of the attitude on the part of American consular officials toward missionaries appeared. Jenkins clearly thought that the work of an American consular office did not include looking after the concerns of an American mission even if one of its members had been murdered. The apologetic nature of his letter indicated he also believed the Department of State shared his thoughts about missionaries. He wrote,

> while the necessity of sending officers from the consulate general to interior points in connection with cases of this sort seriously interferes with the work of this office, I desire to explain that little or nothing can be accomplished unless we have a representative on the spot to bring the necessary pressure to bear on the local authorities concerned. The presence of a man-of-war, whenever it is possible to have one on the spot, is also exceedingly helpful.

Jenkins also repeated the demand Lin Shu-piao had made for $20,000 [Mex.] and noted, "it is understood in Canton that the military forces in Hainan are allied with General Ch'en Chiung-ming and are not under the control of the Canton government. This, however, is a matter which Vice Consul Chamberlain will investigate."[41]

The missionaries in Hainan had had no word if there would be a response from the American government, but as Miss Moninger wrote her family they

> kept hoping a consul or vice consul from Canton would come down to see about the matter and sure enough a grey gunboat steamed slowly into the harbor Wednesday afternoon. We could see her big guns through the telescope but couldn't distinguish her flag. At last a motor boat put down and started ashore, and we could see Old Glory on her stern. Dr. Bercovitz had come on her and the second vice consul, a Mr. Chamberlain. He surely has gone into things thoroughly with the Chinese officials in Hoihow and Kiungchow and yesterday morning he started in to Kachek.[42]

Making the best of a bad situation, the missionaries invited some sixty sailors and marines ashore on the Fourth of July to celebrate the occasion with a game of baseball and a picnic. Miss Moninger discovered at the picnic that the ship's commander was from her hometown of Marshalltown, Iowa, and knew some of her relatives. She reported to her family that the missionaries had "not heard one word from any of the officers or the men about 'one missionary causing lots of trouble.'" Robert and Margaret, the oldest of the Byers children, attended the picnic and were introduced, prompting one of the sailors to respond, "pretty tough. We can't undo what's been done but we will try to prevent its happening again." Some of the missionaries conducted a religious service on the USS *Sacramento* even though Captain Fletcher said he could not say how many of his men might attend. Miss Moninger, who sat in front at the service, judged from the singing that the number was "quite a few."[43] Despite the socializing, the missionaries soon had reason to fear that neither the consul nor the presence of the gunboat was going to hasten a settlement in the Byers case.

In a premature communication, Jenkins cabled Schurman on 7 July: "Progress made thus far is satisfactory suspicious characters have been arrested."[44] This cable was forwarded to Secretary Hughes by Edward Bell of the Peking legation who also noted that "the case is proceeding satisfactorily and . . . the military authorities of Hainan have evinced a genuine desire to lend their cooperation by rendering assistance to Mrs. Byers and by arresting those persons suspected of being implicated in the murder." He reiterated the British consul's opinion that Hainan officials could not be held responsible for negligence in the matter, but could for the general unrest on the island.[45]

In New York, the BFM was concerned that the murder of Byers not harm the work of their other China missions, a view evident in their announcement of Byers's murder, dated 7 July, which was sent to their PCC and China missions. It noted "in many parts of the Kachek district, bandit outrages have occurred throughout the past year, greatly to the distress of the missionaries and to the hindrance of itinerating work. The Mission, however, has not reported any particular danger to the lives of American residents." On the same day from New York, Mrs. Mabel L. Roys, the only woman secretary of the BFM, wrote Miss Schaeffer that they had few details of Byers's death but were praying "it may have been the result of an accident rather than of deep-seated hatred for the Church."[46]

As the news of the murder reached the friends of the Byers family in the United States, expressions of concern were forthcoming. By 24 July Congressman Willis C. Hawley [1st District, Ore.] had become involved when he wrote a letter to the secretary of state about the case. Hawley was responding to a request from his constituent, Wallace H. Lee, president of Albany College, Albany, Oregon, which was Byers's alma mater. On 31 July Joseph C. Grew, as acting secretary of state, responded to Hawley telling him of the actions then being taken.[47]

The Situation on Hainan

In Hainan the missionaries were very concerned about the unstable conditions on the island and, particularly, with resuming their work at the interior stations. Miss Moninger expressed the sentiments of many of her colleagues when she wrote that Chamberlain, Dr. Bercovitz, a military official from Hoihow, and "400 picked soldiers" left on 5 July for Kachek with the "avowed intention of cleaning out the robbers." She continued,

> while on the one hand we feel that justice must be done if there is to be any security for mission work in the interior still we dread the thought of the innocent suffering with the guilty, or perhaps in place of the guilty. That however, is a matter now out of our hands in the hands of Chinese officials.[48]

From Canton, Jenkins informed Schurman in Peking that Chamberlain had written from Hoihow,

> although the Chinese authorities have made promises and attempted to do everything in their power to discover and capture the individuals guilty of the murder . . . little or nothing has as yet been accomplished. . . . [T]he murder of Byers seems to have been unusually brutal. He was dragged out of the compound and shot in the presence of his wife and little son, who also narrowly escaped being killed. . . . [S]uspicion points to the notorious bandit Lin Shu-piao, whom the authorities are endeavoring to capture. A number of bad characters have already been arrested and some have been executed, but even the authorities themselves admit that there is no evidence to show that these individuals had anything to do with the matter.

Jenkins went on to note that "Mr. Chamberlain fears, and in this I agree with him, that the Chinese authorities will practically abandon all efforts in the case the moment Mr. Chamberlain leaves Hainan." Jenkins continued that the Americans could not expect the British consul to pursue the case vigorously, adding, "I fear it will be necessary for our government to detail some experienced consular or other official to return to Hainan to continue working on the case."[49]

The Indemnity Is Requested

In the aftermath of her husband's death Mrs. Byers had to cope with many decisions. Although some in the Hainan mission thought she should remain in China until the birth of her child, she decided to return immediately to the United States. The matter of an indemnity was broached before she departed Hainan when the American consul asked her for her claim. The issue of the collection of the indemnity proved to be the source of great controversy in the months to come among all those involved in the Byers case.

Mrs. Byers reported that many of the Kachek Chinese who were sympathetic to her plight and had sought to comfort her in the immediate aftermath of her husband's murder had expressed the opinion that she should seek support for her children and that an indemnity was justified.[50]

The issue of an indemnity was very complicated as each group and person involved in the case had distinct views on the matter. As a result of the May Fourth Movement which grew out of the 1919 student protests over China's treatment at the Versailles Peace Conference, many young Chinese intellectuals had become increasingly nationalistic and hence opposed the unequal treaties which gave foreigners privileges in their country. Liberal missionaries and mission groups, centered in Shanghai, who were attuned to this change in the Chinese intelligentsia, tended to favor treaty revision and were opposed to anything that smacked of gunboat diplomacy. And many conservative mission groups had given up any claim to indemnities because they thought such requests hindered their work. The Hainan missionaries, because of the location of their mission, were not directly involved with this current of missionary thinking. Although they took yearly vacations away from the island, as required by the medical committee, they tended to go only to Hong Kong, because of the distance and expense of traveling to one of the major mission resorts at Kuling, in the mountains of Kiangsi, or Peitaiho, on the beach in Shantung. Two of the missionaries, generally one man and one of the single women, attended the annual meeting of the PCC in Shanghai, but otherwise only when they were coming and going to and from home on furlough did others visit that city. As a result they did not often come into contact with missionaries from other parts of China or from other missions. They did, of course, meet some missionaries in Hong Kong, but as the others were usually not vacationing but coming and going to and from home they did not spend much time in that city. Thus the Hainan missionaries were not aware of the degree to which nationalism was reshaping the Chinese landscape and altering missionaries' attitudes toward their work. True, there had been an episode of political unrest among the young men at the mission's secondary school in Hoihow, but it was nothing like the student demonstrations on the mainland. China was in the midst of a political upheaval and the Hainan missionaries did not see the larger picture when they so quickly urged that an indemnity be collected for the Byers family, even though among themselves they held different views on the issue. As Miss Moninger pointed out, the issue was, if they sought an indemnity it would be extracted by Chinese officials from the poor people who lived around Kachek, who had nothing to do with the murder, and who had not asked the missionaries to come to live among them, but if the missionaries did not seek an indemnity then the lawless faction in the Hainan population would think they were free to attack foreigners whenever they wanted.[51]

When the PCC in Shanghai heard that the Hainan executive committee had voted to seek an indemnity, they immediately protested that the committee was not authorized to take such action, but that the PCC was. And in New York members of the BFM differed on the issue of an indemnity since it might jeopardize mission work, not only on Hainan but elsewhere in China. Ironically, none of the Presbyterians seemed to realize that when the American consul asked Mrs. Byers for her claim he was following government policy which was always to claim an indemnity, if only to maintain the right to do so.

It is unclear on what day the indemnity was first discussed officially by the mission executive committee and who brought it up. Action by the Hainan mission on the subject is mentioned by Jenkins on 26 July, but the official minutes of the Hainan mission indicated it was discussed on 29 July. In his 26 July letter to Schurman, Jenkins reported that the Hainan mission had passed resolutions seeking an indemnity of $20,000 gold for Mrs. Byers and her children, but again noted that Chamberlain had been instructed not to seek an indemnity at that time. Jenkins wrote that he personally thought an indemnity should be demanded but left the amount to the decision of the legation and the department. He further noted that Chamberlain was seeking "to induce the Chinese authorities to offer a large reward for the arrest of Lin Shu-piao and other bandits" since Chamberlain believed that would "be more effective in securing the capture of these criminals than the present half-hearted search that is now understood to be going on." Jenkins ended by noting he thought it useless to take the case up with the Canton authorities because although Hainan was "nominally under the control of the [General] Ch'en Chiung-ming faction . . . in my opinion the Hainan authorities are entirely independent and such pressure as we may resort to should be applied to them, for it is only through the local authorities that any results can be obtained." However, he noted he was writing to the American consul at Swatow asking that he take the matter up with the general, urging him to use whatever influence he had on Hainan, although Jenkins realized this might be useless. Jenkins also asked legation personnel to "consider the advisability of corresponding formally with the Peking government, which I presume in a legal sense may be held responsible for the outrage."[52]

The official minutes of the 29 July 1924 meeting of the Hainan mission state that the missionaries first sought "the apprehension and punishment of the guilty parties" and second "the settlement of an indemnity." The missionaries were concerned that they would not be able to work in the interior stations until the matter was settled and felt "very strongly that there should be an American consular officer on the ground until this case is satisfactorily settled; and that the presence of a gunboat at Hoihow or Kachek would aid very much to bring about a settlement."[53]

The mission also noted that Dr. Bercovitz had been in Kachek alone since Chamberlain's departure four days earlier and if Bercovitz were not heard from by the following day, the mission would "recommend his return to Hoihow at once." Chamberlain had recommended that the road between the mission buildings in Kachek be closed, but the mission deferred taking any action on the recommendation. The minutes stated,

> in regard to the removal of General [*sic*] Ho [Chia-yu] from Kachek we feel unable to advise. While we favor his removal if there is sufficient force to carry it out, the failure of an attempt to do this would leave the situation in a worse condition than at present. There seems to be a fairly accurate report that one of the General's subordinates is a lieutenant of Lin Shu-piao who is credited with the murder of Mr. Byers. It is also reported that this officer secured his position by the payment of a large sum of money and there is little probability that Lin Shu-piao can be arrested while this lieutenant is in the employ of General Ho.[54]

Mrs. Byers pointed out to the BFM that only members of the Hoihow and Nodoa stations were present at the mission meeting when the resolution on the indemnity was passed. She personally opposed the resolution which, she wrote, "was passed without my knowledge and without any Kachek member being present." (Misses Moninger and McCreery were then in Hong Kong on vacation and Dr. Bercovitz was in Kachek.) Mrs. Byers felt the Kachek members would have opposed the indemnity being raised locally because it would have injured their work, and because

> the amount should be $30,000 instead of $20,000, thus providing an income of $1800 a year besides children's allowances. I argued that I would have to pay $50 a month or $600 a year for rent, and hire help for some years to come. . . . While I am perfectly able to earn my own living . . . I am absolutely unable to earn a living and keep house as well.[55]

The resolutions of the mission were transmitted to Jenkins by Bristow on 1 August and he noted he was "in general agreement" with them. He, too, thought Dr. Bercovitz should leave Kachek and noted that telephone communication was impossible. "It is by no means improbable that the alleged interruption of the line is merely an excuse to prevent communications." Bristow went on to detail for the American consul the political situation in Hainan.

> Colonel Ho Chia-yu was in command at Kachek when the Byers murder took place, and he was the official directly responsible for the protection of the Mission. He had even received a few months before special instructions from Kiungchow to take extra precautions to guard the Mission on account of the increase in brigandage.[56]

Bristow noted that although Ho was clearly to blame,

> no attempt has been made to reprove him, much less to fix the responsibility upon him. Nor has any official notice been taken of the fact that his Lieutenant, Ch'en Yun-liang, was formerly one of the subordinates of the brigand Lin Shu-piao, who is known to be anti-Christian, and is strongly suspected of complicity in the Byers murder. This lieutenant is, no doubt, still in touch with his former chief, and probably keeps him well posted on official plans. Colonel Ho's supine attitude since the murder confirms this idea.

Bristow further suggested that the arrests of Ho and Ch'en Yun-liang were essential, but the missionaries were correct when they pointed out that there "might not be sufficient force available to affect the arrests, even if the Hainan authorities would consent to attempt anything so opposed to their own interests. If Ho got wind of such an intention, he and his men would doubtless join the brigands en masse." Bristow concluded that unless Ho and Ch'en Yun-liang were dealt with

> it seems to me that the whole case might as well be dropped at once, with a possible exception of a claim for indemnity, as promiscuous arrests and executions of unarmed villagers, now taking place, contribute in no way to a settlement, and merely antagonize the people, thus sowing the seeds of anti-foreign disturbances, and prejudicing the future work of the Mission. I do not intend on my own responsibility to demand any action against Colonel Ho. The possibility of a general debacle in the Island, with possible need for forcible intervention, is a problem for the American government to face.[57]

In the United States on 27 July Miss Schaeffer reported to the BFM that she had received a letter from Miss Moninger detailing how the ground had been torn up by Byers's resistance. Miss Schaeffer expressed the opinion that "the motive is greed and not animosity against the church or any individual. All people suffer alike Christian and non-Christian." When the Rev. George T. Scott responded to Miss Schaeffer on 5 August he noted the BFM had received only one letter from Hainan giving them details of Byers's death. He expressed the hope that the other members of the mission were not in danger, adding, "You Christian missionaries in Hainan have troubles enough without having added fears for your personal safety from bandit outrages."[58]

On 30 July from Shanghai where she was about to embark for America, Mrs. Byers wrote Jenkins formally asking that an indemnity be sought. Her letter was written on the advice of the Rev. Tappan and a Dr. Peter, who had recently returned from the United States where he had arranged for the balance of the Boxer Indemnity to be returned to China. The men had urged her to ask for $50,000 and "strongly opposed" the restriction that the indemnity be raised locally, since to do so would allow the Chinese government to "disclaim all responsibility."[59] From the wording and topics referred to in Mrs. Byers's letter requesting an indemnity, it seems likely that it was composed by the Rev. Tappan who signed it as "concurring." The letter reviewed the details of the murder and noted that as the ransom note for $20,000 [Mex.] was found

> we therefore assumed that a desire for ransom money was the only cause of the outrage. When we consider the fact that unpunished outrages against foreigners and missionaries seem daily on the increase; that Chinese officials seem increasingly lax and indifferent in their regard for the safety of foreigners; that despite their apparent indifference for our well being, more and more Chinese, some of them these very officials are yearly availing themselves of the advantages offered by mission schools, by the Rockefeller foundation, by the millions of money given by the American churches and citizens for Christian and altruistic work abroad; and also that America has just remitted to China the balance of the indemnity fund, it would seem imperative that the Chinese government be made to realize its duty regarding the protection of foreigners. In this connection I would call attention to my sworn statement which tells of the behavior of the soldiers sent to guard the house after my husband's death.

Mrs. Byers asked for an indemnity of $50,000 gold, noting that she had four children and a fifth due in two months. She detailed her expenses at $3000 for the trip home; from the BFM she would have received $20,800 in allowances for the children until each was of age; the family's salary until retirement would have been $23,400 (and retirement would have been at full salary) for a total of $47,200. She noted that the United States government estimated her family would need an income of $3000 before it was subject to taxation and that this was about the same amount the BFM would have paid her at home (that amount was $2900), and to produce that amount yearly she needed capital of $50,000 or about the same amount the BFM would have paid the family. She noted she was taking up the matter of the children's allowances with the BFM and if they agreed to pay them, she would then want $30,000 as an indemnity. She closed by noting that she was requesting the indemnity as a private citizen and not as a member of the mission.[60]

Mrs. Byers and her children departed Shanghai 3 August and arrived in the United States on 22 August via the SS *President Pierce*. They were accompanied by the Rev. and Mrs. Ura Brogden who had recently resigned from the Hainan mission.[61] Two days after Mrs. Byers departed China, the official report of her husband's death was sent to the American secretary of state and to Milton J. Purdy, judge of the United States Court for China in Shanghai. The report noted that Mrs. Byers was the executrix of her husband's will and that she had taken all of his possessions with her when she left China.[62]

Pregnant and newly widowed Mrs. Byers with her four children arrived at the San Diego home of her friend, Mrs. Ina Rittenhouse, who would provide free a small house for them to live in for the months to come. Shocked by the brutal murder of her husband, Mrs. Byers did not know that her struggle was just beginning. In the months ahead, with just three weeks rest following the birth of the daughter, she would write constantly to the BFM and to members of Congress trying to spur them to action. Sustained by many friends who could not understand why no action was being taken, she had to deal with their questions while trying to discern the meaning of inaction in Washington and in New York. Events were to move slowly, but Mrs. Byers persevered until the case was finally settled.

3

The Extraterritoriality Case

FROM HER NEW HOME IN SAN DIEGO, CALIF., MRS. CLARA BYERS EMBARKED upon intense letter-writing about her situation just weeks after the birth of her daughter, Georgia, in September 1924. Eventually her efforts resulted in both the United States government and the Presbyterian Board of Foreign Missions (BFM) taking action to resolve the matters of the indemnity for the loss of her husband and the support of herself and her children. Although spurring both organizations into action took many letters and involved a series of convoluted turns she could not have anticipated, Mrs. Byers did not cease her efforts. She repeatedly begged the BFM to pressure the government to take action, and by asking the president of her husband's alma mater; her former employers; and various relatives, friends, and supporters to write their respective congressional representatives, she was able to command enough attention in Washington to move the United States government to action in China after the months of delay that followed U.S. Vice Consul C. B. Chamberlain's departure from Hainan.

Vice Consul Chamberlain Returns to Canton

At the end of July, Chamberlain was ordered to return to Canton where he submitted to U.S. Consul Douglas Jenkins a written report detailing the situation in Hainan. Chamberlain stated that the island was under the autonomous military administration of General Teng Pen-yin, whose headquarters were at Kochow, Kwangtung, on the mainland. Teng was once a subordinate of General Ch'en Chiung-ming, who was then fighting the Canton government, but "the only existing relationship between the two movements seems to be sort of an alliance, as Teng certainly takes no orders from Ch'en."[1]

Chamberlain continued that the officials in Hainan assured him they were entirely independent and owed no loyalty to the Peking government, nor any other government of China. He reported that Chief of Staff Ch'en Tan-shu was the top official on the island which was divided into several military areas. Chamberlain had been told that the officer in charge of commanding troops in each of the areas "actually exercises all authority." In Hainan Chamberlain had informed the Chinese that a "trial before a court with an American assessor would be required for all criminals implicated in the Byers case who might be apprehended." The vice consul also reported that General Ch'en Feng-ch'i, who was headquartered at Hoihow, had dispatched four hundred troops to Kachek on 4 July, and "several proclamations were issued by the Kiungchow headquarters, condemning anti-foreign activity, offering small rewards for the arrest of the murderers of Mr. Byers and giving instructions to subordinate officials to press the case." Chamberlain had left Hoihow on 5 July and arrived in Kachek two days later. He found the area around Kachek "to be in a state of serious disorder with banditry rife." Colonel Ho Chia-yu and his subordinates who were responsible for the area "appeared to be hopelessly inefficient, incapable and corrupt," and the vice consul indirectly attributed Byers's death to them, recommending that Ho be removed from his position.[2]

The vice consul was pessimistic about the Chinese capturing the murderers as he reported that before he arrived in Hainan the officials seemed to have made "no move" in that direction. After his arrival, Ho and the district magistrate, Wang Ta-feng, "offered a reward of $2,000 [Mex.] for the capture of each culprit connected with the murder." Chamberlain continued that "as a disciplinary measure, I insisted that a non-commissioned officer and five soldiers of Ho's command, who had been conspicuous in neglect of duty in regard to the Byers case be punished. They were ultimately flogged, discharged and deported from Hainan."[3]

Chamberlain noted that after General Ch'en Feng-ch'i arrived in Kachek he took charge of the situation and "numerous arrests were made, but no suspects connected with the Byers case were taken." Although Chamberlain wanted the arrest of Lin Shu-piao he noted

> this was not accomplished, due probably to the lack of cooperation between the local civil authorities and the military and the general inefficiency, although Lin was frequently reported to be in the immediate neighborhood of Kachek. It is felt that this man should and could be captured and that his arrest and eventual execution would have the most valuable moral effect through the Island of Hainan.[4]

On 18 July General Ch'en Feng-ch'i had "sixteen men accused of various crimes executed," an action the vice consul found "questionable," so he "caution[ed]" the general that "innocent persons not be punished, as injustice would react against American interests, even though Americans were not directly concerned." The report concluded that Chamberlain left Kachek on 19 July and arrived in Hoihow the following day where he suggested to officials that a reward of $10,000 [Mex.] be offered for Lin's arrest. He also urged that General Teng Pen-yin be advised to come to Hainan to attend to the matter. He noted that Ch'en Feng-ch'i seems "well-intentioned but . . . lacks authority." The vice consul also reported he "learned from Kachek that activity decreased and banditry increased after I left. This was discouraging but anticipated." As a consequence he advised the American missionaries to remain in the coastal cities until the case was settled. Chamberlain anticipated that it would not be quickly settled and finished his report with his opinion that it was "absolutely essential" an American official "familiar with China" be present in Hainan until the case was resolved.[5]

Forwarding this report to Peking, Jenkins noted that the reports of both Chamberlain and H.B.M. Consul H. H. Bristow indicated "the entire island of Hainan is infested with bandits or at least with disorganized troops at outs with the military actually in charge." Both also described local civil and military authorities as "incompetent and disorganized" and expected them to do nothing unless an experienced American official stayed in Hainan until the case was settled.[6]

For his superiors in Peking, Jenkins tried to explain the complicated political situation in Hainan. Repeating the information he had received from Chamberlain, Jenkins wrote that it appeared that General Teng Pen-yin seemed to be in nominal control of the Hainan forces. General Teng was hostile to the Canton government, but friendly to General Ch'en Chiung-ming although it "is safe to assert that General Ch'en . . . exercises no real control on Hainan." General Teng's subordinates were "free agents" according to Jenkins who echoed Chamberlain's opinion that the Americans would accomplish nothing "if we resort merely to correspondence with the nominal commanders-in-chief."[7]

With his report Jenkins enclosed Mrs. Byers's sworn statement about the murder and expressed his opinion that it had been "unusually cold-blooded and brutal" and that the action of the soldiers sent to protect her was "outrageously incompetent and cowardly."

Apparently from talking with Chamberlain, whose written report contained no mention of these sentiments, Jenkins informed his superiors that the missionaries on Hainan were "not prepared to say that Mr. Byers was killed as a result of anti-foreign feeling," but they did feel "there is considerable anti-foreign sentiment amongst the Chinese population." Jenkins continued that the mission schools had had a student strike the previous winter and that a large number of students had left or been expelled and noted, "Some of these students are believed to have had a share in stirring up anti-foreign feeling," although he admitted he had no definite evidence of such activities.[8]

Jenkins thought that important facts about the murder could be obtained if Lin Shu-piao could be arrested. But the consul was not hopeful noting that although no one involved in the Byers case had been arrested there had been "numerous arrests and many executions" as a result of "unsystematic" raids the authorities had conducted in the countryside, adding "it is generally feared that many of those executed were innocent people and that if this practice keeps up the reaction against Americans will be unfavorable, if not actually dangerous."[9]

He also informed the Peking legation that he had been in correspondence with the U.S. consul at Swatow who had responded that General Ch'en Chiung-ming "is no longer in active command of his forces and may not be in a position to influence the Hainan authorities to any great extent." Jenkins cautioned that the Hainan situation was "complicated and difficult" and advised that if another American diplomat were to be sent there he should "be a man of good judgment and one who has already had experience in handling cases of this sort." He then suggested that one of the legation's army language officers or another experienced diplomatic or consular officer be sent.[10]

Jenkins continued that an American man-of-war would be of great assistance in the matter, but noted that Hainan had no safe port and any naval vessels anchored there were in danger of typhoons. Other problems were that Jenkins knew of no officer in the South China Patrol who had experience in dealing with Chinese officials, Kachek was seventy miles in the interior, the trip had to be made by boat and horseback, and the "route is dangerous." Further complications were that there was no reliable telephone communication between Kachek and the port and "the ordinary mails . . . are slow and somewhat irregular" with ten days required for the Canton office to send a letter and get a reply from Kiungchow with even more time required to reach Kachek. The difficulties the consulate had in dealing with the case were further evidenced when Jenkins ended by apologizing that the proper Chinese names were not included in his letter "owing to the absence of the Chinese staff."[11] Clearly, the Byers case was not going to be resolved quickly and smoothly.

While the diplomats were writing official communications about the unstable conditions on Hainan, the BFM received specific information of those conditions. The Rev. William Leverett, a member of the Hainan mission who was home on furlough, wrote on 7 August that he had received a letter from Mrs. Margaret Melrose dated 4 July stating that the Rev. David S. Tappan had telegraphed from Kachek that brigandage was rampant around the town of Tintai, where the largest Kachek out-station was located. According to the Rev. Tappan, the village had been looted, "seventeen mission schoolboys kidnaped and one killed."[12]

The Hainan Missionaries Pressure the American Consulate

The missionaries in Hainan were very concerned about Mrs. Byers's situation and the continuing unrest on the island. On 19 August Dr. Nathaniel Bercovitz wrote to the BFM that conditions were not good on the island and the missionaries hoped the BFM and the United States government would "keep up pressure in the case, for to let such a flagrant outrage go unpunished will mean the jeopardizing of the entire missionary work in all China. We are not seeking revenge, we are seeking adequate protection against outlaws."[13]

Bercovitz wrote the BFM again a week later giving his view of the situation in Kachek since the vice consul's visit. The doctor noted he had shown his letter to the members of the Hainan executive committee before he mailed it. His readers in New York must have been astounded at the level of civil unrest he reported. Clearly, the situation in Hainan was out of control. In the letter Bercovitz noted Chamberlain found that nothing had been done "toward apprehending and punishing the criminals." The military official who was in charge of suppressing banditry had "encouraged gambling and other vices" and was "hand in glove with the bandits" one of whom was now in the employ of the official, having paid $10,000 [Mex.] for the position which he used to oppress the people of his district.

Bercovitz wrote the officials had done nothing to apprehend the murderers and added, the missionaries' situation on the island was "much worse than at the time of Mr. Byers's death."[14]

While the vice consul was in Kachek, Bercovitz noted, "There were wholesale captures of people from villages, and a few thieves were captured with others. But the real bandits all escaped." The doctor added that both the officials and the missionaries knew the location of the bandits who were operating within twelve miles of Kachek while the vice consul was there, but the officials had done nothing to capture them. The doctor continued that while in Kachek with the vice consul the local military official had captured about eighty people, had shot sixteen on one day, and had executed an estimated forty people altogether, adding "some of these were robbers, and deserved their fate," but most were " 'small' robbers, [and] the big bandits, and the men who killed Mr. Byers were not captured." Bercovitz thought there was little anti-foreign feeling in the region since Chinese were the victims of most robber attacks. During the seventeen days the doctor was in Kachek "many villages were raided by bandits, and many people robbed, kidnaped, wounded and killed." He had taken care of wounded people from several of the villages that had been raided, citing among his patients, seven wounded from one village where four men had been killed, and nine wounded in another village where eleven had been killed.[15]

The doctor went on, "From this you can see that the trouble is not primarily against us or against the Christians. I believe that if the proper officials were to be in Kachek peace could be easily restored, and we and the Chinese could live in peace as we have done for so many years." When word from the Hainan mission's executive committee and the vice consul reached Bercovitz urging him to withdraw, he was already preparing to do so because the military official who had been sent to settle the Byers case was leaving, and his departure made it, in Bercovitz's estimation, "absolutely unsafe to stay." As the doctor departed Chinese Christians moved on to the mission compound to protect it. According to these Christians there were only a few "poorly trained" troops in Kachek, sixteen of whom were on the mission compound located about three hundred yards outside the market gates, which were kept closed most of the time since robbers were operating within three miles of the town. The doctor ended by writing, "the local officials are trying to consider the incident closed, and want us to return to the interior and resume work," but he thought that would not be wise even though the station was engaged in an extensive building program adding to the existing structures which were estimated to be worth over $100,000 [Mex.].[16]

Having dispatched his letter to the BFM, Bercovitz sent a similar one to the U.S. consul in Canton on 1 September. In that letter he included more specific details of the brigandage around Kachek. He wrote that he had spoken to many people who had arrived at Hoihow from Kachek and had received several letters from there. These reports stated nineteen men had been kidnapped from cars at Doalou, a market fifteen miles from Kachek; the village of the district magistrate had been attacked, nine people killed, and the police disarmed by a large band of robbers, identified as belonging to Lin Shu-piao's band; and the whole country was "terrorized." Bercovitz went on that the military commander of the Kachek region was still in Hoihow and when the doctor met the commissioner for foreign affairs on the street one day he told Bercovitz the commander was awaiting reinforcements. With the recent defeat of the Hainan governor on the nearby Liuchow peninsula of the mainland, Bercovitz thought the reinforcements would not be forthcoming. He noted, "the officials . . . are not moving a finger to relieve the situation . . . due either to their impotence or because they are in with the robbers. I feel that the latter view has much on its side." Even had Byers not been murdered, Bercovitz wrote, the situation in Kachek was so unsafe that the missionaries would have had to call on the consulate for protection.[17]

Bercovitz continued that during the previous four days different people had come to the missionaries telling them that suspects in the Byers murder were in the Vunsio district. He also reminded the consul that one day while Chamberlain was in conference with the district magistrate a letter had been received from a person who said if soldiers would go to a "certain shop at a certain time in the evening" they could arrest the murderers. The district magistrate had sent the information to his counterpart in the area where the men were supposed to be and that was the last that was heard of the matter. Now Bercovitz reported two men had told another of the missionaries, the Rev. William Stinson, that the men responsible were two Hainan natives and two non-natives, and that two of the men were armed and two unarmed. Bercovitz noted there were more than four hundred robbers in that district, and then added, "We have taken no action on this information because the officials don't seem disposed to do anything in the matter, and we are leaving it to be handled directly from the American Consular office."[18]

He continued that another man from the same district, "a man in whom we have very high confidence, a man who we have known for many years, and who is at the head of the Mission work for that district, and who had not seen the other two men" brought them almost the identical information about the culprits, and noted this was also the information Chamberlain had been given. Bercovitz reported the missionaries did not think the "end of the chase is in sight," but he found the information "very suggestive." The missionaries were holding the information until an American official arrived, for as Bercovitz wrote, "there is no use to pass it on to the Chinese officials without an American official, backed by a warship, on the ground. The only good it would do would be to warn the suspects, if not to give them help in escaping."[19]

In the meantime, the diplomats continued to pursue ways to resolve the Byers matter. On 27 August Jenkins cabled to Peking that the British consul in Hainan had written that Colonel Ho Chia-yu, "military commandant at Kachek whose negligence believed largely responsible Byers murder said to contemplate resigning and leaving Island. Consul and missionaries believe this should be prevented if possible." Jenkins reported he was asking Bristow to do everything proper in the case and also informed the U.S. Minister Jacob Gould Schurman that the British consul suggested the American legation approach the Chinese foreign office as Hainan authorities were then nominally under Peking's control.[20]

This was the second suggestion that the Chinese foreign office be informed of the murder, so the American legation in Peking took it and on 3 September Edward Bell wrote to V. K. Wellington Koo, minister of foreign affairs, about the incident. Koo was informed that although Chamberlain had spent nearly a month in Hainan making "continued and earnest representations" the "Chinese authorities have been 'very dilatory' and had not arrested the murderers even though their names were well known to the officials." He pointed out that prior to the murder, Colonel Ho had been asked to take extra precautions to guard the mission, but he ignored this request and his superiors appeared not to hold him responsible for his actions. Bell continued that he had now learned that Colonel Ho was about to resign and leave the island and wanted Koo's help in preventing that until Ho's conduct had been "thoroughly investigated." Koo was also informed that all local efforts to have the murderers arrested and punished had been fruitless, and, consequently, Bell was "constrained to hold the Chinese Government fully responsible for bringing the murderers to justice and for the fulfillment of whatever other terms of settlement, including financial compensation to the family of the murdered man, may appear to be just to my Government." He also requested that he be informed as quickly as possible what actions the Chinese government intended to take to resolve the matter.[21]

Jenkins in Canton did not know of this action when on 6 September he again cabled Peking that the missionaries and the British consul were urging "action by our Government without delay." He asked for a telegraph on the "prospects of experienced officer and Man-of-War being sent to Hainan in near future." The following day Bell cabled Jenkins that he had contacted Koo about the murder.[22]

On 9 September Bell wrote to the secretary of state informing him of all the recent correspondence about the case and stating he had had no reply to his note to Koo. But on the following day, which was Diplomatic Reception Day at the Chinese foreign office, Bell called on Koo. Bell brought up the Byers murder and the note he had sent "which Dr. Koo said he had read." Bell reported that Koo's response to a question on the status of Hainan Island was "not very clear" but "seemed to indicate . . . there was at least some tenuous connection between the Central Government and Hainan." Bell thought Koo's answer was "a confession of impotence on the part of the Central Government," so informed Koo that "as the Island had nothing to do with the Canton government it would be necessary to look to other means, if the Central Government could do nothing, to obtain satisfaction." Bell also informed Koo that "the American missionaries kept asking for an American man-of-war to be sent" to Hainan. Koo replied that he would investigate the matter and determine what could be done to arrest the murderers, adding that it was a "serious case." Bell asked for a reply from the Chinese government as soon as possible.[23]

The Hainan Missionaries Try In-Person Appeals

While the American government was pursuing these diplomatic measures, the missionaries on Hainan, who were uninformed about them, decided they needed to take more direct measures if the Byers matter were ever to be resolved. In early September the missionaries dispatched H. M. McCandliss, M.D., to Canton, to see Jenkins about the matter. Dr. McCandliss then traveled to Shanghai to attend meetings of the Presbyterian China Council (PCC) where he discussed the matter with other members of his church who were serving in China. In reporting the McCandliss visit to Bell, Jenkins noted it had been three months since the murder and as "conditions are growing steadily worse" in Hainan preventing the missionaries from returning to the interior stations, they want to know "what action they can reasonably expect from our government." Jenkins again asked about the possibility of sending a gunboat and an experienced officer to Hainan. He suggested they could send the USS *Helena* which was expected to return to Canton from the Philippines about 25 September or the USS *Asheville* which he thought would be free to visit Hainan unless it was needed at Shanghai.[24]

Shortly after McCandliss's visit to the Canton consulate, the executive committee of the Hainan mission wrote again to the consul about the conditions around Kachek. They reported their information was from a trusted Chinese who had been in charge of the Kachek compound. He reported confusion throughout the countryside. Every market town and village of any importance had been robbed, some several times. Lin Shu-piao, the leader of a band of over one hundred armed men, was responsible for much of the unrest. Colonel Ho Chia-yu still had two hundred soldiers in Kachek, sixteen of whom were on the mission compound. The colonel had shot four men as robbers, two of whom were over seventy years old and all of whom were known to have been innocent. The Chinese man who gave the missionaries this report had been told by the district magistrate, Wang Ta-feng, the names of the men who had killed Byers. The Chinese informant also related that the names of the murderers had been given by a robber, who had been arrested, to General Ch'en Feng-ch'i who then had the man shot, despite the fact that Vice Consul Chamberlain had asked that all witnesses in the Byers case be detained.[25]

Lin Shu-piao's bandits raided District Magistrate Wang's home village, but Colonel Ho had done nothing and General Ch'en Feng-ch'i had left for another part of the island. Ch'en Yun-liang, who had been one of Lin's lieutenants, joined Ho's army as an officer and later returned to Lin with a large number of arms, even though Chamberlain had asked that Ch'en Yun-liang be watched for just such reason. The Chinese reported Ho was in with the bandits and the missionaries thought that was "probably correct."[26]

The report continued that the bandits responsible for Byers's death were operating seven to ten miles from the mission property. The bandits acted "unchecked" and felt immune from interference by the authorities. None of the demands of Chamberlain had been carried out except the posting of the sixteen men on the mission property which, the missionaries admitted, would be useless if the bandits attacked. The missionaries reiterated that if the Byers murder went unpunished, there would be no safety for the Americans living in Hainan nor for their property valued at several hundreds of thousands of dollars, even though they were protected by treaty.[27]

The lack of action on the part of the American government was beginning to wear on many people. In mid-September Bristow in Kiungchow transmitted a personal note to Jenkins containing a translation made by the missionaries of a Chinese circular which gave the names of the murderers. Bristow noted that "the mission work is all at a standstill until your government sees fit to take some interest in the murder of an American citizen." In sending this note to Peking, Jenkins indicated he knew his superiors would find it "anything but pleasant reading," but added he did not think it had been "sent in an unfriendly spirit." Rather he believed Bristow shared the opinion of the missionaries "that our government has been very slow in taking any definite steps toward securing satisfaction for the murder of Mr. Byers." He ended by expressing the hope that the legation would soon be able to tell him what they planned to do about the matter.[28]

On the same day that Jenkins was sending his message to Bell, Bell was writing to Jenkins in response to the dispatch of 9 September. In his communication Bell regretted there was neither an experienced consular officer nor a language officer available to send to Hainan, as they were needed elsewhere. Bell indicated he had discussed the availability of a warship, particularly the USS *Asheville*, with Admiral Thomas Washington, commander-in-chief of the U.S. Asiatic Fleet, but had learned the admiral could not spare the ship which he needed in Shanghai. The admiral did think once conditions in Shanghai stabilized, he would be able to send a ship to Hainan. Bell ended his note with the information that the Rev. Tappan of the Hainan mission was then in Peking and had called several times to discuss the case. He also noted the Rev. Tappan was about to leave for Shanghai to attend a conference there.[29] (Tappan had evidently remained at Shanghai or Peking after seeing Mrs. Byers embark for the United States as there was not sufficient time for him to have traveled to Hainan and back in the interim.)

On 26 September, three months and two days after the murder, the Department of State informed James Byers of Chula Vista, Calif., of his brother's death.[30]

On 4 October, a month after his first note to Koo, Bell sent a second one stating "the work of the Presbyterian Mission in Hainan is completely suspended owing to the non-settlement of this case. I earnestly request Your Excellency to inform me at the earliest possible moment what steps are being taken to secure the arrest and punishment of the murderers of Mr. Byers." Koo finally responded on 9 October acknowledging the note of 3 September and stating that a telegram was sent to the chief military officer in Kachek asking him to investigate the case and "issue prompt instructions to apprehend the murderers and administer severe punishment to them." Koo also reported he had sent a second telegram urging prompt action after receiving Bell's 4 October note.[31]

In Hainan on 3 October, Bristow sent a message to the Chinese administrator of the island detailing the information the missionaries had sent to the United States consul on 16 September and adding that he knew the chief witness in the case had been executed despite the fact that Consul Chamberlain had particularly requested that the man, Li Tse-hsiang, be kept as a witness for the murder trial. The British consul expressed his amazement that

> the Chinese authorities not only have done nothing to capture Lin Shu-piao and Mr. Byers's murderers, but have actually executed one of the principal witnesses in the case, have allowed an ex-bandit to take a supply of Government rifles to his chief, while the military officials have gone off in other directions, leaving the principal bandit unmolested.

Bristow wrote he felt sure the administrator did not know these facts.[32]

Clearly disgusted with the inaction of the United States government, the British consul sent an English translation of this communication to Jenkins in Canton along with a note which read, "In case you may still be interested in the Byers murder case . . . the only witness so far secured has been executed."[33]

The PCC and the BFM Turn Up the Pressure

The Hainan missionaries had decided that they alone were not going to convince the United States government to do something about the continuing unsettled conditions on the island and so sought reinforcements for their struggle.

Policy matters for Presbyterian missions in China were discussed periodically by the PCC which met in Shanghai. The PCC had been established to function as a clearinghouse for matters of concern to all the church's missions in the country and to establish priorities for filling requests for funds and personnel before they were transmitted to the BFM in New York. It was to the PCC that the Hainan missionaries now turned.

Dr. McCandliss, who had visited the Canton consulate; the Rev. Tappan, who had been at the American legation in Peking; and Miss Margaret Moninger converged on Shanghai in October 1924 to discuss the Byers matter with the PCC at its regular meeting. The Rev. Tappan was the Hainan mission's representative to the PCC. While in Shanghai Miss Moninger wrote to her family that "all this trouble in the north and around Shanghai and in Peking does not look very promising for us as far as getting a consul and a cruiser in Hoihow any time soon."[34]

Just how much the inaction on the part of the American government had disrupted the work of the Hainan mission was evident when Miss Moninger wrote her family that the Canton mission had requested that the PCC assign her to their mission. The transfer did not occur because the executive committee of the Hainan mission refused to approve it, fearing it would be a tacit admission that they would not be returning to the interior and would thus weaken their case with the government. They were also afraid that "the temporary transfer might become permanent." Miss Moninger was acknowledged by her colleagues as an extremely capable woman who was highly skilled at both written and spoken Chinese, so this attempt by the Canton mission to obtain her services was likely seen by the Hainan missionaries as an attempt to skim off one of their best workers during their time of difficulty.[35]

On 10 October the PCC wrote the American legation pointing out that the situation in Hainan had not changed. They noted that in the three months since the Byers murder the bandits were "continually within ten miles from Kachek except when on a raid," and that they seemed to think they were immune from action by the military. Although Vice Consul Chamberlain had visited Hainan none of his requests were met except the posting of a small guard on the mission compound. The missionaries of Kachek and Nodoa had had to withdraw and if the crime went unpunished it would harm the work not only in Hainan, but elsewhere in China. They also pointed out that at the funeral of the Rev. Byers the acting governor of Hainan "spontaneously declared the equity of a claim for punishment of the criminals and of the payment of a suitable indemnity; and other Chinese also clearly recognized that action is to be expected from the American government." The PCC had decided the government needed to exert steady pressure on the Chinese and send a consular officer to Hainan to remain there until the case was settled. The PCC informed the legation they were cabling a shortened version of their letter to the BFM so it could take the matter up in Washington.[36]

On 11 October the Rev. Arthur J. Brown, executive secretary of the BFM, telegraphed the secretary of state that the Rev. J. Walter Lowrie, chairman of the PCC, had informed him by cable that Nodoa and Kachek had been abandoned and the mission property was threatened and that there had been no settlement of the case. The Rev. Brown requested that a settlement be expedited. J. Butler Wright, assistant secretary, writing for the secretary of state, informed Brown on 14 October of the receipt of his note, acknowledging that no one connected with the murder had been arrested, but adding that the noncommissioned officer and the five soldiers who had been sent to guard Mrs. Byers had been punished and discharged. He also said the department would consider any recommendations the legation might make about sending an official to Hainan.[37]

When an advance copy of the minutes of the PCC was circulated among church personnel, it indicated the PCC approved the action already taken by the Hainan mission, and concurred with the policy of the BFM not to seek an indemnity because of the effect it would have on mission work. Because of this policy, the PCC expressed its opinion that the BFM had a special responsibility to take care of Mrs. Byers and her children.[38]

Meanwhile in Canton the beleaguered Jenkins, now pressured not only by the inaction of his superiors in Peking but also by the demands of the Hainan missionaries and the British consul in Kiungchow, had the problem of sending an official to Hainan on his mind when he wrote Bell. Jenkins enclosed the 6 October note from Bristow, which had informed him that the chief witness had been executed and implied that the United States government was no longer interested in the case, and stated "I consider this letter from Mr. Bristow insulting and do not propose to acknowledge it. I feel sure the Legation will approve of my position in this respect." Jenkins went on to inquire if, in view of the pressure he was getting from the British consul and the missionaries, the legation could let him know what it thought of his suggestion to send a consul and a naval vessel to Hainan.[39]

In New York the Rev. Arthur J. Brown at the BFM learned that Minister Schurman was then in the city and so tried to reach him by telephone. Failing that, Brown sent Schurman a letter with a copy of the telegram the BFM had just sent to the secretary of state. Schurman had returned to Washington but got Brown's letter and replied that he had had discussions with Assistant Secretary of State John Van Antwerp MacMurray and a member of the staff of the department's solicitor's office. Schurman indicated no decision had been reached but thought Brown would hear from the department "in due course."[40]

On 20 October the BFM received a cablegram from the PCC "requesting early settlement" of the Byers case, which it referred to its executive committee. On the same day Representative Ernest R. Ackerman [5th District, N.J.] wrote to the secretary of state on behalf of friends of Mrs. Byers, asking about the case and the indemnity.[41]

Following up its cable to the BFM, the PCC sent New York a written report of their lengthy discussions of the Byers matter. They had voted to send a letter to the legation in Peking emphasizing the need to have the criminals brought to justice and the missionaries returned to Nodoa and Kachek, and requesting a consul be sent to Hainan to remain until the matter was settled. The PCC opposed the request for a war vessel to be stationed in Hainan. Two days after that letter was sent the Rev. Lowrie, wanting a response to his earlier cable, again cabled the BFM asking what action had been taken.[42]

Perhaps sensing that the matter was reaching a turning point, in late October Ferdinand Mayer at the legation in Peking transmitted to the secretary of state the dispatches from Jenkins, his instructions to Jenkins of 23 September, and copies of his notes to the minister for foreign affairs along with the reply.[43]

In New York as preparations were being made for the meeting of the BFM's executive committee, the Rev. George T. Scott, the executive secretary, wrote to Mrs. Mabel L. Roys, who was on a speaking tour, about the action the committee might take. Mrs. Roys, the widow of a China missionary and mother of one, had from the start been a staunch supporter of Mrs. Byers claiming the BFM had an obligation to the Byers family. Scott informed Mrs. Roys that the

Rev. Brown was proposing a minute for adoption by the executive committee and noted Brown was "quite adverse to 'urging' the United States Government to do this and that, which largely accounts for the mild, moderate phraseology of the action." Mrs. Roys responded, "I do wish the minute could be less mild. But I bow to Dr. Brown's judgment. 'Urge' is decidedly the thing I feel our Board should do. But perhaps it is more diplomatic to be 'assured' that no urging is necessary!"[44]

After months of inaction by the United States government, the BFM began to exert greater pressure on the Department of State. The Rev. Scott wrote to the secretary of state on 29 October pointing out that two mission stations with valuable American property had been abandoned by consular order because of the "extreme danger" to the lives of the Americans serving them. Scott again asked what action the government was taking and reported the BFM had received another cable from the Rev. Lowrie in Shanghai asking about the matter. Scott noted that the situation "naturally causes deep concern and anxiety" to the missionaries and their relatives, friends, and supporters as well as to the BFM. He asked for a reply by 3 November when the BFM was going to meet again and when "some formal action will doubtless be taken."[45]

The Department of State Acts

The pressure of the BFM and Representative Ackerman, the second congressman to inquire about the case, finally prompted Acting Secretary of State Joseph Grew into action. On 1 November he wrote Ackerman of the department's actions and then cabled the legation in Peking that the BFM reported the Rev. Lowrie of the PCC had suggested to the legation that a consul be sent to Hainan to settle the Byers case. If the legation had received Lowrie's report, Grew wanted their recommendations. Having sent that cable, Grew, mindful of the impending 3 November meeting of the BFM, telegraphed the Rev. Scott in New York that he had

> telegraph[ed] the Legation at Peking to submit promptly its recommendations concerning the suggestion stated to have been made to it by your PCC that a Consul be sent to Hainan for the purpose of taking further measures in the Byers case and obtaining adequate protection for your missions in Hainan.

Before the telegram was sent Grew crossed out a further sentence, "Pending the receipt of the Legation's recommendations, the Department regrets that it cannot see its way to act upon the PCC's suggestions," so that the message was more positive. It seems that Grew, at least, did not want the BFM to formally discuss the inaction of the Department of State in the Byers matter.[46]

The BFM met on 3 November and passed a resolution expressing regret that the Hainan missionaries had had to abandon the Kachek and Nodoa stations due to the "increased lawlessness" following Byers's murder. The BFM's resolution further stated they were "gratified" to know the Department of State considered the matter serious and consequently hoped it would take appropriate measures to guarantee "the safety of the life and property of its citizens engaged in peaceful pursuits in Hainan." Following its meeting the BFM cabled the PCC asking them to keep in touch with the legation in Peking concerning the Byers case.[47] The BFM had carefully omitted any mention of the indemnity in its official statements, since it continued to oppose the collection of one for the death of one of its missionaries, and communicated this position to the supporters of Mrs. Byers who continued to press for an indemnity.

After months of inaction, on 6 November Mayer at the Peking legation suddenly found the personnel to deal with the case. He cabled Washington that he had indeed received the requests for action from the PCC and from the American consul general in Canton. He cited the shortage of personnel for the inaction but wrote that one man was leaving soon for Canton and once he arrived to take over the work, Vice Consul Maxwell M. Hamilton would be sent to Hainan as soon as the navy could provide a ship. Mayer suggested that Hamilton remain in Hainan until the matter was settled, then asked for the concurrence of the department so that he could make the necessary arrangements with the navy and the Canton consulate. That concurrence was cabled by Secretary of State Charles Evans Hughes on 13 November.[48]

Unaware that the United States government was finally going to take action, the Rev. Wilbur Campbell, on behalf of the executive committee of the Hainan mission, wrote on 13 November to the Rev. Charles Patton at the PCC that nothing had changed since the three Hainan missionaries had been in Shanghai to meet with the PCC. The situation around Kachek was still unsettled and Lin Shu-piao continued "wreaking vengeance" on the villagers. The executive committee had written a letter of commendation to Bristow and informally requested the PCC send a copy of it to the British legation in Peking. They also suggested that the PCC get in touch with C. T. Wang who had been one of the secretaries of the Shanghai YMCA when Mrs. Byers worked there prior to her marriage. From Shanghai on 22 November, the PCC telegraphed the American legation in Peking that looting and killing was taking place within a half mile of the now unguarded Kachek compound. The PCC wanted to know what action the United States government was taking.[49]

Mrs. Byers, living in California, had heard nothing of the meeting of the BFM on 3 November when on the 19th she sent a telegram to Mrs. Roys that she would "gladly relinquish indemnity" if they would take the responsibility for supporting her. She also asked if she should have senators bring pressure to bear. Upon receiving the telegram, Mrs. Roys wrote to Mrs. Byers indicating she was leaving for a trip in less than an hour, but stated if Mrs. Byers knew a senator "who can tactfully bring pressure to bear" she should contact him, but cautioned, "you will understand the harm an unwise person might do in this regard. Some senators would in a ruthless way do actual injury to our work if they attempted to play into the game." She expressed "limitless confidence" in Mrs. Byers and felt "perfectly safe in saying, 'go ahead if you think it wise.' "[50]

Then on the 24th, Mrs. Byers wrote again to Mrs. Roys stating that friends in Hainan informed her about conditions there and she felt she must do something to help them, but realized she could not without pressing her own case. She added that some of her friends had written to Senator Selden P. Spencer of Missouri and Representative Ackerman about the case and they had asked her to write them more fully with the details. Expressing a desire to speak directly to both the secretary of state and President Calvin Coolidge, Mrs. Byers wrote, "I have no polite language in which to express my opinion of a government that at the end of five months of 'careful consideration' of a question like this one still does not know what to do." She indicated governments knew what to do when public persons were involved, but if nothing were to be done for a private American citizen,

> then it is a question affecting every American citizen residing abroad. The consul at Canton has shown no interest whatever. The Legation, when Mr. Tappan called, were interested, but did not "know what to do next." Has the State Department no authority to COMMAND the Legation to take action?[51]

Mrs. Byers repeated that Chamberlain arrived on Hainan in a gunboat but it left him there "without any force to back up his demands. Naturally, the officials, who are probably in league with the robbers, did nothing but speak fair words. The United States government is losing more prestige each day that it delays." She reported that the robbers continued to operate in and around Kachek. Expressing Christian forgiveness, Mrs. Byers wrote, "Somehow, I do not feel much bitterness against the men who perpetrated the crime—that is, I CAN say, 'God forgive them for they know not what they do.'" Yet she continued that she did

> feel a bitterness against the Kachek officials, who are laughing up their sleeve[s] at our helplessness and I feel a deep and lasting rage against our government. It seems absolutely incredible that after five months they are still "carefully considering." The truth is that they are utterly indifferent, and will remain so until some political influence forces them to do something.[52]

Mrs. Byers thought that perhaps her friends could bring some pressure to bear on the Department of State that the BFM "as a religious organization, would hardly care to exert. Certain it is that I won't be throwing them any bouquets in diplomatic language if I do go for them. They need some dynamite instead of compliments for what they have done." She continued that she was frequently embarrassed by questions as to why the BFM and the government took no action. Many people had offered to contact congressmen to help, and she had had to explain that the BFM did not want individual help solicited, adding that the questioners did not understand that, either. She suggested that Department of State officials should be sent to sit in Hoihow for five months if they wanted to "carefully consider" as that "might change their viewpoint." Mrs. Byers ended by stating that she now felt that the "exacting of a payment from those who have it—who are not the Chinese Christians—the officials and robbers are in possession of all the wealth in Hainan now—will not harm the work a whit more than the present policy of doing nothing." The arrival of this letter at the BFM was enough to cause them to take action. Mrs. Roys's handwritten note at the top of Mrs. Byers's letter was "Dr. Scott read this and is today writing to State Dept., Dec. 3."[53]

Mrs. Byers also wrote to Senator Spencer noting she knew him to be in sympathy with the work of the mission and she had a "pleasant friendship with his son's family in Canton." She sent him her statement of what had happened and her claim against the Chinese government. She reported that the BFM had agreed to support her, but noted that the larger question was the apprehension of those responsible for the murder who continued to threaten the missionaries. She wrote, "Five months of entreaty to the consulate at Canton, the legation at Peking, and the government at Washington have brought no results whatever." She found their indifference "incredible" and felt it was time they realized they could not evade their duty and she had "a right to demand that the men who killed my husband and [who] are now endangering the lives of the other missionaries be taken into custody at once," concluding "I somehow feel that if Mr. Coolidge and Mr. Hughes were personally approached on the matter, we might get action." She also noted her friends had written to Representative Ackerman and to Mr. Case, president of the Federal Reserve Bank in New York, about the case.[54]

On 26 November Mayer in Peking responded to the Rev. Lowrie at the PCC stating he had sent a cable to the effect that a consular official and a warship were to be sent to Hainan at the "earliest possible opportunity" which was expected to be about 1 January. Mayer noted that the legation was very concerned about the Byers case and conditions in Hainan, but "due to the present extraordinary conditions in China . . . it has been heretofore impossible again to send a Consular officer to the island." However, Vice Consul Hamilton was being dispatched with a warship which was to remain for some time.[55]

The same day that Mayer was writing to the PCC, the PCC was writing to the U.S. consul general in Shanghai, to the effect that there were then no Americans in Kachek, and the mission property there was now reported unguarded. The PCC also informed the consul general that since the telegraph to Hainan rarely worked, they communicated with the missionaries in Hainan by cabling the Hongkong and Shanghai Bank in Hong Kong which then sent the cable by mail to the missionaries at Hoihow.[56]

Mayer in Peking cabled to Hughes on 30 November detailing the plans he had made for resolving the issue. Mayer also telegraphed the commander-in-chief of the American fleet asking for a warship to take Hamilton to Hainan and remain there for several weeks or return from time to time to assist him. The commander-in-chief replied that he had a ship available at Hong Kong on 3 January, and it "can remain a few days after landing the vice consul if necessary but

I do not desire to keep her on an indefinite stay." Mayer insisted it was "useless" to send a consular officer without a warship that could remain in Hainan's harbor for at least several weeks and return from time to time to assist him. Mayer also noted Schurman was planning to meet in Shanghai with Admiral Washington and Captain Smith, the American naval attaché at Peking, and he would discuss the matter there. The diplomats' view that missionaries were not of primary concern to them again surfaced when Mayer noted that Jenkins reported Hamilton was the only experienced assistant he had available and to send him to Hainan for two or three months would "seriously cripple" the Canton consulate at a time when conditions elsewhere in their district were also unsatisfactory. Despite Jenkins's plea that someone else be sent, Mayer decided to send Hamilton, noting that he could find no one else and indicating he hoped Sun Yat-sen's departure for the north would ease the situation in Canton. From Washington on 3 December Hughes cabled his approval.[57]

From Shanghai on 3 December the Rev. Lowrie for the PCC wrote to the American minister in Peking telling him of the continued unrest around Kachek and the withdrawal of troops from the mission compound: "Our American comrades there do not desire the use of violent measures but only such administration of justice as proves the Chinese Government to be caring for the situation and committed to the observance of treaty provisions."[58]

In New York on 3 December the Rev. Scott wrote the Department of State asking that the BFM be constantly advised of the department's actions as many people inquired of them about it, noting these inquiries were "increasingly frequent and insistent." On the same day Senator Spencer wrote the secretary of state asking about the case on behalf of Mrs. Byers. Spencer drew the secretary's attention to the fact of his China experience and that his family had lived near Canton for many years, noting,

> I fully concur in what Mrs. Byers writes that the only possible effective action to be taken is through a determined display of force. The very presence of British gun boats of light draft cruising on the Chinese rivers, gives to Englishmen a protection which, unfortunately, the citizens of the United States do not have in China.

Spencer's letter included a three-page statement from Mrs. Byers detailing the case. She stated that there were thirty missionaries and fourteen children on Hainan, the mission investment was "upwards of one million dollars," and they were currently in "the midst of a large building program." She described the privileged position of foreigners in China by writing that although Hainan had suffered "plundering and killing, kidnaping and holding for ransom" which had grown steadily worse, the Chinese all thought the foreigners were safe from the unrest. She noted, the missionaries had

> come and gone at will, and [had] thought that our immunity was due largely to the bandit's high regard for the strong arm of the American government. Being entirely successful in their attacks upon the Chinese and meeting with no resistance from the officials, the bandits have now grown bolder, and seem to fear no one.[59]

Frustrated by the inaction of the United States government, the BFM was willing to allow Mrs. Byers more freedom to seek action. Replying to Mrs. Byers's letter of 24 November Mrs. Roys wrote that "it awakened responsive chords in my heart. You cannot possibly say anything about our Government and its inactivity and indifference which is profane enough to express my sentiments." She reported that the Rev. Scott had written again to Washington and that the previous evening she had dined with an unnamed former consul general in China to whom she had related the situation, "because I trusted him wholly not to bungle the matter, I presented in detail the awful situation of inactivity in Peking in the face of the dire need in Hainan." She told Mrs. Byers "if you have any influential political friends whom you can trust with so delicate a commission, I hope you will urge them to bring pressure to bear in Washington."[60]

Meantime Hughes wrote Mayer reviewing the case and noting the legation had sent a strong protest to the Chinese government holding it responsible for the resolution of the matter. He added that the districts around Kachek were in "a state of serious disorder with banditry rife . . . the military administration was inefficient and incapable" and had not arrested Lin Shu-piao due to "the lack of cooperation between the local civil authorities and the military and the general inefficiency." He stated that the department felt that the murder of Byers was "due to the inefficient administration of civil and military affairs [on Hainan] . . . and the lack of serious effort on the part of [the] authorities to safeguard the lives of Americans" considering the "state of disorder" and "activities of the brigands" around Kachek. He acknowledged that the loss of Byers's income to his family could be stated at about $45,000 until his retirement and that the family had a "right to be reimbursed for the shock caused by the severance of family ties and the atrocious character of the crime." After serious consideration the department decided that $25,000 gold "would constitute a reasonable indemnity to Mrs. Byers and her children." One of the reasons that amount was decided upon was their desire to "induce" the Chinese government to appreciate the "reasonableness of the demand" and thus "make a prompt settlement of this claim." Mayer responded to Hughes's message on 15 December sending the instructions he had given the naval officers and Hamilton.[61]

As the case dragged on, Miss Moninger in Hainan wrote in late 1924 that the missionaries had learned that Vice Consul Hamilton from Canton was expected to arrive in January to try to settle the matter. "We are hoping that the officials will get busy and produce the men wanted soon so we can go back to the interior stations."[62]

The question of an indemnity for the death of the Rev. Byers continued to be a very difficult one. Jenkins was instructed by Mayer that Hamilton was to go to Hainan and impress upon the Chinese "the gravity" with which the United States government viewed the murder of Byers and the general disorder on the island. Measures needed to be taken to "remedy existing conditions" so that American lives and property would be assured "a reasonable degree of safety." The details of how this was to be accomplished were left to Hamilton since Mayer was unfamiliar with local conditions. He stated that General Teng Pen-yin whose headquarters were at Kochow was in charge of Hainan and the consul was to insist that he personally go to Hainan or delegate full authority to his subordinate on the island to handle the matter. Since the names of the murderers were known, Hamilton was to insist that they be arrested, "a trial held with Mr. Hamilton in attendance," and, if guilty, they be punished. Colonel Ho Chia-yu, the officer in charge at the time of the murder, was guilty of "gross negligence" and Mayer thought he should be punished or at least removed from office, but as the Peking legation had information that he was no longer in Hainan Mayer was unable to give definite instructions. However, if Ho were still in Hainan he "should be . . . dismissed from office in the most public manner possible in order that the public may be aware that such action was taken as a result of his conduct in the Byers case." Mayer viewed Mrs. Byers's request for $50,000 gold as "in excess of the indemnity demanded in other cases of the loss of life of American citizens at the hands of Chinese" so he would not support the demand, but the Chinese government would be asked for a suitable sum.[63]

Secretary of State Hughes directed the American consulate in Shanghai on 15 December to confer with Admiral Washington and Captain Smith with regard to what help the navy could provide in resolving the Hainan matter.[64]

More Congressmen Become Involved

Apparently taking the suggestion of Mrs. Roys to seek help from trusted friends, Mrs. Byers wrote to John B. Brown, superintendent of the Indian School in Phoenix, Arizona, asking him to write his congressman on her behalf, and informing him that Senator Spencer and Representative Phil D. Swing [11th District, Calif.] were interested in the case. Mrs. Byers had written her letter on 13 December and five days later Brown wrote to his congressman Carl Hayden [At Large, Ariz.] asking his help on behalf of Mrs. Byers who had worked for Brown as a secretary twenty years earlier in Morris, Minnesota. Hayden forwarded Brown's letter to Hughes on 23 December.[65]

On 15 December when Hughes replied to Senator Spencer's 3 December letter, he reviewed the action the department had taken and reported that Schurman was due in Shanghai within a few days where he would confer with Admiral Washington and Captain Smith on the action to be taken in Hainan. Hughes took exception to Spencer's statement that British citizens in China were better protected than Americans due to the presence of British warships, by stating that the U.S. Navy also cruised the Yangtze River with its Yangtze Patrol, which was under the command of a rear admiral, and had the South China Patrol in the vicinity of Hong Kong and Canton. "Unfortunately, almost all of the American vessels are of insufficient power and of too great draft to be suitable for the adequate protection of American interests in these parts of China." He further noted that the department supported the request of the navy for "new river gunboats specially designed to meet conditions in China," and that the bill for the appropriation was then under consideration by Congress. Such gunboats, he stated, were "imperatively necessary" to safeguard American interests in China and give them the same protection British and Japanese citizens had. The secretary sent a similar, but shorter letter to Representative Ackerman on the same day.[66]

While Hughes was writing these letters, MacMurray wrote to the Rev. Scott at the BFM informing him that the department had ordered that a naval vessel take a consular officer to Hainan to handle the matter, and that the meeting between Schurman and the naval officers was scheduled. MacMurray also stated that the department was requesting a $25,000 indemnity. The BFM then sent a coded cable with this information to the PCC in Shanghai. Upon receiving the cable the Rev. Patton, representing the PCC, wrote to Edwin S. Cunningham, the U.S. consul general in Shanghai, informing him of the cable from the BFM and offering any help he might desire.[67]

On 21 December Mrs. Byers wrote to Representative Swing about the situation. She asked him to contact the BFM concerning the question of her support and the request for an indemnity. She also wrote there was a second issue involved, namely, "the capture of the bandits and cleaning up of the robber dens, making it safe for the American citizens in Hainan to resume their peaceful occupations." She continued that the mission and the BFM were trying to pressure the Department of State "to send an *experienced* consular officer backed by *authority* to Hainan to compel the officials to capture the men who killed my husband and who are now constituting a reign of terror throughout that region." She reported the consul had ordered the missionaries to the port and then did nothing for six months. She noted the island was only one hundred fifty miles long and one hundred ten miles wide and the bandit homes were well known to the authorities. She wrote,

> There is no reason why they should not be taken into custody except the laxness and indifference of the local officials and the timidity of the military. I personally think probably the local officials have been bought off by the bandits and promised freedom with a share of their loot as the price for immunity.

She related that Vice Consul Chamberlain was only twenty-three years old and the gunboat that had transported him to Hainan had returned to Canton saying it was out of coal. Friends in Hainan reported to her that another inexperienced official was being sent, but "We want an *experienced* consular officer, and enough American force behind him to force the Chinese officials to take notice." She reported that the missionaries were unable to return to their homes and work, "the schools are closed, the hospitals, which normally treat many thousands of patients each year, are also closed, the entire work is disorganized and the American property, worth many hundreds of thousands of dollars, is threatened." She noted the local Chinese were in "constant terror" and expected the American government to come "to the rescue and make the island a safer place to live." She continued that Hoihow was a treaty port and that French, German, and English warships frequently called there, but only two American ships had stopped there in the previous forty years. She also noted there were French and British consulates on the island, but the German consulate had been closed since the war. She pointed out that "if the officials were made to apprehend and punish the head bandits, round up the robbers who are looting in that vicinity, strengthen their military guard and give a promise to keep order in that region, the missionaries could resume their work." She also thought a financial demand would deter future outrages, but was willing to give that up if the BFM would support her. She noted that the BFM was willing to have help in the matter since the Department of State was doing nothing and noted that it would be appropriate if a California representative helped her as there were five Californians in the mission.[68]

On the same day Mrs. Byers wrote to Mrs. Roys telling her that Representative Swing had been contacted by a Mr. Marston, who was a friend of the congressman and "the leading merchant of San Diego, a man well known for his Christian principles." She reported that Representative Swing had told her he was ready to "act aggressively." Mrs. Byers wrote,

> The thing that puzzles me is the fact that though the [BFM] undoubtedly has more acquaintance [*sic*] among influential men in Washington than any private citizen could possibly have, it has not yet been able to get action. Is it because they take the attitude that as a religious organization they do not wish to take an aggressive attitude—that they must deal entirely with weapons that are not of this world?

She indicated she thought the BFM could use its influence with persons in the Department of State, and thought "it would seem an easy thing to get the ear of Mr. Hughes or Mr. Coolidge." She could not believe "these men would be deaf to an appeal." Indicating she was puzzled with the BFM's inaction she expressed her belief that they "could set the whole thing in motion themselves did they but realize the necessity." She had learned the previous evening that Consul Hamilton, who was the son of the pastor of the First Presbyterian Church in San Diego, had written his parents he was going to be sent to Hainan. She also knew Hamilton was only in his twenties and wrote, "I wish it could be branded into the consciousness of the State Department that we need an *E X P E R I E N C E D* man backed up by sufficient *F 0 R C E* to compel the Chinese officials to listen and act. It is no time for soft diplomatic language."[69]

In Shanghai Consul General Edwin S. Cunningham wrote to the Rev. Patton on 22 December saying the conference between the diplomats and the naval officers had been concluded on the 16th and the matter was in the hands of the Canton consul general. Cunningham asked Patton to send him any records the PCC might have that might be of use to Hamilton, who would proceed to Hainan in January.[70]

Schurman cabled to Hughes on 22 December that the navy would transport Hamilton to Hainan during the first week in January. A week later he reported he had instructed Hamilton to request $20,000 gold as an indemnity since there was "consistent failure of the authorities to suppress brigands," failure to "protect missionaries and apprehend criminals," and actual hardship suffered by the Byers family. He noted Mrs. Byers wanted $50,000 gold and the mission board had set $20,000 gold as a minimum.[71]

On 24 December Mrs. Byers telegraphed Mrs. Roys that the Department of State had informed her that they would seek $25,000 gold as an indemnity and asked what the BFM wanted done. Mrs. Roys replied that the action was being taken without consultation with the BFM.[72] (See chapter 5 for a discussion of the BFM's position on the issue of the indemnity.)

Mrs. Byers ended the year by writing to Mrs. Roys that she was surprised that the Department of State had presented her claim to the Chinese government as she had heard nothing more about the matter since she had presented her claim in July to the Canton consulate. She was not even aware that anyone in Washington knew of it. She reminded Mrs. Roys that she had informed the BFM of her action at that time, then added,

> It would be interesting to know just how their minds worked to finally settle upon the sum of $25,000. I was especially anxious that you should not get the impression that any of my friends had anything to do with the presenting of this claim, as I had very definitely told them all that we

> would do nothing whatever in the matter until we got the final [BFM] action on our allowance.

She continued that she was not optimistic about the conference with the naval officials which had been held in Shanghai, because she thought the Department of State was trying to shift its responsibility to Schurman and Admiral Washington. She added, "I hope these gentlemen do not drop it altogether." If the government continued to do nothing, she was in favor of the suggestion of Mrs. Lillian Kelly, a former member of the Hainan mission, that the California churches petition Congress and Coolidge for action.[73]

It had been six months since the murder of the Rev. Byers, but as the year ended it appeared that finally the United States government was going to take action. Mrs. Byers clearly did not think her government would be effective, but she did not know of the many letters and cables concerning the case that had been sent. All those involved in the case hoped it would be resolved in the new year.

4

The Indemnity Is Collected

U.S. CONSUL DOUGLAS JENKINS ON 3 JANUARY 1925 WROTE TO VICE CONSUL Maxwell M. Hamilton giving him instructions from Minister Jacob Gould Schurman in Peking, for the action to be taken in Hainan. Hamilton was to remain on the island until he accomplished his task or until he received orders to leave. He was permitted to travel to Kachek or other places on the island or the mainland, but was cautioned to ensure that "local authorities provide you with a safe and sufficient escort." Since the matter of an indemnity was not yet settled, Hamilton was to make no demand to local authorities for one until "specific instructions are received." However, he was allowed to say that an indemnity likely would be requested. He was cautioned that there was no decision to use force and no "American naval or armed forces will be landed for the purpose of taking part in any expedition" without specific orders from the secretary of state. However, Jenkins hoped the naval commander accompanying Hamilton would fire the customary consul's salute when landing and the commander was permitted to accompany him in his formal call on Chinese authorities.[1]

As the year began, the Hainan missionaries were confused as to exactly what was happening. On 4 January, Miss Margaret Moninger reported that the vice consul and his party were due to leave Canton for Hainan. The missionaries had learned from the BFM that it "would give Mrs. [Clara] Byers a sufficient income if she would make no claims as a private citizen for indemnity," but they also had received "a cable from Shanghai that the Department of State was asking for [a] $25,000 gold indemnity. We do not know whether that is at Mrs. Byers's request or whether the government is doing it itself. If indemnity is collected there is always danger that the innocent bystander will have to pay it instead of the guilty ones."[2]

Vice Consul Hamilton sailed from Canton on 3 January, left Hong Kong on the 5th and arrived in Hainan two days later, but rain and mist prevented him from landing until the evening of the 8th. He later wrote, "a consul's salute of seven guns was fired before I left the ship, but was not particularly effective because of the distance of the ship from the port."[3] The missionaries were told by the consul that he was "sent here directly from Washington, a representative from a friendly power to a friendly power to see about an unfriendly act." They were also told that the indemnity was demanded from Washington as a government matter.[4]

Hamilton later reported that between Chamberlain's departure and his own arrival,

> robber bands pillaged and terrorized the interior districts and the practice of carrying off natives and holding them for ransom became general. Due to the state of terror, there occurred a decided falling off in the planting of crops and the tillage of the soil, while the emigration of coolies to various foreign ports increased. The officials on the island, both civil and military, took no effective measures to suppress lawlessness.[5]

Two days after Hamilton disembarked at Hoihow, the Rev. J. Walter Lowrie, secretary of the Presbyterian China Council (PCC), arrived from Shanghai to attend the annual meeting of the Hainan mission and to offer the missionaries his moral support. Lowrie, who had had forty years' experience in China, stayed in Hainan four months as Hamilton expressed a desire to have "his counsel from the standpoint of the [BFM] and the mission."[6] Because of the mission practice of always leaving at least one person or family at each station when the others departed, all the members of the mission previously had never met together. But with the interior stations temporarily closed and everyone living at Hoihow/Kiungchow all members were able to attend the annual mission meeting held in January 1925. The only members missing were the Rev. William Leverett and Mrs. Byers who were in America and destined not to return to Hainan.[7]

After calls on foreign officials and businessmen on 9 January, Hamilton conferred with the executive committee of the mission. As he later reported to Jenkins communications with the USS *Abarenda* were difficult because the ship's launch could reach the wharf only at high tide which was in the early forenoon and only for about six hours. Captain Davis, Ensign Beard, and four sailors landed on the 10th and accompanied Hamilton to call upon Chinese officials on the 12th, but "no mention [was] made of the nature of the mission upon which I had come to Hainan." The vice consul also called upon Chief of Staff General Ch'en Tan-shu, whose headquarters were at Kiungchow, and whom the consul found "pleasant and affable." The general said he would return the call on the 13th. Hamilton learned that General Teng Pen-yin, who controlled the island, had his headquarters near Pakhoi, on the mainland.[8]

Hamilton also called on General Ch'en Feng-ch'i, who had been elevated to the position of general for police defense, and who was not then on the best of terms with General Ch'en Tan-shu. Hamilton thought Ch'en Feng-ch'i was the real military power on the island and described him as "illiterate, unscrupulous in his methods and generally feared by the populace." When Ch'en Feng-ch'i accompanied Vice Consul Chamberlain to Kachek, he had "terrorized the natives, killed many without seeming to make much effort to ascertain whether or not they were guilty and exacted tribute from the villages through which he passed." Hamilton found that conditions had not improved since Byers's murder and, given the friction between the two Generals Ch'en, there was "little promise for an early return to peace and quiet."[9]

The Rev. Lowrie, who had accompanied Hamilton on his call on General Ch'en Feng-ch'i, also disliked the general. In a lengthy report on his sojourn in Hainan which he sent to the BFM, Lowrie wrote the general had had a number of men "ruthlessly executed," and had collected a "considerable sum of money" from the people.[10]

The arrival of the vice consul was a positive sign for the missionaries and Miss Moninger wrote home that Hamilton seemed to indicate that for the American government to consider the matter settled, the murderers would have to be arrested or proof given that they had left the island, the bandit who had made trouble and "indirectly threatened Miss [Katherine] Schaeffer" had to be captured, the Kachek military official had to be degraded in rank, and the indemnity arranged. Miss Moninger thought only the indemnity would hurt the common people.[11]

Pressures Continue in the United States and China

With the sending of Hamilton to Hainan, the Department of State was anxious that those interested in the Byers case be informed that action was being taken. Accordingly, the acting chief of the Division of Far Eastern Affairs, F. P. Lockhart, informed the BFM of the department's actions on 7 January. On the same day Assistant Secretary of State John Van Antwerp MacMurray wrote to Representatives Ernest R. Ackerman and W. C. Hawley informing them of the department's actions and the amount of the indemnity sought, and Secretary Hughes sent the information to Representative Carl Hayden.[12]

But in California on 7 January some Presbyterian women, unaware of the events transpiring in Washington and Hainan and unhappy with the slow pace of the government, decided to take their own action. Mrs. Lillian Kelly, who with her husband had served in Hainan for nearly a decade earlier in the century, had asked to discuss the Byers case at a meeting of the Women's Missionary Society of the Presbytery of Los Angeles. Mrs. R. W. Cleland, who headed the society, originally tried to prevent the discussion in the absence of consent from the BFM, but Mrs. Kelly and Mrs. Byers arrived at the meeting with the letter from Mrs. Roys in which she suggested Mrs. Byers carefully exert some pressure, so Mrs. Cleland agreed to have the matter discussed, provided that any resolution passed be sent to the BFM for approval before going to Washington. The resolution of the women stated the mission work in Hainan was at a standstill with schools, hospitals, and chapels closed, and Chinese Christians "being killed almost daily." They also noted that the Hainan missionaries had appealed to the Canton consulate, the legation at Peking, and through the BFM to the Department of State to have an experienced consular officer with a naval vessel sent to the island to bring pressure on local officials "to capture the bandits who are terrorizing the island and thus make it safe to resume work in the interior." The women expressed their belief that both "Chinese Christians and the law-abiding citizens in Hainan are bitterly disappointed that America had not come to their assistance long ago," and warned that the "dilatory tactics" of the Department of State were jeopardizing the lives and interests of Americans in China, which they felt would "invite deeper trouble which may eventually interfere with our peaceful relations with that great people."[13]

Mrs. Byers sent a copy of the women's resolution when she wrote Mrs. Roys on 9 January, adding Mrs. Cleland was traveling to San Francisco and could get other church women to bring the matter up. Mrs. Byers hoped that the government was truly going to take action, but if it did not she again wanted to know the BFM's opinion of "initiating a movement in the churches to bombard the President or Secretary Hughes with letters begging them to act." She noted there were now seven Californians in the Hainan mission so she thought the churches would be willing to act on their behalf. She continued, "There seems to be an opinion prevalent that if the government is going to insist that missionaries obey consular orders and desert their stations, they must on the other hand, take steps to render the district safe." She thought if the government took no action the missionaries should be allowed to stay at their own risk, but noted in that case the Department of State needed to make "a clear pronouncement . . . [that it] had no foreign policy of protection" of citizens. She thought it unfair that the British consul compelled the missionaries to live at the port for six months as he has no authority to protect them or change conditions.[14]

Mrs. Byers continued that there was unanimity of opinion among the people she had talked to about the situation, that if it had involved the British they "would have straightened things out long ago." She also noted that congressmen were willing to support her request for an indemnity from the Chinese government but "their ardor cools so considerably when they find out that it is the other thing we want [the territory cleared of bandits], that it lends color to the constantly repeated conviction that the government does not care what happens to its missionaries." She hoped for the future of mission work in China that the government would take some action, because if it did not she feared there would be "no safety anywhere in China."[15]

She also reported she had received a letter from Hainan dated 8 December which said Hamilton would arrive on a battleship about 1 January, but a letter from Secretary of State Hughes, which Senator Spencer had forwarded to her, said this had been decided at a meeting in Shanghai on 16 December. She continued that she was disappointed that Vice Consul Hamilton was being sent as he was only twenty-eight years old, and "certainly does not fill the order for an 'experienced' consular officer." She went on that she did not think any money would be paid but did not see "how any special punishment can be meted out to these brigands unless a fine is imposed. I think, more than other countries, China is affected by what touches her pocket book. It was this that the mission had in mind last summer when they wanted $20,000 collected as a punitive measure." She felt that even if the indemnity were returned to the Chinese "in another form" it would have a "salutary . . . effect upon those lazy, gambling lying officials in Kachek market."[16]

She concluded that the American government was trying to deal with Peking, but she wished "it could realize the fact that Hainan is an entity in itself." She admitted that the island was nominally under the control of Kwangtung province but described it as "really a law unto itself," stating her belief that its distance from Peking meant officials there would not be concerned about the matter. She asked Mrs. Roys to telegraph Mrs. Cleland in San Francisco if the Department of State had not taken any action. Mrs. Roys responded on 16 January, and three days later wrote to Mrs. Cleland, that because of the arrival of the vice consul in Hainan, the BFM thought it was unwise to seek resolutions or letters of support from the churches at that time.[17]

In the meantime another person, the Rev. William S. Abernathy, minister of the Calvary Baptist Church in Washington, D.C., became involved when he wrote the BFM asking about the case. One of his parishioners, a cousin of the Rev. Byers, had told him about it. The clergyman wanted to know if Byers had been a BFM missionary, or one of the Southern Presbyterian Church's. He was concerned because he had heard the murder had taken place in June, the American government had done nothing about it, and the bandits "are openly bragging that they killed an American and no notice was taken of it." On 10 January the Rev. George T. Scott replied to the Rev. Abernathy saying that the earlier consular visit to Hainan was "not conducted with the finality that was desirable," attributing this to the fact that the vice consul was "young and inexperienced." He mentioned the recent conference in Shanghai between Minister Schurman and Admiral Washington and said he hoped the matter would soon be resolved. He also wrote that the BFM was seeing that Mrs. Byers and her children had "adequate support."[18]

The Situation in Hainan

Meanwhile in Hainan the missionaries "had a strenuous week of mission meeting" and then adjourned for three weeks while the vice consul went to Pakhoi to see General Teng Pen-yin. Miss Moninger, the dedicated letter-writer, detailed the missionaries' predicament. She described them as being "up against it" and indicated that some members of the mission were discussing closing one of the interior stations since they did not have enough personnel to staff both of them, as several people were due soon for furloughs and it appeared that the Rev. William Leverett would be unable to return from America because of ill health. She reported that Nodoa was the most likely to be closed, but that Mrs. Margaret Melrose, who had served that station since the 1890s, said she would resign and go home if that happened. Yet Miss Moninger thought Nodoa would be easier to close since it had two ordained native pastors who could do the work, while Kachek had none. Also, as the murder had taken place in Kachek it was important for the missionaries to return there as soon as possible to "save face." She indicated that they were happy Dr. Lowrie was visiting so he could "help us in our puzzles."[19] Yet as long as the Byers matter remained unsettled, the missionaries were unable to make any definite plans for the future.[20]

Meanwhile, the local authorities told Hamilton there was little likelihood that General Teng would soon visit the island, and as the vice consul thought it was useless to try to deal with local officials, he went to Pakhoi to see the general. Hamilton reported that Teng was commander-in-chief of eight districts including two, Kiungchow and Yichow, in Hainan. Although Teng had direct allegiance to General Ch'en Chiung-ming, he also recognized the authority of the Peking government and was in communication with it.[21] Before departing Hainan to visit the general, Hamilton wrote to Canton that the missionaries had received word from their PCC in Shanghai that the Department of State had decided to seek an indemnity of $25,000 and asked that official confirmation of the amount be sent to him.[22]

Hamilton's query about the indemnity snailed its way through the diplomatic channels until it reached Schurman who cabled Hughes on 23 January asking that he cable either Peking or Canton with the Department's position on the indemnity. Hughes had mailed a letter of instructions on 6 December and cabled Schurman about it on 6 January, but these had been either overlooked or not received by the legation, hence Schurman's repeated request for instructions concerning the indemnity.[23] On the 27th Hughes cabled the legation in Peking that an indemnity of $25,000 gold was sought, noting a larger sum could be justified, but this amount was decided upon to "induce prompt settlement."[24]

Meanwhile, Hamilton went to Pakhoi, arriving there on 14 January. The Rev. Lowrie, who was accompanying the consul, reported that they traveled from Chinchow to Pakhoi as General Teng Pen-yin's "invited companions."[25] They met with the general several times and he admitted he was responsible for the conditions in Hainan and acknowledged the concern of the American government over the Byers murder and the continued unrest on the island. The general promised to take immediate steps to correct the situation and issued orders to Generals Ch'en Tan-shu and Ch'en Feng-ch'i making them fully responsible for the capture of the murderers and the protection of the Kachek mission. Ch'en Feng-ch'i was to proceed to Kachek and put down "all the bandits" in the district and arrest Lin Shu-piao. Instructions, which called for the murderers "to be captured and the bandits defeated and punished without delay," were given to Hamilton by Teng for transmission to Ch'en Feng-ch'i. The consul also reported that General Teng agreed that Colonel Ho Chia-yu should be punished, but first assigned him to help in the capture of the murderers, after which a punishment would be carried out. The matter of an indemnity was broached to General Teng who first suggested it be collected from the Canton government or the central government, but then agreed to "the principle that an indemnity was just and should be paid by him." The general did not mention a specific amount for the indemnity, indicating he wanted to visit Hainan first.[26]

The extreme difficulty of resolving the case was evident when Hamilton learned from the acting French consul in Pakhoi that General Teng had had a meeting with some of the leaders of the Pakhoi community, described by the foreigners as the "Pakhoi Chamber of Commerce," on the question of an indemnity. The French diplomat reported that one of the general's representatives told this group that an indemnity of $60,000—presumably Hong Kong currency—had been demanded. (In reporting this Hamilton assured his superiors he had asked no specific sum.) According to the French diplomat, the men had been "advised that the general was not afraid of the American gunboat, whereupon the chamber decided unanimously that not a cent of the indemnity should be paid." The Frenchman also told Hamilton that General Teng was actively anti-foreign, but Hamilton had personally seen no evidence of it. The general promised to visit Hainan after Chinese New Year, and, although Hamilton realized this might have been an "effort to postpone action," he thought it was best to allow the general time for a visit. Because of the approach of Chinese New Year, Hamilton left Pakhoi for Hoihow to await the general's visit, indicating if he did not appear, Hamilton was prepared to return to Pakhoi. Writing to Jenkins in Canton, Hamilton indicated he thought it would be difficult to get Colonel Ho punished, and a request for an indemnity would cause trouble, so he had not pressed either point. He added that the navy was threatening to withdraw the USS *Abarenda* to duty near Shanghai, but he thought it was advisable to have the presence of a ship in Hainan waters until the matter was resolved and asked the captain Lt. W. C. Calhoun to convey this to Admiral Washington.[27]

Jenkins forwarded Hamilton's reports of 13 and 26 January to Schurman in Peking on 3 February and indicated he had received the telegram stating the indemnity was to be $25,000. With the reports, Jenkins indicated, that in view of General Teng's meeting with the Pakhoi Chamber of Commerce and his lack of fear of the American gunboat, it was going to be very difficult to collect an indemnity or to have Colonel Ho punished. Schurman in turn transmitted these reports to Hughes in Washington.[28]

While awaiting General Teng's return to the island, Hamilton met "almost daily" with officials in Kiungchow and Hoihow for discussions which were "friendly but unsatisfactory," as no efforts were being made to arrest the murderers.

> It became increasingly apparent that the administration of affairs on the island was so helplessly corrupt and inefficient that no improvement could be expected unless General Teng visited Hainan or entrusted the administration as well as the prosecution of the Byers case to more responsible and capable officials.[29]

At this point another American consul, C. J. Spiker of Swatow, entered the case at the request of Jenkins. Spiker sent to Hughes a copy of the dispatch he had sent to General Ch'en Chiung-ming. Spiker's predecessor had requested the general's help in the Byers case on 30 July 1924 and the general had responded on 15 August. Spiker noted that as General Teng was General Ch'en's subordinate he asked Ch'en to issue "fresh instructions . . . to effect a speedy settlement of this case," stating that to do so would maintain the friendly relations their two countries enjoyed. The general was informed that a $25,000 indemnity was being requested, and noted

> I can assure you that my Government will not allow this brutal outrage to go unpunished, and I am confident that you as a friendly high official of a friendly Government, will exert every effort to bring this most unfor-

tunate case to a satisfactory conclusion through your subordinates in Hainan.[30]

In late January Miss Moninger reported that the consul said he thought he would have to return to Pakhoi after Chinese New Year "to poke at the general some more before he accomplishes anything." Then on 8 February she reported the situation was beginning to wear on everyone including the captain of the gunboat. She wrote that the missionaries were "very doubtful" they could return to the interior, that Hamilton was "very discouraged" and was planning to return to the mainland if the governor did not soon arrive on the island, but that the USS *Abarenda*'s captain, Lt. Calhoun, who had been staying ashore with the Standard Oil man, was in worse condition. Miss Moninger reported the captain "was pretty nearly half-seas over [i.e., drunk] when he came to lunch at Mrs. McCandliss's the other day," and added "I guess the marines are not having much shore leave, which is just as well under the circumstances."[31] Hoihow, it must be noted, offered little amusement for sailors which would not have complicated the situation. The port lacked even a hotel, hence the captain's accommodation with the businessman. Vice Consul Hamilton and his wife most likely stayed with the British consul's family, as they did not reside with any of the missionaries. The Rev. Lowrie was, of course, accommodated by the missionaries.

The National Christian Council (NCC) of China Opposes the BFM's Action

A request for a gunboat to protect missionary rights and an indemnity for the loss of a life were touchy subjects to many in the missionary community in China, as the Presbyterians were to learn from the NCC. The NCC was composed of representatives of most of the Protestant mission groups working in the country, but generally represented the more liberal side of the mission movement. One of the NCC's secretaries, Rev. E. C. Lobenstine, wrote the BFM asking about their request for a consular official in a gunboat to go to Hainan and about the request for an indemnity. Lobenstine was opposed to both. He said there was "clear recognition of the difficult situation" of having workers in a "country where conditions are very disturbed." However, he pointed out that growing Chinese nationalism was causing many Chinese to question the privileged status foreigners held in China. He also indicated there was a "growing opinion amongst thoughtful, spiritually minded Chinese Christians that we missionaries should not keep silent" in cases such as the Byers's where the BFM appealed to the American government to send a consul in a gunboat to investigate the matter and secure compensation. He cited the charge that the missionaries could only propagate their religion with the help of their privileged position, and noted that the action of the BFM did nothing to counteract that charge.[32]

Lobenstine pointed out there was a "sharp division" among the missionaries over the correct thing to do, but after traveling in north China he had the impression that the money taken in the Boxer Indemnity for lost lives and property and to compensate Chinese Christians had done more harm than good. He thought that among the mission community there was a growing consensus that financial compensation should not be sought from the Chinese government when a missionary was murdered. If compensation were needed, he felt, it was the responsibility of the sending board to provide it. He continued,

> The intimate connection between gunboats and missionary preaching and education has always seriously complicated missionary work but never to anything like the extent to which this is true today. We are face to face with a much more difficult situation than has thus far confronted us and shall need to revise some of our ideas and plans in the light thereof.

He stressed he did not write to be critical of the action, but to express the impression it made on him.[33]

Following up this letter with another on 19 February Lobenstine indicated he had talked to the Rev. Charles Patton, who was a member of the PCC as well as NCC's executive committee. Patton told Lobenstine that Mrs. Byers had pressed the claim for an indemnity, not the BFM which was also opposed to sending a gunboat. Lobenstine reiterated he had not written to be critical, but was concerned about the last sentence in the BFM's report which said, "The PCC and the Mission will desire to continue to urge that proper and adequate measures may be taken by the United States authorities in China with any advisable pressure by these authorities upon the appropriate office in Washington." Lobenstine pointed out that the

American missionaries were going to have to rethink their relationship with their government on such issues as things they had done previously were clearly not going to be acceptable to the Chinese in the future and "it is important that both the Board and the Missions should be extremely guarded both in their actions and in formulating their policies in regard to matters like those referred to in this Minute."[34]

When the Rev. Scott replied to the letters of Lobenstine on 17 March he regretted that the BFM's China Missions Letter left the impression that it had urged the government to send a gunboat to Hainan because that is "exactly what the Board declined to do." He pointed out that the American government had informed them that it would "follow whatever course it believed wise in interpreting the rights of American citizenship overseas," but that the BFM had tried to make it clear to the government that its actions in protecting American rights and citizens "should be, if possible, a help rather than a hindrance to the Christian enterprise." Scott indicated there were many opinions among the BFM members on this issue as Lobenstine acknowledged there were many among the China missionaries. On the same day a note was added to the upcoming China Missions Letter that the BFM wished to make clear that they had asked the government only to take steps that would allow the reopening of the evacuated stations.[35]

Some Decisions in Hainan

Yet despite Lobenstine's reservations the matter was in the hands of the American government, Hamilton was in Hainan, and the indemnity was requested. Hamilton, in consultation with the missionaries, finally made some decisions about the compound at Kachek even though the matter with the Chinese government continued unresolved. Miss Moninger reported, Hamilton was "still pegging along on the Byers case but doesn't seem to be getting anywhere very fast." She did note, however, that the mission's executive committee, in consultation with both the Rev. Lowrie and the vice consul, decided that the Kachek mission property had to be walled in before anyone would be permitted to live there permanently. She described this as a "terrible blow," and noted the large size of their property meant the cost would be tremendous, and could not be done until the BFM raised the money.[36]

Vice Consul Hamilton was patiently awaiting the arrival of General Teng who was expected in Hainan about 10 February, but when he had not come by the 17th Hamilton decided he was not coming and returned to the mainland to talk with him.[37] In cabling Secretary of State Hughes of this development Schurman noted the consul general at Canton had telegraphed that it was evident the Chinese authorities were endeavoring to evade action and cautioned if Hamilton were not successful on this trip to see the general the department "must consider other means" of settling the case.[38] Fortunately for the Chinese, the general decided to resolve the matter and the Americans did not have to pursue the "other means."

Returning to the mainland Hamilton, with a company that included the Rev. Lowrie, the USS *Abarenda*'s second officer, a Chinese interpreter, a cook, and twenty Chinese soldiers with an officer escorting, traveled to Chinchow where the general then had his headquarters. The Rev. Lowrie reported, "The situation seems to be . . . about as difficult as imaginable," and then summarized the case in eight points: 1. Nothing had been done to settle the case after Vice Consul Chamberlain left Hainan. 2. The brigand chief thought responsible for Byers's murder was "roaming at will, kidnaping and blackmailing far and near." 3. Vice Consul Hamilton arrived in Hainan and then went to Pakhoi to see General Teng who promised to visit Hainan after Chinese New Year. 4. Hamilton visited Teng's chief of staff every day in Hoihow, but could not learn when the general would arrive in Hainan and so decided to return to the mainland to see him. 5. Hamilton had been directed by the American government not to use force but pursued his "unpromising commission" with "self-control, decision of character and persuasiveness." 6. Hamilton avoided public association with the Hainan missionaries but asked Lowrie as a "more detached party" to assist him with some of the "delicate questions" that might arise and Lowrie, knowing the BFM was pressing the case in Washington, "did not feel at liberty to decline." 7. Teng was "of pirate and brigand origin himself" and Hamilton found him "rather irascible" on the first visit. Lowrie thought if the general became irritated at their return, the visit might end quickly, otherwise he believed persistence might pay off. 8. Hamilton had been authorized to insist that the murderers of Byers be "caught, tried in his presence, and punished"; to have the responsible officials degraded, and to collect $25,000 gold paid to the American government "not as indemnity, but as 'mercy money.'" Lowrie acknowledged that a British consul would have settled the matter more quickly, but pointed out that he thought the American approach was "preferable." He noted that although Hamilton was only about thirty years of age, he spoke Mandarin and was "well fitted to present matters in the light that appeals to the Chinese mind." Patton, in turn, sent the BFM the gist of this letter.[39]

The Rev. Lowrie would later write to the BFM that "neither the Mission nor I presented any request for indemnity money." He also reported "all the negotiations were conducted in a cordial spirit of comity and at the close there existed between the parties participating mutual relations of personal goodwill which can but prove of advantage to the Mission and the Christians in the future." Lowrie praised Hamilton whom he termed "eminently wise" and possessed of "great patience, tact and courtesy coupled with firm determination." He thought Hamilton accomplished all that could have been done considering the "recognized policy of the United States government to refrain from threatening violence and only employ methods of persuasion in conferences with China over such questions as this."[40]

Summing up the situation in Hainan, Lowrie noted the local populace was neither anti-foreign nor anti-Christian and the missionaries had good relations with all groups of people on the island. He noted some of the middle school students "seem swayed by Bolshevist principles," but added that was also true elsewhere in China. Away from the cities, bandits, who were ex-soldiers of the armies that had contended for control of the island for several years, continued to be a problem. He noted General Teng might not succeed in pacifying the island, but thought that at least the men of the mission could return to the interior, although everyone's safety would be increased should Lin Shu-piao be arrested. The mission compounds at Kachek and Nodoa were to be surrounded by "substantial" walls or fences.[41]

Once Hamilton returned to General Teng's headquarters, the matter took a surprising turn when the general offered an indemnity of $20,000 [Mex.]. Hamilton informed his superiors that he thought the general could raise that sum if the American government agreed to accept it. Upon receiving this news, Schurman telegraphed the secretary of state urging that the offer be accepted if it were paid immediately since there was the possibility that General Teng would be replaced by someone who had no responsibility for Byers's murder, which would make collecting an indemnity much more difficult. He noted that Colonel Ho had been punished and

General Teng promised to continue his efforts to capture the murderers and ensure the safety of the missionaries in the interior. Schurman continued, they could use only persuasion to convince Teng to pay the indemnity and thought that persisting in demands would only result in a complete refusal on his part. He also noted at the current rate of exchange the amount Teng was offering was $45,000 silver which was the amount the military governor of Hunan had paid following the murder by some of his troops of the American Reimert in 1920. Schurman noted the Byers case was different as there was no way to compel Teng to pay as his soldiers were not responsible for the crime. The minister then reviewed past extraterritoriality cases noting that $25,000 gold had been paid by the central government when Hicks was murdered in 1912, O'Brien in 1918, and Coltman in 1922, and $5000 gold each was accepted for five Americans killed in Lienchow, Kwangtung, in 1905 and for five others killed at Hsianfu in 1911. Further, he stated that the diplomatic community thought a precedent for such cases had been set by the $20,000 silver asked for the death of a Britisher in the Lincheng Incident. Accordingly, Schurman suggested the department accept Jenkins's recommendation and authorized Hamilton to negotiate the best terms possible, but with the understanding the minimum not be less than $30,000 silver.[42]

Indemnity, Indemnity—Who Wants the Indemnity?

When the news of the offer of the indemnity reached the United States events moved swiftly, and comically, as Mrs. Byers and the BFM each reacted as if someone had handed them a live bomb which each tossed quickly to the other in the hope that it would somehow land at the Department of State without either of them having to take the responsibility for getting it there. The situation was complicated by the fact that although President Calvin Coolidge was sworn in for his second term as president on 4 March, Hughes was replaced as secretary of state that day by Frank Kellogg. It was 3 March when Hughes received word from Schurman that Jenkins thought General Teng might be induced to increase his offer. Schurman asked that Hamilton be given the authority to negotiate any amount between $20,000 and $30,000 [Mex.].[43] Hughes then telegraphed Mrs. Byers in California that the Chinese had offered $20,000 silver and that "both Consul and Legation recommend that in view of local political conditions" that amount be accepted as a minimum for negotiations. She was asked if she were willing to accept this settlement and to telegraph an immediate reply.[44] Unfortunately, Hughes's telegram was sent collect, so instead of being delivered promptly, it was put in the mail for delivery to Mrs. Byers's rural address, so she did not receive it until 4 March.

Meanwhile, on 4 March, Peking time, Schurman again cabled the Department of State about the indemnity stating that the general insisted the amount could be increased, but that if it were accepted it could be raised in fifteen days. Schurman cautioned those in Washington that the "apparent collapse of Ch'en Chiung-ming forces is quite possible. General Teng may also fail in the near future." Accordingly, he "earnestly advised" the offer be accepted as soon as possible.[45]

Once she received Hughes's telegram on the 4th, Mrs. Byers immediately replied that the decision was the BFM's to make, adding that she had telegraphed the BFM to contact him. She then telegraphed Mrs. Roys the text of the telegram from Hughes, indicating she had wired Hughes that the decision was in the hands of the BFM and that she had asked that they respond to him at once, adding "my personal opinion is that offer should be accepted."[46] The following day, 5 March, Mrs. Roys telegraphed the Department of State that the BFM took no responsibility on the question of the indemnity, noting the decision lies "wholly with Mrs. Byers," although Mrs. Byers had telegraphed the BFM that she thought the offer should be accepted. On the same day Mrs. Roys telegraphed Mrs. Byers to the effect that she regretted Mrs. Byers had told Hughes that the matter "lies in the Board's hands," as the BFM could not take that responsibility.[47]

Mrs. Roys then wrote to Mrs. Byers on 6 March stating she was "considerably disturbed" that Mrs. Byers had wired Hughes that the decision was in the BFM's hands. "I regret exceedingly that I did not present unmistakably the attitude of the Board, which is that in all matters concerning indemnity for life individual missionaries must act as American citizens and the Board will in no way take official action dealing directly with the Government." She realized Mrs. Byers wanted to defer the decision to give the BFM time to send word to Washington, but "the fact of the case is that this is the very thing which the Board is absolutely unable to do," and keep within its historic policy of not asking for an indemnity for a life. She indicated she was "counting definitely on your appreciation of the position in which the Board finds itself."[48]

Once Mrs. Byers received that letter she telegraphed Mrs. Roys: "My claim being already waived according to agreement with Board I thought decision no longer in my hands." She continued that she was wiring Hughes that she no longer wished to make a claim because the BFM had agreed to support her family. Mrs. Byers then cabled Hughes that as the BFM had made adequate provision for her "it will not be necessary for me to ask indemnity through Government agency and therefore I do not wish to make any personal claim."[49]

The following day Mrs. Roys again wrote to Mrs. Byers saying she was finding it difficult to make the BFM's position clear and to understand Mrs. Byers's position on the question. Mrs. Roys reiterated that the BFM could not move as a board to claim an indemnity for a life, but gave the "utmost freedom" to individuals to do as they thought best. She then added that Mrs. Byers's 4 March telegram indicated that she wished the money to be accepted, which the BFM had reported in its telegram to Hughes. Mrs. Roys then wrote, "I am puzzled to know what element entered into your thinking to induce you to telegraph Mr. Hughes on March 6th that you do not wish to make any personal claim." Of course, Mrs. Roys realized that the BFM had made the commitment to provide for the Byers family, but then continued, "I do not feel that the question now is a matter of your *making* personal claim but a matter of your accepting the payment made in response to the claim presented by the U.S. Government I see quite clearly a distinction—Do you not agree with me?" She thought that Mrs. Byers's telegram to Hughes was not sufficient for the government to cable to China to stop the process and believed it would become a matter of whether or not Mrs. Byers accepted the money that had been collected. She went on, "I am puzzled about the whole matter because obviously you believe that the payment of a claim will bring about a better state of things in China."[50]

Mrs. Roys wrote that since Mrs. Byers had indicated she thought the offer of the Hainan authorities should be accepted, and she had previously expressed her reluctance to have the BFM provide support for her family, those at the BFM would understand that by accepting the indemnity Mrs. Byers was doing so to release the BFM from that part of its financial obligation to her family. Mrs. Roys expressed her sorrow that such a misunderstanding had come between them since she thought they saw "eye to eye in all the complications of this distressing question," but indicated she was guided in her thoughts by Mrs. Byers's statement that the indemnity ought to be accepted. Mrs. Roys indicated that although she was unable to confer with the Rev. Scott, who was out of the office, she thought it best to see how the Department of State reacted to the conflicting messages before doing anything else.[51]

All this correspondence clearly perplexed Mrs. Byers for on 7 March she wrote to Mrs. Roys saying she was "impaled on the horns of a dilemma." When she received Hughes's 2 March telegram on 4 March, her first thought was she could do nothing without the approval of the BFM as she felt in accepting their support she had waived her claim to the indemnity. She thought the Department of State had so "scaled down" the amount they had asked for that it would be "negligible." When she received the second message from Mrs. Roys she was "more perturbed than ever," but decided if her choice was between acting against the policy of the BFM and "offending the State Department" she had to do the latter, and so sent her second telegram. She thought Vice Consul Hamilton would be displeased after all his work, but she noted she had no way of knowing what the State Department would do, and she was sorry Hughes had not received the message before leaving office. She concluded by saying she was not surprised at the attitude of the Board of Ministerial Relief, which had recently declined to help the Byers family, and she realized that the money from the indemnity would just about cover that amount.[52]

Mrs. Byers had no way of knowing that her 6 March telegram was received by the Department of State at 3:04 a.m. on 7 March, and that Secretary of State Kellogg had cabled to Schurman in Peking at 6:47 p.m. the previous day authorizing Hamilton to negotiate the indemnity with $20,000 silver as the minimum.[53] Also on 7 March an unsigned cable from Peking to the secretary of state urged Teng's offer be accepted and the balance of the indemnity be sought from the Chinese central government, noting if control of Hainan changed hands, Hamilton would be able to accomplish nothing. The cable's sender feared that no further indemnity would be collected from the central government, but urged the department to reply directly to Jenkins by cable with their decision. Kellogg replied on 9 March that he had cabled on the 6th that $20,000 was acceptable, but the balance needed to be demanded from the central government.[54]

Mrs. Roys's letters about acceptance of the indemnity left Mrs. Byers bewildered, as she wrote again on 17 March explaining her actions. After reviewing all the communications she had had with the BFM on the matter, when she received Mrs. Roys's 6 March telegram, Mrs. Byers realized she had to make a decision, so she and her friend, Mrs. Ina Rittenhouse, took all the correspondence and went to La Mesa, California, to consult the Rev. and Mrs. McKelvey and Miss Kirby, Mrs. McKelvey's sister, who "are the clearest headed people I know." The Rev. McKelvey had been the pastor of the Presbyterian Church in Plainfield, New Jersey, for thirty years and Miss Kirby had been the secretary-treasurer of the Plainfield Trust Company for many years.[55]

After spending the entire afternoon carefully reading all the correspondence, they came to the unanimous decision that Mrs. Byers's opinion on the indemnity had nothing to do with it being collected. They decided that while the BFM "implied that the money could be accepted, the whole tenor of the Board's thought and policy was directly opposed to the receiving of a money payment." She continued that all along she had not wished the collection of an indemnity to harm the work of the mission in Hainan, yet they had concluded

> there was no distinction between *our* pressing the claim or the government pressing it, in its ultimate effect upon the work in Hainan. The fact that the money was demanded *for* me would be the thing that the Chinese would see. Ultimately it would make no difference to them what the agency who did the collecting.

She felt that some of the paragraphs in the letters from the BFM suggested that the money might be accepted, but they understood it had to be the decision of the BFM to do so. Then she specifically cited Mrs. Roys's 7 March letter which read, "Since this represents your conviction I do not see why you personally should not accept the payment. . . . I am quite sure that should you accept the payment the Board would wholly understand your doing so with the purpose of releasing the Board from that much of its financial obligation to you" which gave her a different view of the situation and had she had those statements earlier she would not have wired to Hughes the second time. She could see the distinction Mrs. Roys made "between *making* a claim and *accepting* what was offered," but "not in the effect such a claim would have upon the work. If the Chinese government should *offer* me, not as the result of outside pressure, but spontaneously, a sum of money, I would see a distinction clearly in its effect upon Hainan. Such a procedure however is beyond imagination." She also noted that she and the BFM had not agreed on the damage to the mission work the indemnity would cause, but she deferred to the BFM's judgment as she felt it was not a topic she could continue to discuss.[56]

Mrs. Byers concluded that whatever distinction anyone wanted to make, if the government collected the money it would need to be disposed of. She then wrote, "If the Board really feels that coming in this manner I might take the income of it and thereby lessen their grant to me, I would have no hesitancy in accepting it in that way." (The BFM copy of this letter shows someone, probably Mrs. Roys, underlined this sentence and added the marginal note, ***"YES!"***) Mrs. Byers ended, "My whole effort has been to find out just what the Board really wanted."[57]

Mrs. Roys replied on 23 March to the effect that "the Board would not in any sense misunderstand your accepting the grant, coming as it does without any pressure being brought to bear by you personally or by the Board." She also noted that the current situation in China was a perplexing one to many involved with mission work and that they were having an interdenominational meeting on the subject the following week.[58]

Vice Consul Hamilton Returns to Hainan Accompanied by General Teng

While the BFM and Mrs. Byers were trying to decide what to do about the indemnity, Hamilton was still in Pakhoi where he convinced General Teng to travel to Hainan while they awaited word on the American government's acceptance of the indemnity offer. At the beginning of March, Miss Moninger wrote her family that the USS *Abarenda* arrived in Hoihow harbor followed by a Chinese gunboat, "so Mr. Hamilton has evidently brought Mr. Teng back with him, which looks much like a victory for our side." She expressed her desire that the general go to work and clear up the bandit problem.[59] A week later she reported that Hamilton; Mr. Byrd, one of the officers from the USS *Abarenda*; Dr. Bercovitz; and the Revs. Lowrie and Tappan; along with the Rev. David Thomas, who had recently returned from furlough with his family, left for Kachek on 6 March with General Teng and his commissioner of foreign affairs. The missionaries at the port were anxious to know what they might be able to accomplish as the vice consul had said "very distinctly" the action was not "a re-opening of the station for mission work, but just a removal of consular headquarters from Hoihow to Kachek." Miss Moninger also reported the missionaries had given a dinner party for the vice consul, his wife, two of the officers of the USS *Abarenda*, and some of the other foreigners who lived in Hoihow.[60]

A week later Miss Moninger wrote that the men had found the mission compound in Kachek in good shape. She also wrote that the local Chinese newspaper had reported that the general had promised to do four things: "make reparation for the breaking of American treaty rights, put up a memorial stone for Mr. Byers in the church, catch the men who killed Mr. Byers, and catch the head bandit chief there, Lin Shu-piao." She added that the local people knew an indemnity of $50,000 [Mex.] had been demanded, and that the missionaries were having some difficulty making it known that it was "the government and not the church nor Mrs. Byers who is after the money," adding that the missionaries would be happy when the matter was resolved.[61]

The indemnity matter was an important one to the missionaries as Miss Moninger had indicated. They knew there was a likelihood that those from whom the money was demanded would not be those directly responsible for Byers's death and the demand itself would make it difficult for the missionaries to continue their work. Before long, the missionaries at the port had news from Kachek that the money was being demanded from the local market, and had resulted in a protest meeting, as the market people had not killed the Rev. Byers. She also reported that the French consul had received a letter from a man who claimed he and seven others had been "paid $364 [Mex.?] to kill Mr. Byers and had been offered money to kill another foreigner but they knew it was wrong so they [were] leaving for foreign parts!" The French consul had sent the note to Dr. McCandliss asking if "the writer was a lunatic, a wag, a scoundrel or a friend." Dr. McCandliss had turned the letter over to Vice Consul Hamilton, but the missionaries thought it was designed to convince them that Byers's murderers had departed for Singapore.[62]

The death of Sun Yat-sen in March 1925, unfortunately, did nothing to ease the political turmoil of China. From Hainan Miss Moninger wrote there was likely to be fighting as General Teng was not a Sun man. She hoped he would settle the Byers case "before he skips to parts unknown to live in luxury on the money he's squeezed out for himself while being an official, . . . but if the Byers case isn't settled before he leaves I'm afraid it never will be! Unless the new official would do it in a hurry just to show his superiority."[63]

Miss Moninger continued that Dr. Bercovitz, the Rev. Tappan, and Mr. Byrd had returned from Kachek, but the vice consul had forbidden them to talk about the situation so the other missionaries were uncertain what had happened. She again added that the indemnity was going to

> make it very hard for us to preach the Gospel when money payment has been demanded from people who did not ask us to come in the first place and from those who had nothing to do with the murder of Mr. Byers. Of course the idea is that such a proceeding would prevent any further accident, but the weak point in that reasoning is that the enemies who did the deed aren't the ones who have to pay the money.

(Although Miss Moninger reported that the vice consul did not talk much, she also wrote that in the midst of these difficulties, Vice Consul Hamilton, General Teng, his deputy, and the Rev. Lowrie attended the laying of the cornerstone for the Hainan Christian Middle School.)[64]

While these events were transpiring, General Teng sent a lengthy letter to Consul Hamilton reviewing the facts of the Byers case. He stated that the murderers of Byers were bandits. He noted that upon arrival at Kachek he had ordered soldiers to guard the roads, and to search out and exterminate the bandits. "According to the daily reports made by my military officers, some of the bandits have been captured alive, some have been captured in a wounded condition, and some killed, and no efforts are being spared to pursue the remaining bandits who are fleeing in all directions." He continued that he had ordered the Rehabilitation Bureau in Hainan and each commanding general to have all military and civilian officials organize militia and make a house-to-house search for bandits and to bring to justice the bandit leader, Lin Shu-piao, within two months' time. After that was accomplished the local officials would be held responsible for maintaining order, and would be dismissed from office if any incident occurred. He noted that as the United States and China were friends he had ordered soldiers to protect the mission properties in Kachek, Nodoa, Kiungchow, and Hoihow, but after the bandits were suppressed these troops would be withdrawn. He added that the missionaries at Nodoa and Kachek could return to their stations to carry on their work. He noted that Colonel Ho had not given protection before the murder and did not settle the case promptly and that he was punished according to Chinese law, but noted he was left in his post to help in the capture of the murderers and was ordered to put up a $10,000 [Mex.] reward for their capture. Regarding the indemnity and the Americans' claim that the amount of $25,000 gold was paid elsewhere in China, Teng wrote, "I have the honor to state that the treaties contain no such provision and that the amount of any indemnity is not fixed." He noted he was able to give only $20,000 silver because of "the [poverty] of the land and people of Hainan." If the Americans agreed to request the balance from the central government, the matter could be resolved quickly, but if they could not accept his offer they should take the matter up with the central government.[65]

Hamilton replied on 3 April, indicating he had reviewed the details of General Teng's statement. He then noted that he knew the general desired to maintain friendly relations between the United States and China, that he had personally visited the scene of the murder, and that the people of the Kachek region had suffered heavily because of the Byers murder and because of the bandits. Accordingly, Hamilton accepted the indemnity in the amount Teng offered and requested it be paid to the American legation in Peking. The following day Schurman informed Kellogg of Hamilton's action.[66]

Once Hamilton accepted the offer, Teng announced he would leave Kachek. According to Miss Moninger, Vice Consul Hamilton and the Revs. Lowrie and Thomas arrived in Kiungchow at 4 p.m. on Sunday having left Kachek that morning. At 9 p.m. the previous day General Teng announced he would leave Kachek at 6:00 A.M. the next morning, so Hamilton informed the general that he, too, was leaving. Miss Moninger reported that $20,000 [Mex.] had been agreed upon as an indemnity and was to be paid that week. She thought that once the transaction was completed, the missionaries would be permitted to return to the interior stations as a mission meeting had been called and the Rev. Lowrie was planning to depart for Shanghai the following week.[67]

Vice Consul Hamilton left Hainan for Hong Kong where on 15 April he received from General Teng's representative a bank draft of $20,000 local currency, which he gave to Consul Jenkins the following day. Hamilton then returned on the 18th to Hainan aboard the USS *Hulbert*. In transmitting the bank draft to Schurman, Jenkins related that General Teng had promised to rid Hainan of bandits by 1 June and to capture Lin Shu-piao, and that Teng had several thousand troops on the island pursuing bandits, a number of whom had been captured and executed. His hand-picked guard was stationed at the mission compounds. Additionally, Jenkins reported that construction of a motor road between Kachek and Hoihow had been completed and it was now possible to travel between the two places in five hours, which he said would greatly facilitate the maintenance of order. He continued that the missionary community wanted Vice Consul Hamilton to remain on the island, pointing out that if he left "all efforts to capture the bandits will cease and since Lin Shu-piao, the bandit leader, will still be at large, he may be expected to attempt reprisals on the Chinese converts, if not on the missionaries themselves." Jenkins also wrote that much had already been accomplished in the matter and the American government was not able to maintain a consul and a naval vessel in Hainan indefinitely. He pointed out that the consulate had responsibilities to missions and American interests in other parts of the district and if they left Hamilton in Hainan until the matter was resolved, he could be there for months or maybe years. Accordingly, Jenkins requested Schurman's permission to recall Hamilton.[68]

Mayer relayed summaries of the two cables from Jenkins to the secretary of state saying that Hamilton could do nothing more in Hainan and if the missionaries still believed Kachek to be dangerous they should be advised not to return to the interior stations. Mayer concurred with Jenkins's request to recall Hamilton, but pointed out that they still wanted to press for bandit suppression. Kellogg approved the request.[69]

Trying to Return to Normal

In the United States on 20 April, Mrs. Byers wrote to Secretary of State Kellogg explaining that she had declined the indemnity as the BFM had made an allowance for her and her children only on the condition that she make no claim against the Chinese government. However, as the Department of State had made the claim on her behalf, the BFM was willing to have her accept the money as it would be used to offset part of their support of her family. Then on 7 May, newspapers reported the government had secured an indemnity for Mrs. Byers. Some reported the amount at $20,000 and others at

$10,000 making no distinction what sort of dollars they meant. The next day Mrs. Byers was informed by an assistant secretary of state that an indemnity had been collected and was asked what she wanted done with the money.[70]

Meanwhile, the missionaries on Hainan attempted to resume their work. Miss Moninger reported that after a long meeting of Vice Consul Hamilton, the Rev. Lowrie, and the mission's executive committee, the Revs. Tappan and Thomas went to Kachek to build a concrete fence with sentry boxes around the compound and to install lanterns. Dr. Bercovitz was expected to accompany the Rev. Lowrie and the vice consul to Kachek to inspect the work. Those who served in Nodoa were allowed to return there as soon as the Steiner family returned from Hong Kong. In reporting this news, Miss Moninger noted they were all so happy, but

> we are almost holding our breath for fear some hitch will come again. As a matter of fact, bandits are very bad all around Kachek again and the governor doesn't seem to be making any efforts whatever to stop them. Either he is paid to let them alone or else he doesn't care enough about the island to make an effort to clean things up.

She also reported that news from Kachek indicated a dozen young boys and a three-year-old child had been kidnapped in the area around the town. She also wrote that in Hoihow, the Rev. Tappan had given a dinner party for the male missionaries, Vice Consul Hamilton, General Teng, Rev. Lowrie, the deputy governor, the district official, and some local businessmen, with the hope that some of them would give money for the school.[71]

But despite the desire of the missionaries to return to their work, unrest, not related to the Byers case, erupted. Age-old antagonism between the Hakkas and Limkos in the area around Nodoa resulted in several villages being burned and the vice consul forbade any of the Americans to travel there.[72]

On 28 April Vice Consul Hamilton was ordered by Jenkins to return to Canton, but he was also instructed to caution General Teng that his departure did not mean the American government did not continue its interest in the situation. He pointed out that should Lin Shu-piao be arrested, he "anticipated" that the consulate would be informed immediately, as they wanted to send a representative to the trial as agreed upon. General Teng was urged to communicate frequently with the consulate concerning his progress in Hainan.

Jenkins suggested that the missionaries be advised not to return to Kachek or Nodoa unless it was deemed safe for them to do so, as the American government could not guarantee their safety beyond the seaport. He wrote that if the missionaries returned to the interior "in spite of unsettled conditions, they will do so at their own risk."[73]

The Vice Consul's Final Report

Hamilton left Hainan on 7 May and reached Canton on 10 May where two days later he submitted to Jenkins a lengthy report on his activities on Hainan. In his report Hamilton stated that General Teng promised to capture and punish the murderers, but Li Tse-hsiang, who had made a statement to authorities that Lin Shu-piao was responsible for the murder, had been executed by authorities shortly after Vice Consul Chamberlain left Hainan. Other than Li's statement, Hamilton noted "very little evidence has been procurable as to who the actual murderers were" as there were no eyewitnesses, and "the absence of clues makes it impossible to make absolutely definite accusations."[74]

Hamilton also noted that the testimony of Li Tse-hsiang, in which he named five men of Lin's band—Li Tse-ying, Li Tse-hsiung, Huang Hui-wen, Su Chung-t'ai, and Huang Chung-hua—as the murderers, had been sent by General Teng to the consulate in a dispatch dated 4 August 1924. According to this dispatch, the purpose of the kidnapping was to raise money by collecting a ransom. Hamilton noted it was chiefly because of this testimony, and the fact that Lin Shu-piao had threatened to burn the mission and had personally threatened Miss Schaeffer, that the crime was attributed to him and his followers. The consul noted that General Teng was still working on capturing Lin Shu-piao and his followers.[75]

The vice consul continued that Colonel Ho had been negligent in the protection of Mrs. Byers, and acknowledged that the colonel's efforts to arrest Lin had been unsuccessful. But he noted that as the colonel was "an intimate associate of General Teng, it did not seem advisable to press for a vigorous punishment of the colonel, which, if it could have been obtained, would have alienated General Teng, upon whose friendliness and sincerity of effort depend the future safety of the Americans on the island." Ho was punished by having his rank removed and having to offer $10,000 silver for the capture of Lin Shu-piao. The consul reported that there was no evidence that Colonel Ho has ever exhibited any anti-foreign feeling or action, but rather his faults were "carelessness, inefficiency and general incompetence."[76]

Although Teng had promised to eliminate the bandits from the island and worked at it while Hamilton was in Kachek the task was harder than anticipated and the Consul noted these efforts had nearly ceased. Hamilton also wrote that the indemnity of $20,000 Shanghai currency was accepted due to the "poverty of the people of the Kachek region, where the indemnity was collected," adding that the money was collected by General Ch'en Feng-ch'i when he accompanied Chamberlain to Kachek in July 1924 through "heavy levies from the people."[77]

Hamilton thought General Teng was "a man of reasonably sound ideas. Unfortunately, many of his subordinates are corrupt and inefficient." He reported Teng had been friendly to him and seemed to want good relations with the United States. Teng's visit to Hainan with Hamilton was the first time the general had been there in twenty months. Hamilton did not know if Teng had the "actual power or is a big enough man to actually clean the island of bandits," but noted he seemed to be a better friend of the United States than he had been at the outset of the negotiations. The vice consul thought the general's "friendliness and honesty will cause him to carry out his promises so far as he is able." Hamilton suggested that the American legation send the Chinese foreign office a note of appreciation for what Teng had done and was trying to do as he thought it would "stimulate" Teng to continue on the case. Hamilton also wanted the Chinese foreign office to tell Teng that the United States was "deeply concerned" that he capture the murderers and "suppress lawlessness on the island of Hainan."[78]

After following Vice Consul Hamilton to the island, Teng reorganized its administration. General Feng Ming-kai was brought from the mainland and made rehabilitation commissioner, a post Teng had previously held. In the absence of Teng, Feng was the highest official on the island and Hamilton wrote that he "appear[s] to be honest and of a decidedly superior type to the corrupt and inefficient military leaders who have had actual control on the island for over a year." The "undisciplined" soldiers of the island had been replaced by "a somewhat more efficient and better class of soldiers" who had been brought from the mainland, and Teng promised to build a barracks and keep a permanent garrison at Kachek. The commander of the Kachek garrison was Colonel Teng Po-ch'i, a youthful nephew of General Teng, who Hamilton said "appears to be honest and friendly." He noted the new road to Kachek would make "mission life at Kachek less isolated and less dangerous."[79]

Hamilton also detailed the specific recommendations he had made to the members of the mission. These included informing Chinese officials of their specific routes when trips into the interior were planned, but, for the moment, itinerating trips were to be curtailed. The interior stations were to have two male foreigners at them at all times. Lights and fences were to be installed and in Kachek the public road through the compound was closed by orders of Teng. The missionaries were advised to keep the Consul General at Canton informed on all matters relating to their safety, and they were advised to withdraw when unsafe conditions prevailed. Male members of the mission were now permitted to return to the interior as the missionaries had decided to reopen both the Kachek and the Nodoa stations. Hamilton noted that the missionaries continued to fear for their safety since Lin Shu-piao had not been captured and they thought he would take vengeance on the missionaries because the anti-banditry activities of General Teng were aimed at Lin. Hamilton again visited Kachek on 5 May to talk with the male members of the mission who had already returned.[80]

Hamilton's report also took note of the assistance of the United States Navy. From 5 January to 2 April the USS *Abarenda* was in Hainan. The ship's captain Calhoun was commended for the "fine spirit" in which he fulfilled "a monotonous and irksome assignment of duty." The captain or one of the officers accompanied Hamilton to almost every interview with Chinese officials. The USS *Hulbert* maintained the duty in Hainan from 7 April to 20 April.[81]

The vice consul also acknowledged that the Rev. Lowrie had been with him at almost all interviews with Chinese officials and he was "in entire sympathy with the basis upon which the negotiations have been conducted." Hamilton concluded that "the settlement of the Byers's case . . . is far from ideal," and noted Teng still needed to capture and punish the murderers, including the bandit leader, Lin Shu-piao, and to protect American lives and property.[82]

The Diplomatic Case Concludes

After nearly a year at the port, the missionaries were allowed to return to Kachek, but the description of their return, written to her family by Miss Moninger, would hardly have reassured anyone:

> Miss Schaeffer, Miss [Caroline] McCreery, two women servants, a kitten, lunches, suitcases, traveling bags and a chauffeur were in one Ford, with a soldier "boy" on each running board, their fingers on the triggers of their wicked-looking pistols. Mr. and Mrs. [Samuel] Ensign, their woman servant, their baggage, a chauffeur and two soldier guards (same as above) were in the second Ford. . . . [Miss Mc]Creery said their soldier guard was very courteous and very obliging all the way.

Miss Moninger also noted that the Thomas and Bercovitz families were planning to return to Kachek the next week and that the first returnees had had fifty-two callers on their first day at the compound. She also noted that the continued unrest around Nodoa kept anyone from returning there for the time being.[83]

From Kachek Dr. Bercovitz reported that he was building a concrete wall around the mission compound and that four men and an auxiliary officer were stationed on the property. He thought the mission would be well protected "provided the present men in power stay in power," but acknowledged if there were a change of government, the missionaries would have to come to an understanding with the new officials. With regard to the attitude of the people he met, he wrote, "I find that the paying of the indemnity was the best thing which could have been done, as it has shown them all that the killing of a foreigner was not a paying proposition, and it is that which appeals to the Chinese mind." He said many people admitted there was justice in the indemnity, and many thought the American government had been very lenient about the amount as they had "expected a much larger sum to be collected." He thought the "position and prestige" of the Americans were "practically restored to what they were before Mr. Byers was killed," and added that

> it was never a matter of religious persecution, but simply an act of outlawry, and had to be settled on that basis. And as a result I feel that the work will go on better than ever before, for not the least of the apologetic for Christianity is what is accomplished in the way of establishment of law and order and suppression of crime. I mention all this because of a certain amount of sentimentalism in some quarters in regard to prosecution of the case, whereas what was demanded was simple justice for ar unusually hideous murder.

He went on that the man responsible for the murder was still at large, but officials said they were watching him. Bercovitz stated the man had killed more than one hundred fifty people so "it would be no miscarriage of justice if he were to be executed, as he and his followers have terrorized the region for a long time."[84]

Meeting in Hoihow on 27 May, the Hainan mission voted their thanks to Vice Consul Hamilton for his handling of the matter, which they noted he did without "leaving a feeling of rancor among the Chinese officials."[85]

In the United States Mrs. Byers sent the Department of State instructions for the transmission of the indemnity to her bank and asked if she might have a copy of Chamberlain's [*sic*] report. "I have received no direct information and would much appreciate learning just what he was able to accomplish in the punishment of the bandits and making conditions safer for the Americans there." She thought he had done a good job and recognized "securing . . . even such a small sum as $20,000 [Mex.]" was difficult.[86]

The indemnity amounted to $10,862.10 and was sent to Washington on 18 May 1925. Mayer, in writing to the secretary of state, expressed his opinion that the indemnity already collected was a "considerable sum" and "in view of the notorious inertia as well as bankruptcy of the Peking Government, it will be impossible to collect any compensation from the latter without bringing a greater amount of pressure to bear than the circumstances of the case would seem to warrant." He continued that he had made no demands on the Peking government for a definite sum and would not do so until the department instructed him to. He did intend to continue to "press the Chinese Government for the suppression of banditry on Hainan island and I have instructed Mr. Jenkins to do likewise with the local authorities."[87]

On 10 June Joseph C. Grew, under secretary of state, wrote to Mrs. Byers concerning the transmission of the indemnity, but refused to send her a copy of their report saying it was not "appropriate." He did, however, give her a general summary of what had transpired. The money and the report were still on Mrs. Byers's mind and the following day she again asked about them, again naming Chamberlain as the person she thought was in Hainan.[88]

On 1 July Mrs. Byers was informed that the Treasury had been asked to draw a check in her favor, and on 11 July she sent three copies of her signature as required to receive her check and thanked the department for the information on Hamilton, but she also wanted to know the results of General Teng's promise to suppress banditry and if the murderers had been caught. "I heard a report that the bandit chief had been given a position as official in the regular army. It is hard to believe that there would be such a travesty of justice. It is what he was aiming at for a long time, and if he has been thus bought off it but means future trouble."[89]

On 18 July Mrs. Byers informed Mrs. Roys that the Department of State told her the amount was $10,862. She also asked if Mrs. Roys knew why the missionaries had returned to Kachek when the bandit chief was not captured and why the papers reported they had fled. (In a letter that reached the BFM, Miss Schaeffer wrote from Kachek on 22 June that the missionaries had been back at the station for five weeks. But at the end of the letter was the note, apparently added at the BFM, that the women and children had evacuated the island on orders of the American consul in Canton.) Mrs. Roys replied indicating she did not know why the missionaries had fled again, but she thought, correctly, it was due to the anti-Christian agitation following riots in Shanghai.[90]

On 26 August the check was sent to Mrs. Byers and she was again given a summary of what had transpired between Hamilton and General Teng and told that Colonel Ho had been demoted and required to post a reward for the capture of Lin Shu-piao. The same day she again wrote to Washington about the money, noting she had been informed that it was paid to the Canton consul on 1 April and she was dependent upon the money for her support. On 3 September she received the money.[91]

So the American government's involvement in the Byers case ended. It had succeeded in collecting an indemnity which Mrs. Byers finally received, but it was not sufficient to support her family until the children were grown and for that support she had to depend on the BFM. Throughout the long months during which she had dealt with the American government, she was also in constant contact with the BFM over that support.

5

The BFM and Support of the Byers Family

LIFE CHANGED RADICALLY FOR MRS. CLARA BYERS ON THAT JUNE NIGHT when her husband died in her arms on the mission compound in Kachek. Suddenly a widow and still in shock, Mrs. Byers felt the Board of Foreign Missions (BFM) would make some provision for her family, but this was far from a foregone conclusion. Presbyterian missionaries in China were not required to have life insurance, nor was any provided by the BFM, although the Rev. Byers did have a personal policy of $1000. The church expected that when one of their employees died, even by violence, the surviving family members would find ways to support themselves either by employment or by depending upon relatives. The church did have a Board of Ministerial Relief, but it offered only nominal sums largely to aid destitute retired clergy and it was unwilling and unable to undertake the support of Mrs. Byers and her five minor children.

Unaware of how difficult her protracted struggle with the BFM was going to be, Mrs. Byers found a staunch ally in Mrs. Mabel L. Roys, who was an executive secretary of the BFM's Foreign Department and the highest-ranking woman at the BFM. Although the two women had not met at the time they undertook to resolve this matter, Mrs. Roys was a steadfast supporter of Mrs. Byers's cause before the BFM and even became a confidante to whom Mrs. Byers poured out her concerns.[1] It is likely neither of the women considered herself a feminist. Mrs. Byers had been in Hainan, trying to maintain the American lifestyle all missionaries sought to re-create in China so that their children would feel at home when they returned to the land of their parents, when the women's suffrage movement finally succeeded in getting women the right to vote in the United States. Mrs. Roys worked full-time at the BFM and likely had little time for feminist activities even though she certainly would have been knowledgeable about them. It was Mrs. Roys who eventually swayed the male-dominated BFM with her argument that it had a moral obligation to support the Byers family and to do otherwise was unChristian, to say the least.

The reluctance of the BFM to immediately accept responsibility for the support of the Byers family complicated the indemnity issue which was in itself a particularly vexing problem as all concerned realized. Shortly after the murder, the Hainan mission's executive committee had voted in favor of asking for an indemnity, both to demonstrate the consequences of killing a foreigner and as compensation for Mrs. Byers and her children. U.S. Consul Douglas Jenkins in Canton was unaware of the position the BFM was taking against the continued support of the Byers family, so assumed it would provide for her even though he favored collecting "reasonable compensation" from the Chinese.[2]

The bureaucrats at the BFM, aware of Mrs. Byers's grief, nonetheless contacted her almost immediately for instructions concerning her finances. Russell Carter, the BFM's associate treasurer, wrote her while she was still in China asking what he should do with the $125 in children's allowances then owed to her. In the past the BFM had been depositing the children's allowances in the Greenwich Savings Bank in an account in her husband's name, but the bank would no longer accept them. She also was informed she had a balance of $3607.46, and interest of about $36 in that account. Carter also wanted to know if the Rev. Byers had had a will.[3]

On her journey homeward across the Pacific, Mrs. Byers wrote the BFM some of her thoughts about the indemnity and the situation in general. She thought that the Chinese expected that an indemnity would be collected, "partly as a punitive measure and partly in my behalf." She also noted the local Chinese had offered the Agricultural College, which was next door to the Kachek compound, as a memorial, but the missionaries refused it.[4]

Dr. Nathaniel Bercovitz, writing as Mrs. Byers's personal physician, informed the BFM that she had never been a robust woman, and had been able to live in Hainan only with the help of her servants. He emphasized that alone she might be able to support herself, but did not see how she would manage with the added responsibility of her children. He stressed the "real need for an indemnity" and indicated "something will have to be started so that there will [be] no hitch in getting [it]."[5]

The diplomatic aspect of the indemnity question was the subject of a 19 August telegram from Jenkins to Minister Jacob Gould Schurman, in which he gave Mrs. Byers's request that the indemnity be

$50,000. He followed his telegram with a letter, in which he relayed the increased demand, but pointed out that Mrs. Byers was willing to reduce it if the BFM provided for her family's support. While admitting he was "not familiar with claims of this sort," Jenkins thought the $50,000 demand was unreasonable, adding that $20,000 or $30,000 should be sought.[6]

Mrs. Byers Is Asked How Much Support She Needs

At the BFM Mrs. Roys's concern for the Byers family was first evidenced in early September when, in her official capacity, she wrote to Mrs. Byers indicating that she thought the $3000 Mrs. Byers estimated she needed to live on each year was insufficient. Mrs. Roys wrote that she hoped Mrs. Byers would "stand back of the request for $50,000." (A signed, handwritten, but undated, marginal note of Mrs. Roys added, "This is [Rev. George T.] Scott's opinion and was mine at first. Later I changed my opinion and felt *no* indemnity should be asked.")[7]

Mrs. Byers had suggested to the BFM that any indemnity collected could be held in trust for her, but Mrs. Roys replied that such an arrangement was "unwise." She informed Mrs. Byers that the BFM would meet on 11 September and indicated she had not had a chance to talk with the others but she personally felt that the BFM "may wish to stand quite aside and allow the Chinese Government to face securely its responsibility to you in this matter." She indicated that this did not reflect upon Mrs. Byers personally or how the members of the BFM felt about her situation, but, "In matters where governments are involved you realize, as a missionary, that the [BFM] may think it wise not to become involved."[8]

The Rev. Scott followed up Mrs. Roys's letter with one of his own, in which he told Mrs. Byers, "We, of course, must make every effort to settle this involved question with justice and fairness to all concerned and in a way in which the Christian principles involved will be acted upon for the furtherance of the missionary cause."[9]

From California Mrs. Byers, awaiting the birth of her fifth child, wrote Mrs. Roys asking what she should do about her travel expenses. The mission had paid the Rev. Byers's salary through the end of June and she had left Kachek on 26 June. She then spent three weeks in Hoihow waiting for her belongings to be shipped from Kachek, and arranging for steamer passage to Hong Kong and then home. Less than three months a widow, Mrs. Byers was already in financial difficulty even though at its September meeting the BFM's executive committee agreed to pay her children's allowances until they were twenty-one, unless she requested they end earlier. The committee also decided to extend to Mrs. Byers a single missionary's home allowance until the end of the year and if she were still in financial need at that time they would consider extending the allowance.[10]

The BFM Reviews Past Extraterritoriality Cases

The BFM discussed at length what Mrs. Roys termed, "The perplexing problem of the wisest course in regard to an indemnity." After discussing the pros and cons as well as the BFM's historic policy in such cases, Mrs. Roys wrote, "There seemed to be a unanimous feeling that while the [BFM] adheres to its policy not to accept indemnity for the lives of missionaries, it nevertheless has no jurisdiction over any individual who chooses as a private citizen to make such a demand." In reviewing the historical cases she noted that during the Boxer years the BFM accepted no indemnity for the loss of missionaries' lives, but the brother of one victim asked and received an indemnity as a private citizen. The same was true in the Lienchow case in 1905; the BFM accepted no compensation, but some of the relatives and dependents of the victims shared in the indemnity the United States government collected.[11]

In formally discussing the Byers case the BFM took note of the action taken in 1905 regarding the Lienchow case. At that time the BFM had declared that

> if it accepted any indemnity, it would only be for the actual cost of replacing destroyed or damaged property, and that in no case whatever would the [BFM] receive indemnity for the beloved dead, nor would it accept indemnity of punitive character, the [BFM] holding that the value of the blood of those who laid down their lives for Christ's sake should not be estimated in dollars and cents.

The BFM acknowledged that it spoke only for itself, and had no control over what others might do. In the Lienchow case, the BFM believed no one suffered a financial loss and it was "deplorable" for those who did not suffer financially to seek compensation as that was "inconsistent with the spirit which led the beloved martyrs to consecrate their lives to missionary work." But as noted previously Minister Schurman indicated that $25,000 had been collected for the five adult Americans killed at Lienchow, and the money had gone to their survivors.[12]

Mrs. Roys emphasized that the BFM could speak only for itself and "the Cause it represents," not for any individual, and acknowledged that Mrs. Byers had submitted a claim for an indemnity while still in Hainan at the request of American Vice Consul C. B. Chamberlain. Mrs. Roys wrote, too, that the BFM was "perplexed" at the action of the executive committee of the Hainan mission in requesting an indemnity of $20,000 gold to be "raised locally," since they had not sent the resolution to the Presbyterian China Council (PCC) before sending it to the consulate. Mrs. Roys also noted Mrs. Byers's statement that had there been a Kachek member on the executive committee, the resolution would not have been approved because of the fear of the damage its collection would do to their work. Mrs. Roys further noted that the BFM was awaiting word from the PCC on what action they would take with regard to the Hainan resolution.[13]

Some members of the PCC thought the Hainan mission's executive committee wanted to supervise the collection of the indemnity themselves. An attempt to explain the committee's actions was made on 23 August when the Rev. Wilbur Campbell wrote the PCC. He stated the action was taken because the vice consul, upon arriving in Hainan, had asked the missionaries to state their views regarding the situation. Only after Chamberlain returned from Kachek did he tell the missionaries that he would not ask for an indemnity, and that such action had to be taken by the Peking legation. Once they had that information, Campbell explained the Hainan executive committee "had not the least thought of doing anything further in the matter locally." Campbell further cautioned that "since there was a decided difference in the opinion of the committee from that of Mrs. Byers especially in the details of the case the committee did not wish record made of this action." He concluded that the Hainan executive committee did not wish to ignore either the PCC or the BFM in the matter.[14]

Mrs. Roys expressed her opinion to the Rev. Patton that the Hainan mission did not have any "liberty of action" in demanding an indemnity without consultation with the BFM, but added, "in the case of an individual, I feel Mrs. Byers has full liberty to make any demands she chooses as a private citizen." However, she felt "no missionary can ever be 'merely a private citizen,'" pointing out that the effect on the Chinese would be the same whether the claim were made by a private citizen, by the BFM, or by the mission. Mrs. Roys continued that she was concerned that the allowance for the Byers children was only about half of what Mrs. Byers would need to live on and the Board of Ministerial Relief made maximum grants of only $300 per year. Mrs. Roys also noted that some had said Mrs. Byers's situation was no different from that of any widow with children whose husband had died in the service, but she found a flaw in this argument because the BFM's policy of not accepting an indemnity because of the "highest spiritual considerations . . . unavoidably inhibit[ed] the freedom of action of Mrs. Byers." Mrs. Roys also wanted to insure that "no slightest pressure" would be used to influence Mrs. Byers's decision in making a claim on the Chinese government.[15] Interestingly, Mrs. Roys did not include in this letter any mention of Mrs. Byers's statement that she opposed the action of the Hainan mission executive committee because the amount they requested was too small.

The BFM had received a cable on 15 September from the PCC saying there was no cause for anxiety among the missions because of the Byers murder. The Women's Committee of the BFM met on the 15th and received a report from the foreign department on the Byers matter. The report noted there was an anti-foreign boycott in Canton in part due to the appearance there of the infamous sign once displayed in a Shanghai park "to the effect that 'dogs and Chinese must keep out'" which, the report stated, had "greatly aggravated the hatred and resentment of the Cantonese" toward foreigners. However, the report indicated that the Chinese made distinctions between missionaries and businessmen and were not discriminating against the missionaries.[16]

Mrs. Roys and Mrs. Byers Correspond on the Indemnity Issue

The question of Mrs. Byers's situation was discussed at length and the majority of the secretaries of the BFM approved of her request for an indemnity. However, Mrs. Roys was opposed and gave a list of her reasons. They were: 1. No value can be put on a human life; 2. It "violates the basic principle of missionary consecration: the willingness to lay down life if need be is inherent in missionary consecration"; 3. Mrs. Byers as a private citizen could make such a request, but in the eyes of the Chinese, she was seen as a missionary, not as a private citizen; 4. Although many saw a distinction between compensatory and punitive damages, the BFM had never asked for punitive damages, and the local community which was asked to pay the damages would not make the distinction; 5. Although some saw it as future protection for missionaries, an indemnity would in fact "arouse and deepen rather than remove hatred of the foreigner"; 6. Any indemnity collected would not come from those who killed Byers and "the officials would levy heavy taxes on a local community already oppressed beyond reason." The officials would extort more than requested and keep the rest for themselves; 7. The action of the executive committee of the Hainan mission would set the work back at least a decade and cause "bitter resentment and hatred"; 8. Mrs. Byers's situation needed to be resolved by paying her children's allowances and her salary through the fiscal year and by bringing pressure to bear on the Board of Ministerial Relief to "adequately care for the widows of ministers and missionaries."[17]

In informing Mrs. Byers of this discussion Mrs. Roys wrote that she believed Mrs. Byers would have months to decide what should be done. She also noted that Mrs. Byers was free to do anything as a private citizen, but asked, "If the way should be open for you to have a living income aside from any payment from the Chinese government," would you not prefer that?[18]

Mrs. Roys also clarified the situation with the Byers children's allowances and told Mrs. Byers that if she needed money the treasurer's office would advance it to her. She also wrote that salaries were ordinarily paid until the missionary left a station and then travel allowances were paid, but it was assumed that the person would spend only a short time before taking passage. Since Mrs. Byers had spent three weeks in Hoihow before departing Hainan, she was asked to send a full explanation of why it took her so long to receive her belongings from Kachek and to depart from Hainan.[19]

Mrs. Byers responded indicating that on the question of asking the Chinese government to pay for the support of her family, "I seem to see both sides of the question with about equal clearness." She indicated the BFM had taken the action she expected them to take and agreed there was "no such thing as an 'indemnity' for precious lives lost." Yet she also realized that the BFM was "limiting my own freedom of action," and as long as she was partially supported by the BFM she wrote, "I cannot feel free to do anything that is contrary to [BFM] policy or take any steps that the [BFM] feel might hinder their work."[20] It was this belief on the part of Mrs. Byers that was to cause the numerous telegrams and confusion concerning the indemnity the following March.

That the Chinese probably would not see the distinction between asking as a private citizen and asking as a missionary for compensation, Mrs. Byers readily acknowledged. She knew, too, that to demand compensation would hinder the mission work. She said there were several other factors that she wanted the BFM to consider and asked if at the time of the Boxers any families with young children had been left in the same financial circumstances as she was. She wrote, "There ought logically to be a distinction between asking for the support of a family of five small children and asking for an 'indemnity' for either the loss of property or the lives of missionaries." She reiterated that the Chinese assumed that some provisions needed to be made for the children and wrote, "The more time that elapses before some definite action is taken the more difficult it will be."[21]

Although she had lived more than a decade in China, Mrs. Byers now expressed the opinion that Chinese officials would not be able to raise the money for an indemnity by oppressing the people of the Kachek area because, she said, "they haven't got it." She further stated that "the Christians themselves are hardly likely to suffer much in the levy as they are among the poorest." She clearly thought "the amount, if raised in Hainan, would of necessity come from the gambling receipts and customs and general taxes, or from the squeeze which the officials have already collected." Moreover, she believed the officials who were responsible for conditions in Hainan needed to "suffer financially, [as] it is by far the most potent method of getting them to ferret out the brigands and make the robbers themselves divide the loot they have been piling up these last few years from robbing markets and rich men."[22] Little did she know that money had been extracted, from the same Kachek populace she thought did not have it, by General Ch'en Feng-ch'i when he had accompanied Vice Consul Chamberlain to the scene of the murder in July, or that General Teng Pen-yin would demand more money, from the same people, when he visited Kachek with Vice Consul Maxwell M. Hamilton.

Mrs. Byers also related that one of the Chinese elders of the Hainan church had expressed the idea that if Byers's death made the officials clean up the island, making life "safe for the many people who have been terrorized for so long, he would not have died in vain." She then cited a letter she had received from Dr. Bercovitz who wrote that over one hundred people had been killed by bandits since 1 July. The doctor thought the difficulty was not the indemnity, but the inaction of the American government. In the two months since the murder the government had done nothing, so that people were "boasting that a foreigner was murdered and nothing was done about it, so anything can be done to anybody with impunity." She acknowledged there was not a general anti-foreign feeling in Hainan, but noted the American government's inaction reflected upon the work of the mission and on "the Chinese Christians to their severe detriment." She cited the fact that the mission schools were closed and the missionaries were living in crowded condition at Hoihow and Kiungchow, and added, "The Chinese Christians would greatly prefer that the American government would strike some terror into the hearts of the rulers of the island so that their own affairs would be improved."[23]

She found it difficult to believe

> that a peaceful American citizen should be set upon at his own front door, bound, dragged off, and then deliberately killed for no reason except a desire for ransom; that a threat to destroy all the buildings unless ransom was given should be sent to the missionaries; that the people in the streets should boast that since one foreigner had been killed and nothing done about it, now they "could kill off the rest of them,"—that all these things could be done and the American government take no action seems to me both incredible and intolerable. It is true that a gunboat brought down the Vice Consul, but it sailed away without doing anything.[24]

Mrs. Byers was distressed that as Vice Consul Chamberlain was not yet twenty-four years old "his youth spoke against him to the Chinese." She then urged the BFM to pressure the government into action. The Rev. David S. Tappan's sister had written her that he had been in Peking to see the American minister, but, as the minister was away, had seen his next-in-charge. Mrs. Byers wrote, "Our representative was very much interested and interviewed him thoroughly but 'didn't know what to do next.' And that seems to be the general attitude."[25]

In explaining the action of the Hainan executive committee, Mrs. Byers wrote that Vice Consul Chamberlain did not expect to see her again as she was preparing to leave and so had asked her to submit a claim before she left the island and to have "some member of the mission . . . sign the claim with me, as approving." She had written her claim and gave it to the chairman of the executive committee the Rev. Campbell, saying that it was tentative. The committee met soon afterward and discussed her request without her knowledge and then handed her their resolution.

> My resolution was in the form you have it in your office, asking for $50,000 the principal to go to the [BFM], and the income to me. Theirs was for $20,000 raised locally, with the understanding that the [BFM] should continue the children's allowances. They wanted the amount raised locally as a punitive measure. I objected to this being so specified, but I was unable at a subsequent meeting of the committee, which I attended, to change their minds.

She also noted that the Rev. Tappan, Hainan's PCC representative, said the resolution needed to go to the PCC before it was presented to the consul.[26]

She added that she supposed the BFM knew that the Nodoa missionaries always carried guns when they traveled, but the Kachek people never did, adding that the area around Nodoa had always been "infested with a much rougher class of thieves." She cited a number of items stolen from the Nodoa missionaries in the previous few years, including Dr. Clarence Salsbury's microscope, X-rays, and a saddle, and reminded the BFM that the Byers's own baggage had been stolen on the way to the mission meeting in Nodoa in 1919. She continued that when robbed "the missionaries . . . [went] after the robbers and forced them to return the stuff or a money equivalent, and their methods have been successful. If they had waited for action from the PCC before settling the question locally it would have probably been impossible to settle it at all." She thought the robbers of the Nodoa region had "quite a wholesome respect for the missionaries in the vicinity." Acknowledging that her case was a much bigger question, she thought that, as there were three people from Nodoa on the executive committee which passed the resolution, it was logical to think they would view some punitive measure necessary.[27]

Mrs. Byers went on that she had left Hainan without giving the vice consul her request. She felt if the BFM continued the children's allowances, she should ask for $30,000 instead of the $20,000 the mission requested, but wrote, "I was too heartsick to want to think about it at all, and after one intimation that I was asking for a private fortune I felt I could never bring the subject up again." When she got to Shanghai all of her friends were insistent that she make some request and that "a just claim . . . was necessary for the protection of foreigners in the future," so she wrote out the one she sent to the consul and to the BFM. Since she had not heard from the government she assumed the question of the indemnity, like the "whole Hainan matter," had been pigeon-holed.[28]

If it were "finally decided that it were expedient to push the claim with the Chinese government," Mrs. Byers wrote that she felt unable to do it alone, as she had "neither the strength nor the heart to do it," yet she knew it should not be postponed, for the more time that elapsed, the more difficult it would be to collect the indemnity. She then questioned why the BFM, with its contacts to men in public life and its legal department, did not act. If they did not want to do it on behalf of the BFM, she asked that it be done on her behalf, adding that if the BFM could not do that,

> I would like an expression of opinion from them as to whether they think an effort on my own part to secure the money would be attended with disastrous results to mission work. That is, while they grant my right as a private citizen, to take any steps I want to, would they regret such an action on my part and feel that I had acted unwisely and in opposition to their wishes?

She also noted that there was a unanimity of opinion in the scores of letters she had received that the Chinese government needed to provide for her family. She thought it was too big a decision for one person to settle and was awaiting news of the decision of the PCC and the opinion of the BFM.[29]

Mrs. Roys responded stating that the BFM's executive committee was to consider the "perplexing matter" on 3 November, but assured Mrs. Byers that "one of two things is going to happen without fail: The [BFM] will see to it that you have adequate support, or it will give itself to securing that support for you from the Chinese Government." An undated handwritten note, and a typewritten note repeating part of the handwritten one, both in the BFM's files, record that the issue of an indemnity was discussed at the 3 November general meeting. The notes request the American government take immediate steps to secure the safety of mission work on the whole of Hainan, request the government to work for the "proper punishment" of Byers's murderers, and ask the BFM to provide for the support of Mrs. Byers, supplementing the maximum grant from the Board of Ministerial Relief. The handwritten note also mentions referring the matter of the indemnity back to the executive committee.[30]

Mrs. Roys Writes the BFM Members About the Indemnity

In New York on 6 November William D. Murray, attorney at law, wrote to the Rev. Robert Speer at the BFM, saying he had been contacted by a friend to see if he could help get the Department of State to act in the Byers case. Murray wanted to know what the BFM had done because he did not want to interfere with its work. Although Murray's letter had not mentioned any financial help, when Mrs. Roys replied to him on 10 November, she thanked him for his offer to help with "financial aid secured through the State Department." She also promised to let him know what action the BFM took on the matter at its 17 November meeting. Murray then wrote to James M. Speers, who was a member of the BFM, asking him to support the matter of Mrs. Byers. He again mentioned that a friend had written him about the case, this time stating he was asked to help secure financial aid for the widow. He concluded his letter by stating he doubted if the American government would be able to secure any money from China. In replying to Murray, Speers sent him the resolution of the BFM and stated their position: they would not seek an indemnity because it would hinder the work of the mission. Speers forwarded Murray's letter to the Rev. Scott, noting that Murray was an elder in a church and an active Christian worker, and was also the vice chairman of the international committee of the YMCA and chairman of its foreign department committee.[31] The BFM had carefully omitted any mention of the indemnity in its official statements, since it continued to oppose the collection of one for the death of one of its missionaries, and communicated this position to all the supporters of Mrs. Byers, who continued to press for the indemnity.

On 14 November Mrs. Byers telegraphed the BFM asking if the government were taking any action as "influential friends offer assistance if government still inactive." She suggested she could enlist the aid of several congressmen and wanted to know what action the BFM had taken at their 3 November meeting. Mrs. Roys responded by telegram the following day saying the BFM was in close touch with the Department of State, had cabled the PCC to pressure the legation to action, and would "strongly advise against using personal influence in Washington or enlisting congressmen's help."[32]

Mrs. Roys then followed the telegram with a letter, sending Mrs. Byers the text of the BFM's minute from the 3 November meeting. Mrs. Roys noted that the Rev. Scott had sent her the wording while she was on a speaking trip and both of them felt it was "far too mild and anemic, but we were advised by those familiar with the affairs in Washington that it would be a grave mistake to use more forceful language." She thought requests for help from other persons would weaken the case as the BFM was officially approaching the Department of State about the matter. She remarked that Mrs. Byers had not mentioned the payment of money to her by the Chinese government and noted, "In the [BFM] there is every shade of opinion from that of the highest idealism which even for property damage would accept no indemnity to that of the hard-headed business man who would have the [BFM] claim from the Government a large indemnity for the life of one of its missionaries." She again assured Mrs. Byers that the BFM would provide for her and her children whether or not any money was received from the Chinese government. She stated, "freedom of action in this matter lies wholly with the individual." Personally, she wrote, she felt an indemnity would seriously harm the work that the Rev. Byers had devoted his life to because it would be collected from those who were not responsible for his death. Yet she felt that those responsible needed to be punished and pressure brought to bear on the Hainan authorities to "preserve the peace and protect foreigners and foreign property."[33]

One of the BFM members, W. Reginald Wheeler, was unable to attend the meeting on 17 November, but wrote to formally express his opinion. He felt it was not right for the BFM to seek an indemnity and not right for an individual to make such a request or for the BFM to encourage them to do so. He also thought that in adopting such an "ostensibly high-minded policy" the BFM had to be responsible for the widow and children. At the 17 November meeting the BFM took action and Mrs. Roys again telegraphed Mrs. Byers that they feared an adverse impact on the work of the mission if she requested an indemnity, but recognized her right as an individual to do so. "Should you relinquish this right [the BFM] will see that adequate financial provision is made for you."[34]

On the 18th Mrs. Roys responded to Murray saying, "since there is no central government [in China] at present," any money would be collected locally from those "wholly innocent" of the crime. She sent him the details of the BFM's meeting and added the PCC had voted unanimously that it was inadvisable to seek an indemnity. She added that the BFM was in contact with the Department of State.[35]

Mrs. Roys again reassured Mrs. Byers on 18 November that the BFM would "adequately" provide for her, explaining "adequate" to mean adequate both in the amount and in the time limit. There was a time limit on children's allowances, but not on hers. Mrs. Roys had approached the Board of Ministerial Relief for their maximum grant which the BFM indicated it would supplement. She then asked Mrs. Byers to state the figure she would need each year to maintain her family. Mrs. Byers was then receiving $175 per month and Mrs. Roys wanted to know if that were adequate. Mrs. Roys indicated she was going to ask the BFM to advance Mrs. Byers's allowance from that given for single missionaries to two-thirds or three-fourths of the amount given for a husband and wife. The BFM also gave grants of $25 per month for rent, provided that was at least two-thirds of what the person spent. She also asked if Mrs. Byers needed a supplementary grant to cover her medical expenses, incurred at the time of her daughter's birth. Mrs. Roys also wanted to know if the action of the BFM on 17 November met with Mrs. Byers's approval.[36]

Mrs. Roys ended the letter by citing the case of the London Missionary Society (LMS) whose property in Tsaoshi, Hupeh, was looted by Hunan bandits in June 1923. Although there was no loss of life the mission residences and part of the hospital were burned, along with two-fifths of the town. The LMS had accepted an indemnity in 1900 for damage done by the Boxers, but had since decided the resentment over indemnities was so intense they would no longer request them.[37]

Mrs. Byers's Living and Medical Expenses

Mrs. Ina Rittenhouse, in whose cottage the Byers family was living, also wrote to Mrs. Roys detailing the medical costs Mrs. Byers had when her daughter was born, along with the costs of nurses for six weeks and a woman to help with the housework. She noted that Mrs. Byers's aunt had come to stay, so the cost of help was expected to be cheaper than anticipated. Mrs. Rittenhouse indicated that Mrs. Byers had been very disappointed not to hear of the BFM's action after the 3 November meeting and noted there had been "disquieting letters from the field," to the effect that the American government was doing nothing about the case. Mrs. Rittenhouse also had a letter from a Presbyterian minister, who was a friend, and who had written a congressman about the situation. She indicated most of Mrs. Byers's friends urged her to press the case with the Chinese government and could not understand why she did not.[38]

Mrs. Rittenhouse said she understood the position of the BFM and agreed with it. Yet the letters from the field made Mrs. Byers think she should do something to help those missionaries still in Hainan, even though she knew to do so meant pressing her own claim, too. Mrs. Rittenhouse wrote,

> Word from the [BFM] as to what they could and would do for her had been vague, the recommendation of the PCC that she be given what would amount to $2100 per year for two years was not very reassuring, friends were very insistent that she take steps in her own behalf. You can see what a dilemma she was in.

She continued that Mrs. Byers was reassured by Mrs. Roys's second telegram saying the BFM would "undertake to care for her if she waived her claim." Mrs. Rittenhouse felt the BFM needed either to help Mrs. Byers make a claim with the government or to take the responsibility for her support. She thought Mrs. Byers would not be able to work for at least ten years, and by then her eldest son would be grown, but "if he is to go out to the field in his father's place, he cannot support his mother and younger brothers and sisters." She also said she felt it would not be proper for Mrs. Byers to have to live from year to year waiting for the BFM to vote her an allowance, stating such a situation would be uncertain "as new people came in who did not have the same interest in her case. Also that it would be somewhat humiliating as some would be sure to arise who would criticize the use of so much of the [BFM's] money for what will then be a half-forgotten case."[39]

On 12 December Mrs. Byers wrote to Mrs. Roys about her needed expenses. She was then living rent free in the cottage of Mrs. Rittenhouse, but as it was too small for the family she knew she would have to move soon. She estimated she would need $3000 a year for minimum expenses and $3500 if she were to employ someone to help her with the housework. She mentioned that three years earlier while on furlough they had had many things, including their rent, donated and spent $2600, but "ran behind in our tithe and had to make it up on the field when we returned. . . . My husband did most of the housework. I think you will agree with me that most missionaries save something on the field and spend it when on furlough."[40]

She related the economic condition of various people she knew in southern California from a local minister to Mrs. Rittenhouse's gardener and most were not able to live on $3000 per year. She reported that some of the local church people wanted to establish a memorial fund for her and she expressed her reluctance to accept any money from the Board of Ministerial Relief, because she knew there were retired men and women who needed that money. She expressed her desire to "drop the entire 'indemnity' question" if the BFM would provide for her support. She also reported that Senator Selden P. Spencer was taking the matter up with the Department of State.[41]

A note in the BFM file on the allowances for the Byers children indicated that for the five children Mrs. Byers would receive $1100 in 1925 with increases until 1934 when she would receive $1500.[42]

On 23 December Mrs. Byers telegraphed the BFM to ask how she should respond to the government which had informed her that they were making a claim to the Chinese government on her behalf. A handwritten note by Mrs. Roys on this letter questioned if the BFM needed to ask the Department of State not to press the claim, since to do so would harm the work of the mission. Although the telegram arrived in New York at 1:30 p.m. on 24 December Mrs. Roys had apparently already left the office for she responded on 26 December saying she had received the telegram that morning. She telegraphed Mrs. Byers that the Department of State had acted without consulting the BFM whose next meeting was 19 January. Mrs. Byers was advised, "In the meantime my personal suggestion would be to await outcome."[43]

Mrs. Byers also reported receiving a letter from Mrs. Lydia Lord Davis of Oberlin, Ohio, whose husband had been killed by the Boxers, leaving her with three small children. She said she had accepted the money from the Chinese government, used it to support and educate her children, and if she had to do it again would do the same. Mrs. Byers asked that the arrangements for her financial support be put in the form of an agreement so that when there was a change in the secretaryship she would not have to ask again, and would not be dependent on a yearly appropriation. She wrote, "I would like to have the question settled definitely once and for all . . .

keeping any aspect of the question before me is very hard emotionally . . . [and] very exhausting."[44]

The BFM Agrees to Support Mrs. Byers and Her Children

The year closed with Mrs. Roys writing to the Rev. J. C. R. Ewing of Princeton, New Jersey, who was a member of the BFM, telling him of Mrs. Byers's request for $3500 per year in support. She indicated that the executive committee would discuss the matter on Friday morning, but thought,

> We shall not reach unanimity of agreement as to the [BFM]'s responsibility to meet this requirement in full; but with the action of the [BFM] as explicit as it is, I plan to propose to the Executive Council, in case of a disagreement of opinion, that the whole matter be referred back to the Foreign Committee to define what they meant by "adequate financial provision."

She asked if she might speak personally to Ewing on this "perplexing situation," adding, some of the BFM members were more in agreement with her on this issue than were some members of the executive committee. She also informed him of the Department of State's request for $25,000 gold in indemnity. She hoped Mrs. Byers would receive $1100 in children's allowances, $300 from the Board of Ministerial Relief, and the balance from the BFM. She also thought that at some time in the future Mrs. Byers would "herself release the [BFM] from any financial obligation to her."[45]

On 1 January the Rev. Ewing responded to Mrs. Roys indicating he would arrive early for the meeting and stating he felt the Foreign Work Committee and the BFM had "left the details of the relief for Mrs. Byers very unsettled." Mrs. Roys responded the following day with the decision of the executive committee to grant Mrs. Byers the allowance of a married couple ($1800) and the children's allowances ($1100) and the Board of Ministerial Relief grant ($300). She added, "Dr. [Arthur J.] Brown and Dr. Speer both opposed the recommendation; Dr. Speer feeling that Mrs. Byers should apply for and insist on indemnity and Dr. Brown considering that she should have only the home allowance of a single woman, namely, $1000. With these two exceptions everyone in the Executive Council voted favorably." The following day Mrs. Roys wrote to Miss Jean Mackenzie of New York City stating that the needed $300 for Mrs. Byers would "without doubt be given by the Sage Legacy Committee." She also wrote,

> Dr. Speer stood solidly against any grant whatever for Mrs. Byers, feeling that she should apply for indemnity. Dr. Brown voted in the negative for the home allowance as suggested, feeling it too large a sum. With the exception of these two votes, the entire Council of secretaries from both the Home and Foreign Departments voted approval of the action.

On 5 January the executive council approved a minute to formalize the action for Mrs. Byers, stating that any funds received from Peking or a memorial fund would be applied to the BFM grant. On 9 January Mrs. Roys wrote to the Rev. Charles R. Erdman to tell him of the decision about the money for Mrs. Byers and the minute of the executive committee. She repeated the opposition of Rev. Speer and Rev. Brown. She related that the matter was twofold. First was the matter of the BFM's policy on indemnity. She presented the Rev. Erdman with the historic position of the BFM and again stated that while Mrs. Byers might ask for an indemnity as a private person, "no missionary would likely do anything in a private capacity which the [BFM], as a Board, would feel unwilling to do." She informed him of the Department of State's request for $25,000 and noted if it were paid, "Mrs. Byers will undoubtedly accept it [and] this will relieve the [BFM] of its obligation." She also mentioned the proposed memorial fund. She pointed out that the executive council's minute clearly indicated that funds from Peking or a memorial fund would take the place of the grant from the BFM.[46]

Mrs. Roys went on that the second aspect of the case was the BFM's policy toward the widows of men who died on the field. She pointed out that whatever was done for Mrs. Byers would become a precedent for such cases, adding,

> The women of the [BFM] feel strongly that up to this time we have not provided in an adequate way for the widows of our missionaries. The principle that a woman left alone with a family can get on with a single woman's allowance, whereas a man widowed must have either two-thirds or the whole of a married man's allowance, is tragically far from the truth.

She then added, "I shall be deeply grateful if the Byers's case opens up the whole question of a more adequate provision for the wives of those who have given their lives in the service." She continued that she felt so deeply about the issue that she had gathered "all the necessary data . . . such as exact wording of the BFM's historic policies on indemnities; Mrs. Byers's own statement and the testimony of others as to her present needs; and the report of the Department of State as to its recent action." She asked the Rev. Erdman if he thought it would be a good idea to send this material to the members of the BFM before the scheduled meeting. The Rev. Erdman responded to Mrs. Roys on 14 January that if the government did not succeed in getting the $25,000 and if the memorial fund were not raised, he was in favor of paying Mrs. Byers $1800 a year, stating, "not because it is 'a married man's home allowance' but because it is a sum which I feel we should try to pay to any person in her condition and circumstances." He, too, hoped the BFM would use this as a precedent for other widows of missionaries in similar situations. He admitted he had never thought much about indemnities, but saw the difference between one demanded by the BFM and one secured by the government by its own action.[47]

Mrs. Roys prepared a nine-page, single-spaced report giving the particulars of the BFM's historic policy on indemnities, what had transpired in the Byers case, and Mrs. Byers's request for adequate support in the amount of $3500 per year and sent it to the BFM members on 14 January so that they might review it before the 19 January meeting. Mrs. Roys summed up the situation: "Three issues are involved. I. The [BFM]'s policy as to indemnity on life; II. The amount which the [BFM] is willing to grant Mrs. Byers; III. The [BFM]'s policy as to its financial obligation to the wives of men who have died in the service." Regarding the first issue she said they needed to consider the attitudes of Mrs. Byers, the PCC, and missionaries on the field. She noted, "Mrs. Byers's letters reveal her earnest desire to conform to the [BFM]'s policy of not claiming indemnity for life. She is unwilling to accept indemnity if the Chinese Christians or the poor are taxed. She is willing to accept a payment only if it is exacted as a punitive measure from the guilty parties." Mrs. Roys also noted that the PCC was unanimous in its opposition to asking for an indemnity for a life, and wrote, "The sentiment of missionaries on the field seems increasingly opposed to indemnity. Resolutions against any pressure on China for the 'right' of missionaries were considered at both Kuling and Peitaiho [missionary resorts] during the past summer." She repeated that the request for an indemnity by the executive committee of the Hainan mission was issued without submitting it to the PCC and the action was taken without a member of the Kachek station present. She wrote,

> The question of indemnity raises the following questions: Will it insure safety to our missionaries? Will it result in the guilty being punished? Can indemnity be collected, as Mrs. Byers hopes, from gamblers and corrupt officials? Will it deepen the present mistrust of the West which Anti-Christian forces are encouraging? Will it yield an aftermath of resentment and bitter hatred? Will it set back for a generation the work in the very community where Mr. Byers gave his life? Will it disillusion the students and the churches in America whose idealism in missionary consecration is as high as the teachings of Christ about counting life not dear? Is there significance in the fact that the [LMS] which recently had its compound at Tsaoshi in [Hupeh] looted and burned, including the destruction of residences and part of the hospital, refused unanimously to accept any payment for the destruction of its property because of the harm done to its evangelistic work by the acceptance of indemnity for property in 1900?

In considering Mrs. Byers's financial need, Mrs. Roys pointed out Mrs. Byers was a semi-invalid and her children were in ill health and she needed to furnish a modest home. Mrs. Roys recognized that her third point, support of all those widowed on the field, introduced a new matter which the BFM needed to consider.[48]

A Memorial Fund Is Proposed

In January Mrs. Lillian Kelly, who was working in California to have Presbyterian women's groups write to congressmen about the case, was also seeking to establish a memorial fund for Mrs. Byers and other women who might one day need it. Mrs. Roys thought such a permanent fund would be a good idea, writing, "It has been heart-breaking to me since coming to the [BFM] to see how inadequately our Board provides for the wives of men who give their lives in the service." Mrs. Roys also wrote to Mrs. Kelly indicating her support for the memorial fund, but wanted those involved to take care that it did not "undercut the income of the [BFM] by diverting money which would otherwise go to the regular budget. . . . This would work disastrously, in that it would cut off the salaries of missionaries on the field and do endless harm to the work already established."[49]

On 19 January the Women's Board sent Mrs. Roys a check for $150 for Mrs. Byers and the BFM, on the recommendation of the Foreign Committee, adopted the minute for the support of Mrs. Byers in the amount of $3500 per year, adding the provision that it begin that day. Mrs. Roys telegraphed the news to Mrs. Byers. The following day Mrs. Roys's secretary wrote to the Rev. Erdman telling him of the action and noting there were no negative votes in the Foreign Committee although Rev. Ewing, Rev. Speer, and Rev. Brown spoke against the measure. On the 21st Mrs. Byers telegraphed her thanks to Mrs. Roys. Two days later Mrs. Roys wrote to Representative Phil D. Swing to tell him the BFM had taken care of the support of Mrs. Byers, adding, the BFM felt there was "a very definite distinction between an indemnity which is *demanded* by our Board and an indemnity which is *secured* by the government at its own instance for the life of an American citizen."[50]

On 24 January Mrs. Roys wrote to Mrs. Byers about "how great a burden of perplexity and anxiety I have carried because of the many issues involved in this matter." She indicated that she previously had not wanted to tell Mrs. Byers, but it was the most important issue she had faced since joining the BFM three years earlier. "I wish you could have felt the deep concern of every member of the Board for your welfare. I was especially eager to have the entire matter *settled*." She indicated that the minute passed without a dissenting vote. She noted that each child's allowance would increase by $100 when the child reached the age of ten. Because of this, she asked if Mrs. Byers would agree to take a corresponding decrease in the $1800 when that occurred, so that "I may leave the file of letters bearing on this whole arrangement in such clear shape that were I to be taken out of the office in any unforeseen way there would be no misunderstanding whatever between you and the Board." She indicated that if Mrs. Byers got an indemnity and turned it over to the BFM the proceeds could be used to reduce the BFM's payment. The same could be done for any memorial fund.[51]

Mrs. Roys wrote that the next China Mission Letter would contain a note about the arrangement, but not the dollar amount involved as she did not think it was wise to publish it. She noted there were other women who had been widowed on the field who had not been provided for in the past and she did not want to stir up hard feelings.

She also noted that she had written to Representative Swing saying if an indemnity were paid it would go directly to Mrs. Byers.[52]

Mrs. Byers responded saying she "went completely limp" upon receiving the news of the BFM's action and had her first good night's sleep in many months. She wrote, "In my heart I feel sure that I owe this all to you, for had it not been for your vigorous handling and sympathetic backing I am convinced no mere 'Board' would have done the very generous thing they did." She also noted,

> I am ready to do anything the Board wishes about that claim of the Government for $25,000. They have never written me a line about it. I suppose they would not care to back down tho [*sic*] I'm quite willing to write them that I will waive it. In absence of advice from you I've done nothing.[53]

This absence of advice from the BFM was largely responsible for the conflicting telegrams sent to the Department of State on 4 March.

On 1 February Mrs. Byers wrote that she hoped the memorial fund would materialize and was willing to consent to have it structured so that women who came after her might also benefit. She asked that the $1800 for her be maintained and the children's allowances not increased so that when the children were grown she would still have the $1800 a year for herself. She indicated she would leave to the BFM the disposition of the indemnity if it were collected. She knew the BFM was opposed to receiving such a payment and asked if the government should not be told of their position, noting that if the money were collected

> the reaction on the Chinese psychology would be the same as if it were collected by the Board or the mission. . . . If a Chinese has a dollar taken from him he doesn't care especially *how* it was taken. It is the fact of its going that distresses him. If the government paid it out of public moneys [*sic*] it would be somewhat different.

She indicated her willingness to tell the government she did not want the money, but she thought the government would do what it wanted to.[54]

On 25 February Mrs. Roys advised Mrs. Byers to do nothing about the government's request for $25,000, as she did not think such an action was wise and "I am quite sure the [BFM] would not wish to do this." Mrs. Roys continued to believe that the matter would be dropped unless both Mrs. Byers and the BFM pressed it vigorously.

She noted that word was coming from various sources other than Presbyterian ones concerning "the whole question of the wisdom at this time of demanding indemnity from China and thus strengthening the anti-foreign feeling and deepening the mistrust of the Chinese in our disinterested friendship." On the following day, the Rev. Orville Reed at the Board of Ministerial Relief informed Mrs. Roys that they could pay Mrs. Byers nothing, noting "the vast majority of our annuities paid to widows are paid to those who have no other income whatsoever." Mrs. Roys informed Mrs. Byers of this telling her she would ask for $600 from sources outside the BFM, instead of the $300 she had planned to request. On 11 March the Sage Legacy Committee voted $600 a year for the support of Mrs. Byers as long as she needed it.[55]

The BFM Tries to Establish a Position on Indemnities

Mrs. Byers's situation clearly caused many on the BFM to consider the entire question of treaty rights, extraterritoriality, and indemnities, and the position of the Presbyterian Church vis-à-vis them. Some months after the BFM's decision regarding the support of the Byers family, Harold A. Hatch, who was a trustee of the American College for Women in Constantinople, wrote Speer his views of the church's stand on the unequal treaties in China, urging that the Presbyterian Church "completely reject for itself" reliance on those treaties that he said would "hinder in a large measure the success of our great Cause in China." Hatch believed that unless the BFM "repudiate for itself utterly and entirely all these unequal treaties" and urge the American government to do likewise, then it would be better to turn all missionary work in China over to the Chinese churches and give them support. He believed that the Christian Church needed to reject the philosophy that the end justified the means and build "with the Christian Method upon the rock of the Christian Faith."[56]

Hatch was likely the author of an eight-page statement, "Some Tentative Considerations Researching Indemnities," that survives in the Speer archives at Princeton Theological Seminary. Although this statement is unsigned and undated, it refers to the Byers case and other correspondence preserved with it suggest it was written in late 1925.[57]

The author indicated that the indemnity question was part of the larger church-state issue—a problem that had never been solved. Although ideally "a free church in a free state" was sought, such a condition had never existed, and the author noted that missionaries could not enter British India without the permission of the British and in China they had not been able to own land until that right was conceded by treaty. He could see two extreme positions—missionaries could be employed by the government of their own countries, such was the case of chaplains of the East India Company; or they could completely dissociate themselves from their native states by becoming citizens of the countries they wanted to serve. Although he cited the case of individuals who had sought this path in Chile and Japan, he thought most would never consider such an option. Even if one adopted new citizenship, one would still have to deal with the laws of the new country when there was a loss of property or life. Yet he wrote that this, too, could be overcome if the individual decided in advance to passively accept all things and claim no rights. He cited Paul who had both exercised his rights as a Roman citizen on occasion while ignoring those same rights at other times.[58]

On the question of indemnities for lost property Hatch thought it was only fair that the person who had taken or destroyed property needed to make restitution. As to loss of life, he stated the BFM had already taken the position that it had not suffered as the result of the death of a missionary, so it had decided not to seek compensation. He cited the case of the U.S. Consul Major Imbrie who had been killed in Teheran. Although acknowledging that Imbrie was not a missionary, Hatch argued that if it were right in that case then it was also right to seek an indemnity for the loss of a missionary's life. If it were wrong to accept an indemnity for a missionary's life, then it had to be wrong, not on principle, but out of "expediency and wisdom for the sake of the missionary cause." He argued that if it were wrong to seek an indemnity for the life of a person then for the sake of consistency it must also be wrong to seek compensation for the loss of property.[59]

Acknowledging that the case in China was different due to the extraterritorial clauses in the treaties, Hatch argued that if Chinese lost property in the United States they did not seek compensation from the government, but rather did so in the law courts. Then he argued that perhaps it was not wise for missionaries to seek compensation for lost property, arguing on the biblical teaching that if a man takes your cloak give him your coat, too. Yet he acknowledged as long as the laws of human societies were involved, theft, fraud, and general mayhem should not be allowed. He further pointed out that the loss of life generally involved governments, or more specifically the lack of government action to protect foreigners as provided for under treaty provisions. In the Byers case he particularly cited the action of the PCC disavowing an indemnity for the Rev. Byers's life, but the collection of it, nonetheless, by the American government. He wrote that as the Chinese willingly paid the indemnity and the PCC and the Hainan mission "pressed so urgently for political action of the United States to secure the establishment of order and the punishment of crime that it would not be possible to isolate and weigh separately the effect of the . . . indemnity paid to Mrs. Byers."[60]

Hatch then summed up his argument by stating that as the American government would, of its own accord, collect an indemnity, the fact that it was not asked by the survivors would be lost on the people from whom it was extracted. The demand for protection and the establishment of order by the BFM and missionaries in the field would work more hardship on the people than would a "reasonable indemnity," which he thought was the "best and surest and most powerful method of restoring order." He also noted that if the BFM was to discourage surviving relatives from accepting indemnities or if the dependent relatives refused to accept an indemnity, then the issue of how the dependents were to be supported still remained, as it had in the Byers case. If the BFM did not accept an indemnity, but then paid for the support of the dependents from mission funds, was the BFM not "transfering the responsibility for the indemnity from those who were guilty of the crime and liability and laying it upon missionary contributions, surely not made for such purpose." If the BFM thought such use of mission funds justified, he then asked why it should be limited only to those who met violent deaths. He questioned if those who died of disease or suffered mental breakdowns that necessitated returning home, might not similarly have their dependents supported, particularly since those who died of disease would have no recourse to a governmental indemnity. He concluded that he thought the collection of an indemnity would be no more "evil" than the actions taken by the American consul as had been described in Rev. Lowrie's letter of 22 April 1925. He thought there was much more danger in engaging in punitive measures which he believed the government needed to inflict.[61]

In March 1926 Speer, noting he had been on the field for most of the winter, responded to Hatch's letter concerning missionary problems in China and Turkey. Speer expressed his opinion that the American treaties of 1858 and 1903 with China could only be called "unequal" if one ignored the historical facts. He maintained the treaties were not forced upon China and were not maintained by force. He claimed that Chinese in America had the same rights Americans had in China, although he did note that some states limited the rights of aliens, particularly the right to own land. He also acknowledged that the "new psychology" made it wise to revise the treaties, but even revision suggested they were not unequal. In the treaty revision he thought they should secure "recognition of the inviolable principles of universal religious liberty." If Hatch had referred to the extraterritorial provisions when he called the treaties unequal then Speer would agree they were unequal and he maintained the missionaries had never sought those privileges and "do not need them and never have needed them."[62]

Speer continued that he held

> unequivocally the doctrine of the New Testament and of the Reformers, Calvin and Knox, that the State is a divine institution, that it is under obligation to obey the law of Christ, that Christ is not Lord of individuals and the Church only but of the whole of human life and that the true business of the State is justice and righteousness.

He believed that the state needed to promote freedom of religion as much as freedom of trade. He noted he supported the League of Nations because he thought it would develop international law which would guarantee religious freedom and noted that in the past the Evangelical Alliance had sought the same goals.[63]

On the question of a missionary's relationship to governments, Speer noted it was impossible to separate the person from any government. He cited many cases where missionaries had served various governments when they established diplomatic relations, or had acted as consuls or vice consuls, or in other ways such as helping to defend people from "the traffic in liquor and fire arms." He stated that it was a fundamental principle that a nonmissionary Christian in a foreign country could occupy a status different from a missionary Christian. He also believed that foreigners who went to live in other lands as missionaries needed to go "with their eyes open and prepare to accept the conditions which they find there," but if the

> conditions there are inhuman and unjust, inflicting wrong upon foreigners, or natives, or both, if the laws are indefensible and intolerable, they ought to be changed and more humane and enlightened governments have the right and duty to seek by just and peaceable measures,

> or by the organized public opinion and constraint of the world through a World League to secure rational and humane laws. It is right to seek universally righteous laws, both national and international and all people, whoever they are and wherever they are, have the right to desire and enjoy such laws.

He thought that fundamental among such laws was the "right of religious liberty." He went on to acknowledge that such theoretical arguments obscured the practical question, namely,

> the confusion of our unselfish spiritual religious enterprise with the great ambitions and self-seeking of western trade and its support by western governments and with the evils and injustices of western civilization. Christian missions must completely disentangle themselves from all this and stand out clear and pure.

But he noted Americans missionaries would always be Americans and they could not become "Chinese, or Indians, or Africans, no matter how they live or talk or what they eat or wear," as they could surmount many conditions by love and service, but not the reality of who they are. He believed that the West had given Asia both good and evil and that current nationalistic sentiments had emphasized the evil more than the good.[64]

Speer concluded his argument by stating it was the duty of Christians to speak out against wrongs and seek to redress for injustices whether they were by their own governments or by foreign governments either against the missionaries or against their own people. The major question was what missionaries should do in countries "where religious liberty is denied or abridged." Should the missionaries expect their own governments to gain for them the right to preach the gospel or should they "go ahead and preach with all the wisdom and prudence they can command but still fearlessly and take the consequences?" He acknowledged that Western governments had a problem with this and believed it was the duty of the missionaries to "avoid creating troublesome problems for their governments," but added they were "certainly . . . justified in exercising the right of freedom of religion as merchants are to exercise the right of freedom of trade and the governments themselves must determine what their duties are in consequence." An even more difficult issue was what were the missionaries to do when their consuls "advise or even order them to follow a course of abstention from missionary work, or abandonment of mission stations?" He believed that missionaries ought never ask for the protection of consuls and ought never to ask for gunboats or military protection. "Missionaries can get along best without any political interference and they wish none. All they have a right or desire to ask is the common enjoyment of the rights of life, property and conscience, which ought to be secured to every human being everywhere."[65]

It was obvious from the positions stated by Hatch and Speer that there were no easy solutions to the question of what should be the relationship of missionaries to governments—both their own and those of the countries they served. Although Speer was secretary of the BFM he had never been a missionary so his views of the situation were those of an American whose only contact with missionary problems had been through letters and his occasional visits to the various fields. What was clear was the BFM could develop a policy of supporting the dependents of men who died on the field, but they could not have a clear-cut absolute policy on how to handle governmental problems, if their missionaries died by violence.

As the question of indemnities continued to reverberate within the BFM, in June 1927 they sought to pass a resolution that stated it was their policy neither to claim nor accept any indemnity for the loss of a missionary's life. However, at the same time the BFM acknowledged the responsibility of the church at home to support the surviving dependents. With regard to indemnities for property, the proposed resolution stated that in these cases the BFM would consider if a government had taken property or if it had been destroyed by the "remissness of governments," or if the circumstances were such that a claim could be made against the American government. The resolution also stated that the BFM did not "lay down any general rule" but that each case needed to be decided "with reference to right Christian principles." They were also opposed to an indemnity which would "be levied on the innocent or in the locality where the loss occurred in any way that might injure the Christian cause."[66]

Mrs. Byers's Life in the Aftermath of the BFM's Decision

In the years after the BFM voted to support the Byers family and the indemnity was collected by Mrs. Byers she continued to write from time to time to Mrs. Roys and others at the BFM about the Hainan mission and her finances. For example, on 2 March 1926

Mrs. Byers wrote that she wanted to give up her $600 grant from outside sources, that is, the Sage Legacy Committee, and reduce by $300 the yearly appropriation she got from the BFM. Upon receipt of this letter Mrs. Roys wrote to Miss Schultz, Miss Lepper, and Miss Hodge, all at the BFM, telling them of Mrs. Byers's request. Mrs. Byers then received $1500 a year from the BFM for herself, plus her children's allowances. Mrs. Roys wrote,

> This voluntary action of Mrs. Byers justified my unshakable confidence that she would in no circumstance ask for or accept one dollar more than her actual needs. I shall take every means to have these facts made known for I do not like the undercurrent of suspicion that Mrs. Byers extorted from the [BFM] as large a sum as possible and is living in extreme luxury.[67]

Some people at the BFM apparently thought Mrs. Byers's grant could be reduced from time to time. Many letters to Mrs. Byers from Miss Ruth Elliott at the BFM between March and May 1927 suggested a reduction in her grant would help, especially as the BFM expected a deficit in their budget for that year. While trying to decide what to do, the BFM held up Mrs. Byers's May check and the financial strain was clearly evident when she wrote Mrs. Roys about it:

> I sometimes wonder if after all I should not make some arrangement with a children's home for [my children] and go to work myself. Of course this would shift the load from the [BFM] to the state or other public agency and the children *should* be more of an asset to the church when grown if raised the way I am trying to do it than if committed to institutional hands. The one argument in its favor is that I can do office work more easily than housework and I would save the price of help in the bargain. I can argue for it but I can't convince myself of the wisdom of such a course. And yet plenty of women do have to do it. Who am I that I should balk?

Mrs. Roys quickly replied that Mrs. Byers's current check, which had been delayed, was then on its way to her and added,

> Please do not ever contemplate making an arrangement to put your children into an institution in order that you may be able to find a position for yourself. The biggest service you can do for the world is to give those blessed children the care and upbringing which you alone are able to provide for them.

She concluded that Mrs. Byers should consider the wording of the BFM's minute on her case in that it was not a gift from the BFM that she received but adequate support for herself and her children which was "gladly voted."[68]

But problems continued and Mrs. Byers again wrote to Mrs. Roys in July asking her to straighten things out. Mrs. Roys reported,

> You will laugh I think if you knew how many checks have been made out and destroyed until finally late last evening I secured the enclosed check which I believe is the accurate amount due you. One of the assistants in the Treasurer's office, in a final effort to clear the matter, bore into my office a tome so large that we could hardly get it on my desk. With this before me and with pad and pencil as though I were teaching a class of elementary arithmetic I explained at great length the present situation in regard to your remittances. You would have had checks for various amounts larger than this if I had not interfered with my ruthless arithmetic, but such a procedure would have entailed settlement later and I was eager to have the slate clean so that from now on there will be no possibility of mistake.

On 22 July Mrs. Lucy Lepper Shaw wrote to the Rev. Speer about Mrs. Byers's situation and the likelihood of a settlement from an uncle's estate which would decrease her need for the BFM's grant. She noted Mrs. Byers "is exceedingly conscientious and careful in her accounts and I believe we can rest assured that the [BFM] will be relieved of all financial responsibility just as soon as it is possible for her to do so." In October Mrs. Byers asked that the BFM reduce the grant to her to $150 per month.[69]

The correspondence that survives in the BFM archives on the Byers case ends with the October 1927 letter, except for a few letters written in the 1940s, one of which concerned the clarification of the citizenship of the Byers children who had been born in China.

Clearly, the BFM found the need of Mrs. Byers to have some way to support herself after her husband's death a perplexing issue. The BFM did not have life insurance for its missionaries and did not require them to have their own policies. Prior to the Byers case the BFM had no policy for handling the needs of women who were widowed while on the field and had children to support. As Mrs. Davis's letter to Mrs. Byers indicated such women had to depend on the BFM voting them some compensation on a yearly basis, which, as Mrs. Davis, who had been widowed during the Boxer Uprising of 1898–1900, indicated could be a lengthy ordeal. In Mrs. Roys, Mrs.

Byers found a champion who felt that the policy of the BFM needed altering. Mrs. Roys, herself widowed while in China, spend many hours corresponding and talking with the male members of the BFM, finally convincing them that they had an obligation to make some permanent arrangements for Mrs. Byers and her children while they were minors. Mrs. Roys's work was made more difficult by the great differences of opinion among the members of the BFM regarding the issue of seeking an indemnity. Yet through hard work and dedication to her cause Mrs. Roys managed to convince her male colleagues on the BFM that they needed to "adequately" support Mrs. Byers and they voted that compensation. That dissenters among those at the BFM remained is evident from the letters over the years which asked Mrs. Byers to request a reduction in her grant, but Mrs. Roys steadfastly held to her position that the grant was voted to Mrs. Byers—it was not a gift. From the surviving letters it is clear that the BFM maintained its commitment to Mrs. Byers, and her minor children, through the 1940s and probably until the end of her life. In later years Mrs. Byers was employed in the library of the San Anselmo Seminary in California, which her husband had attended.

6
Conclusion

HAINAN'S REMOTE LOCATION WAS A MAJOR FACTOR IN THE EXTRATERRITORIALITY case that followed the murder of the Rev. George Byers in Kachek in 1924. The murder had occurred in a remote town five days' travel from the nearest American consulate, so any official sent there was, of necessity, going to be gone from the consulate for quite some time. American consular officials clearly did not think the murder of an American missionary to be of grave concern; rather it was a distraction from what they considered their work and several expressed such sentiments in their official correspondence. Hainan's remote location affected the missionaries, too, because they were not up-to-date on the issues of the church's attitude toward the extraterritorial provisions of China's treaties with other countries.

Hainan, like most of China, had seen increased violence as a result of the political chaos that wracked the country in the early twentieth century. The missionaries in Hainan were aware of the potential dangers they faced, but they believed the extraterritoriality clauses in America's treaties with China protected them. Yet when violence around Kachek increased to an unprecedented level they took the extraordinary step of asking the British consul at Hoihow, who acted on their behalf, to ask the Chinese military to better patrol the area. They certainly realized they were likely victims for kidnappers since they knew missionaries on the mainland had been kidnapped and held for ransom. They even discussed among themselves the best course to take should a kidnapping occur and Mrs. Byers admitted she wondered when her family's time would come. Despite the unrest, the missionaries did not alter their lifestyles: they continued their travels about the island, they moved their silver dollars openly, and they left the Byers family alone at the Kachek compound while the others went on vacation. After the Rev. Byers was killed, the Hainan missionaries did not question the wisdom of gunboat diplomacy—they wanted a gunboat and a diplomat in Hainan until the matter was settled to their satisfaction, which meant until peace was restored so that their work might continue. No evidence survives to suggest any of them ever questioned the summoning of the consul in a gunboat, although their colleagues in Shanghai thought such a request clearly inappropriate in the new climate of Chinese nationalism. Mrs. Byers, certainly, had no problems with summoning a gunboat, and she clearly believed the Chinese who had embraced Christianity would not object to the Americans taking military action in Hainan if it would "clean out the bandits," regardless of the consequences such action might cause the Chinese Christians. Dr. Nathaniel Bercovitz shared her view as he expressed the sentiment that one of the benefits of Christianity was the establishment of law and order and the suppression of crime. Miss Margaret Moninger even termed the arrival at Hoihow of the Chinese official in charge of the island as a "victory" for the missionaries. Their expressed feeling probably represented the majority opinion among the missionaries in Hainan, who as a group sent the Rev. David S. Tappan and Dr. H. M. McCandliss to plead their case at American consular offices in Canton and Peking. None of the missionaries appeared to realize that the position they were taking, that is, trying to extend the extraterritoriality clauses of the foreign nations' treaties with China to restore order in the countryside for the benefit of the Chinese people, particularly those who had converted to Christianity, was one that had been common in the nineteenth century, particularly among Roman Catholic missionaries for whom France acted as protector, but was relatively rare among Protestant missionaries and little resorted to in the twentieth century.

Throughout the case the Hainan missionaries and Mrs. Byers insisted the major problem was the unrest on the island. Mrs. Byers had indicated that some of the bandits were what Phil Billingsley called "occasionals," that is, farmers or ex-soldiers who had taken to thievery. But Lin Shu-piao and his gang were surely "regulars" by Billingsley's classification of bandits. The men of his gang were not "occasionals" who took to banditry to avoid starvation, but rather were professionals who plundered many villages and held young and old alike for ransom. They were not interested in the Rev. Byers specifically as they would have tried to kidnap any foreigner who happened to be available and for whom they might hope to gain a sizable ransom. These bandits simply took advantage of the collapse of China's central government and civil order to take what they could for themselves. The missionaries wanted the arrest of Lin who they believed was responsible for the Rev. Byers's murder *and* they wanted the restoration of order. Many of the missionaries purported to speak for the Chinese, or at least the Chinese Christians, in requesting the United States government take action to restore that order. However, the surviving correspondence of the American consular personnel clearly indicates that from the beginning they had no intention of landing the marines to aid the missionaries in having a peaceful place to work.

Hainan, like other parts of China, in 1924 was caught up in the aftermath of the collapse of the Ch'ing dynasty and the 1911 Revolution. Because the missionaries lived on the remote island of Hainan they did not have the perspective of viewing the country as a whole for nowhere in China in 1924 was there the kind of stability the Hainan missionaries sought. Many missionaries, including some of those living in Hainan, thought the 1911 Revolution had brought to China a democratic government similar to that of the United States and thus they had difficulty understanding why China, thirteen years later, did not have the peace and tranquility of the United States. This simply was not the case as China's revolution produced chaos not order. Chinese nationalism was emerging during these years and, although many missionaries taught their version of nationalism in the schools they ran, what took shape in China was definitely anti-Christian, a fact few missionaries understood in 1924. The realities of China in 1924–1925 simply meant, as they always had, that in the absence of a strong central government capable of keeping order bandits and scoundrels did as they pleased, mostly at the expense of Chinese, but in this case at the expense of the Rev. Byers's life. The United States government had not taken any action to "clean out the bandits" as the missionaries had wanted, because to do so would have been tantamount to an act of war and indeed might have precipitated one. Many of the diplomats and members of Congress, as well as others, recognized this as a problem—witness Mrs. Byers's statement that "ardor cooled" when people realized her desire for the United States government to make Hainan a safe place for the missionaries to work.

With the collection of the indemnity from General Teng Pen-yin, the Byers case was closed by the United States Department of State. The consul permitted the missionaries to return to their interior stations of Kachek and Nodoa, even though in the latter case another problem of chronic unrest kept the missionaries from returning immediately. That the missionaries returned to their stations, even though there was still a risk, clearly indicates they had made accommodation to the China in which they chose to live. The case had not been resolved, only those innocent of Byers's murder had been executed, but by then the missionaries knew that the collection of the indemnity and permission for them to return to Hainan's interior were going to be the only solutions to the case. Then two years after the Byers murder, the missionaries were faced with more political turmoil. Lin Shu-piao, who had never faced any charges in the Byers murder, entered the Kachek market at the head of a "peoples' army" of former bandits to hold it until Cantonese troops could arrive. He sent his card to the missionaries and announced he had been designated by departing soldiers to protect the missionaries. Promising no harm to the Americans or their property, he actually sought medical attention in the mission hospital.[1]

"Indemnity, indemnity, who asks, gets or demands the indemnity" best describes the intricate machinations of the BFM concerning the issue of the compensation sought from the Chinese by the American government for Mrs. Byers. Among the missionaries in China there was no unanimity of opinion about indemnities nor was there any among the members of the BFM, as Mrs. Mabel Roys indicated. Mrs. Byers thought an indemnity could be collected from the opium-smoking, gambling officials she so disliked and truly believed the people of the Kachek region, particularly the Christians, were too poor for the officials to try to extract money from them. The BFM did not want to officially demand a payment for the loss of the life of one of their missionaries, which accounts for much of their foot-dragging in the early months of the case. Mrs. Roys, who had originally supported seeking an indemnity, changed her mind and even reviewed the entire history of various Christian missions and indemnity questions dating back to the Boxer Uprising to reinforce her case that they were harmful to the work of the missionaries. Yet the same Mrs. Roys is astounded that Mrs. Byers, then reassured of adequate support from the BFM, waived any claim for herself when the Department of State asked if the indemnity they were offered met her requirements. Little wonder that Mrs. Byers declared herself confused and sought the help of the clearest thinking people she knew to sort through all the letters she had had from the BFM on the subject. It finally dawned on Mrs. Byers that the BFM would not seek an indemnity on her behalf if it had to request the Department of State to collect it, but it would certainly allow Mrs. Byers to accept the indemnity already collected by the government, because the BFM could then reduce its support of the Byers family by that amount! Since the government had collected it as a matter of principle, the money would go into the general funds of the United States if Mrs. Byers did not accept it. She finally concluded the BFM wanted her to have it to save them money, not as compensation for the loss of her husband's life. Asking her long-time correspondent Mrs. Roys if this were a correct assessment of the situation, Mrs. Roys penciled onto Mrs. Byers's letter *"YES!"*. At last Mrs. Byers had it figured out. She cabled the secretary of state that she would accept the money, and by doing so she reduced her dependence on the BFM.

It is perhaps ironic that while the Americans engaged in philosophical discussions on the pros and cons of indemnities, the Chinese clearly thought one was due Mrs. Byers. In the two days she was in Kachek after the death of her husband, Mrs. Byers reported that many of the Chinese who came to express their sorrow expected some compensation to be paid to her, and at the funeral of the Rev. Byers such sentiments were also expressed. Certainly, the Chinese officials thought an indemnity would be asked for and when General Ch'en Feng-ch'i accompanied Vice Consul C. B. Chamberlain to Kachek in July to investigate the murder he extracted money from the Chinese along the way. General Teng also expected an indemnity request and, in fact, brought the matter up before the Americans officially asked for one. Although the Rev. Tappan and the others who advised Mrs. Byers in Shanghai before she departed for home pointed out to her that a request of $50,000 was less than passed across the gambling tables of that city each night, it was not from the gamblers, nor the officials whom Mrs. Byers so despised, that the money came, but rather from the hard-working Chinese of the Kachek region where the Rev. Byers had worked and died.

The other issue of this case—Mrs. Byers's struggle with the BFM to provide support for herself and her family—is interesting for what it says about the Presbyterian Church in 1924 and its attitude toward women in her situation. Her strongest supporter, Mrs. Roys, steadfastly refused any thought of the BFM asking the United States government for an indemnity in the case, but just as tenaciously insisted the BFM had an obligation to support Mrs. Byers and sought to make her case a precedent for any other woman who found herself in a similar situation. Mrs. Roys's struggle against the male-dominated BFM appears to be a David vs. Goliath, or more correctly a Mabel vs. Goliath, contest in which Mabel eventually wins because she is right. For all their squabbling and quibbling over the indemnity and the amount of money they should provide for Mrs. Byers and her family, it is noteworthy that when the final vote was taken at a meeting of the BFM, it was unanimous in favor of Mrs. Byers's support. Christian charity, alas, did prevail among the members of the BFM. The two women, who undoubtedly would have denied theirs was a feminist issue, succeeded in asserting their position as people who sought and eventually received equal treatment from the male-dominated institutions they had had to confront. Without the actions of Mrs. Byers and Mrs. Roys there is no doubt that the issue would have gone quietly away. The BFM would have acquiesced in the "blood of martyrs" argument and provided little or no support for the Byers family.

The American diplomats in China clearly did not want to spend time on an extraterritoriality matter concerning the death of one missionary. Their work, as they saw it, was to help businessmen, not settle matters concerning missionaries who insisted on living in remote parts of China where unrest was rife. Forced by political pressures from both the BFM and congressional representatives, the United States government finally found a consul, albeit a very young one, and a ship to take the consul to Hainan. For the settlement of the case it was fortuitous that Vice Consul Maxwell M. Hamilton was uniquely qualified with the patience and perseverance to deal with the Chinese officials. Even though discussions on treaty revisions, which would have eliminated the extraterritorial rights, were taking place among many groups concerned with China in the 1920s, the United States certainly would have collected an indemnity in the Byers case if only as a matter of policy and to preserve its right to do so in the future. But Mrs. Byers's letter-writing campaign spurred the American government to action and got the indemnity paid to her rather than to the United States Treasury.

The work of the Hainan mission resumed after the indemnity was collected and Vice Consul Hamilton withdrew even though the man thought responsible for the crime, Lin Shu-piao, was never arrested. The murderers were thought to have fled the island, but the unrest continued unabated. The summer after the Byers murder, in the aftermath of strikes on the Chinese mainland, the Hainan missionaries fled to Haiphong, French IndoChina, for six weeks and in 1927 when civil war wracked much of China the missionaries again withdrew from the island. Each time they resumed their work when more normal conditions returned. The missionaries all knew the names of those who had probably murdered the Rev. Byers and in

1935 Miss Moninger wrote that she had accompanied the Revs. David Thomas and Arthur French and a Chinese pastor named Ngou to a Christian ground-breaking ceremony at the home of the man who was supposed to be the go-between, appointed to collect the ransom, when the kidnapping was planned. The man had fled to Singapore and the villagers said he "can never come back home."[2]

The Hainan missionaries always maintained theirs was one of the safest locations in China and they were right. Although the mission existed for just over fifty years, none of the women, and only five of the men died on Hainan. Two of the men died from illness and two as the result of accidents. Only the Rev. Byers, who had struggled so ferociously against his attackers, died by violence.

Notes

Chapter 1: The Murder and the Milieu

1. Robert Byers, Interview with author, Des Moines, Wash., 29 March 1997; the Rev. George D. Byers's murder was reported in the *New York Times* (1 July 1924): 23; and in *Chinese Recorder* 55 (1924): 531. (Hereafter *CR.*)

2. American Presbyterian Mission, Hainan, Thirty-first Annual Meeting, 1923, Kackek, *Minutes,* (Shanghai: Presbyterian Mission Press, 1923), 1. (The missionaries also asked for the protection of Chinese and the release of a Chinese who had been kidnapped.)

3. David S. Tappan wrote an account of the Rev. Byers's life which appeared in the *Hainan NewsLetter* (August 1924) and was subsequently distributed by the Board of Foreign Missions (BFM) and then published as "The Martyrdom of the Rev. George D. Byers of Hainan," *The Presbyterian Magazine* 30 (October 1924):485–86. In it he mentioned that the Rev. Byers had kept a diary of his Christian life and in 1911, after five years in Hainan, had lamented he had "won so few souls for my Lord and Master." Tappan added that in the next twelve years the Rev. Byers had baptized "hundreds." As the Rev. Byers was one of only two ordained men at the Kachek station he likely did baptize many of its members, who numbered several hundred by 1924.

4. Clara Byers to George T. Scott, aboard the SS *President Pierce,* 10 August 1924, BFM, RG82, Presbyterian Historical Society, Philadelphia. (Hereafter BFM.) (All subsequent references to Byers are to Mrs. Clara P. Byers unless stated otherwise.)

5. Phil Billingsley, *Bandits in Republican China* (Stanford, Calif.: Stanford University Press, 1988), 13–14, 174–75, refers to both the Lincheng Incident and missionaries taken by bandits. For an account of the bandit situation in North China see Elizabeth J. Perry, *Rebels and Revolutionaries in North China, 1845–1945* (Stanford, Calif.: Stanford University Press, 1980). For accounts of the Lincheng Incident see Michael Nozinski, *Outrage at Lincheng: China Enters the Twentieth Century* (Macomb, Ill.: Glenbridge Publishing, 1990) and Chan Lau Kit-ching, "The Lincheng Incident—A Case Study of British Policy in China between the Washington Conference (1921–22) and the First Nationalist Revolution (1925–28)," *Journal of Oriental Studies* 10 (July 1972): 172–86. For accounts of the missionaries kidnapped and killed see Kenneth S. Latourette, *A History of Christian Missions in China* (New York: Macmillan, 1929), 815–21. Byers's murder was reported in the press at the time it occurred, but Latourette's history contains the only mention of it in a scholarly work that I have been able to locate. The entire reference is a sentence and a half: "That same year George D. Byers, an American Presbyterian, was killed by bandits in Hainan" (817); and "Occasionally an indemnity was collected— . . . $20,000 silver

[paid] by the Chinese general controlling Hainan for the death of Mr. Byers" (818).

6. "Bandit Record Since the Lincheng Outrage," *The China Weekly Review* 2 (16 February 1924):412.

7. The British consulate had been established at Hoihow in 1876, but it was considered a terrible post to have to serve. The Chinese government refused for years to allow the diplomats to purchase land and construct suitable buildings, finally relenting only in 1901. In fact, the Presbyterian missionaries secured land at all three of their mission locations before the British diplomats were able to move from their extremely sub-standard building, a partially enclosed structure which had previously been a rope storehouse, and which had one room that served as both office and living quarters. One consul begged for a housing allowance stating the first floor of the building was under water several times a year. To support his plea he enclosed a letter from the mission's Dr. H. M. McCandliss who said the building was not suitable for living quarters. P. D. Coates, *The China Consuls: British Consular Officers, 1843–1943* (Oxford: Oxford University Press, 1988), 236–37; and Ernest Bennett to N. R. O'Conor, Kiungchow, 18 December 1894; McCandliss to Bennett, Kiungchow, 10 December 1894, United Kingdom, Public Record Office, Foreign Office, "China: Consular Papers."

8. H. H. Bristow's father H. B. Bristow had also been a British consul in China and the younger Bristow was married to the daughter of a China missionary family. See Coates, *The China Consuls,* Appendix II, 511.

9. Maxwell M. Hamilton to Douglas Jenkins, Hoihow, 13 January 1925, National Archives, "George D. Byers" File 393.1123, RG59, Papers Relating to the Foreign Relations of the United States, China, Washington, D.C. (hereafter NA.); Margaret Moninger to Mother, Kiungchow, 5 April 1925, Margaret Moninger Papers, RG39, Presbyterian Historical Society, Philadelphia. (Hereafter MP.)

10. Edwin M. Borchard, *The Diplomatic Protection of Citizens Abroad, or The Law of International Claims* (New York: Banks Law Publishing, 1925), 446.

11. John K. Fairbank, Edwin O. Reischauer, and Albert M. Craig, *East Asia: The Modern Transformation* (Boston: Houghton Mifflin, 1965), 337.

12. Godfrey E. P. Hertslet, *Hertslet's China Treaties: Treaties etc. between Great Britain and China and between China and Foreign Powers . . . in Force on the 1st of January 1908,* 3rd ed., vol. 1 (London: His Majesty's Stationery Office, by Harrison and Sons, 1908), 542–45; and George W. Keeton, *The Development of Extraterritoriality in China,* 2 vols.(1928; reprint, New York: H. Fertig, 1969), 1:285–86. The pursuit-of-pirates provision in the 1858 United States treaty exceeded terms of the earlier British treaty. For the full text of the United States treaties see Charles I. Bevans, comp., *Treaties and Other International Agreements of the United States of America, 1776–1949,* vol. 6: "China" (Washington, D.C.: Department of State, 1968–76). "Treaty signed at Tientsin, June 18, 1858," 659, 662–63; and "Treaty signed at Shanghai, October 8, 1903," 695, 703–4. For a discussion of how these treaties were implemented see Frank E. Hinckley, *American Consular Jurisdiction in the Orient* (Washington, D.C.: W. H. Lowdermilk, 1906), 118–24.

13. For a discussion of some of the extraterritoriality cases involving nonmissionaries, foreign-educated Chinese, and foreign companies in China see American Chamber of Commerce of Tientsin, *Memorandum of the American Chamber of Commerce of Tientsin Relative to Extraterritoriality in China* (Tientsin: n.pubs., 1925).

14. Billingsley, *Bandits in Republican China,* 5.

15. For an account of the Chinese political situation in the early twentieth century see Jonathan Spence, *In Search of Modern China* (New York: W. W. Norton, 1990), chapters 12–15.

16. "Editorial," *CR* 55 (1924):485–87.

17. For an account of how one family in Chengtu, Szechwan, negotiated the warlord issue to go on vacation see John K. Fairbank, *The Great Chinese Revolution: 1800–1985* (New York: Harper and Row, 1986), 180.

18. "Editorial," *CR* 43(1912):65–66.

19. Harold A. Hatch[?], "Some Tentative Considerations Regarding Indemnities," [n.d.] Robert E. Speer Papers, Princeton Theological Seminary, Princeton, N.J. (Hereafter SP.) This is an unsigned, eight-page statement which refers to the situations in China and Persia and mentions the Byers case. Later correspondence from Speer seems to indicate the author of this statement was Harold A. Hatch. See also Ernest F. P. Scholes, "Changing China's Status Amongst the Nations and the Missionary's Status in China: A Plea for Delay," *CR* 57(1926):322–28.

20. For confirmation that American diplomats in China viewed missionaries as nuisances as well as a discussion of the missionary concerns vis-à-vis extraterritoriality and treaty revision in the late 1920s see Paul Varg, "The Missionary Response to the Nationalist Revolution," in *The Missionary Enterprise in China and America,* edited by John K. Fairbank (Cambridge: Harvard University Press, 1974), 311–35. Extraterritoriality and how it was implemented was the subject of many scholarly books and articles early in the twentieth century. See, for example, Charles Cheney Hyde, *International Law Chiefly as Interpreted and Applied by the United States,* 2 vols. (Boston: Little, Brown, 1922); Westel W. Willoughby, *Foreign Rights and Interests in China,* 2 vols. (Baltimore: Johns Hopkins Press, 1927); and Min-chien T. Z. Tyau, *The Legal Obligations Arising out of Treaty Relations Between China and Other States* (Ph.D. dissertation, University of London; reprint Taipei: Ch'eng Wen Publications, 1966).

21. Latourette, *A History of Christian Missions in China,* 815–16. The Machle family victims are mistakenly identified here as Mackle. Official correspondence on the Lienchow and other, earlier extraterritoriality cases can be found in NA, Department of State, U.S. Consulate, Canton, *Despatches from U.S. Consuls in Canton, 1790–1906* (Washington, D.C., 1947), microfilm; U.S. Embassy, China, *Despatches from United States Ministers to China, 1843–1906* (Washington, D.C.: 1946–1958), microfilm; and *Numerical and Minor Files of the Department of State, 1906–1910,* file 167, Washington, D.C., microfilm. See also *CR* (1914):251, 593. In addition to the CIM mentioned above, missions that had decided after the Boxer Uprising to forego indemnities included the London Missionary Society (see chapter 5).

22. Cited in *CR* 50 (1919): 65.

23. "Missionaries and International Relations," *CR* 54 (1923): 569.

24. Ibid.

25. "Editor's Outlook," *CR* 54 (1923):375–76.

26. T. Z. Koo, "Letter to the editor," *CR* 54 (1923): 499. An ordained minister, Koo was a secretary of the YMCA and a delegate to many international church conferences. See Kathleen L. Lodwick, *The CHINESE RECORDER Index: A Guide to Christian Missions in Asia, 1867–1941* (Wilmington, Del.: Scholarly Resources, 1986), 1:262–63.

27. Paul L. Corbin, "Letter to the editor," *CR* 54 (1923): 499; E. E. Aiken, "Let-

ter to the editor," *CR* 54 (1923): 756–57. Mission affiliations are from Lodwick, *The CR Index* 1:3, 99.

28. Thomas Barclay, "Letter to the editor," *CR* 54 (1923): 619; Lodwick, *The CR Index* 1:24.

29. R. B. Whitaker, "Letter to the editor," *CR* 54 (1923): 757–59; Lodwick, *The CR Index* 1: 511.

30. John Hind, "Letter to the editor," *CR* 55 (1924): 53–54; Lodwick, *The CR Index* 1:211.

31. D. W. Crofts, "Letter to the editor," *CR* 55 (1924): 194–95; Lodwick, *The CR Index* 1:105.

32. "The Church in China and International Arrangements: Some Chinese Christian Opinions," *CR* 55 (1924): 241–43; Lodwick, *The CR Index* 1:78–79.

33. "The Church in China and International Agreements: Brief of Conversation with a Member of the Government Board of Agriculture, and a Graduate of Nanking and Michigan Universities," *CR* 55 (1924): 243–45; D. E. Hoste, "The Christian Attitude Towards Present International Agreements," *CR* 55 (1924): 245–51; Lodwick, *The CR Index* 1:211.

34. "K," "Letter to the editor," *CR* 55 (1924): 261–62.

35. "Discussion on Extrality," *CR* 55 (1924): 411.

36. G. G. Warren, "Extrality," *CR* 55 (1924): 442–45; Lodwick, *The CR Index* 1:503.

37. "Editorial," *CR* 54 (1923): 635–36.

38. Ernest F.P. Scholes, "Changing China's Status Amongst the Nations and the Missionary's Status in China: A Plea for Delay," *CR* 57 (1926): 323.

39. Tyler Dennett, "Extraterritoriality and Missionaries in China," *The Christian Century* 39 (May 1923): 626.

40. For Americans this was not an issue until the twentieth century as the United States was itself a mission field of the Roman Catholic Church until 1905 and thus was unable to send its own missionaries to China. See Caspar Caulfield, *Only a Beginning: The Passionists in China, 1921–1931* (Union City, N.J.: Passionist Press, 1990), 213–15, on the murder of three Passionist priests and their converts in Hunan in 1929. The decision not to seek indemnities came in "Instructions given by the Apostolic Delegate to Bishops having to deal with Questions of Indemnity" issued in Peking, 2 August 1927, and contained in NA, "Walter Coveyou," file 393.1123, RG59.

41. Marshall Broomhall, *The Jubilee Story of the China Inland Mission* (London: Morgan and Scott, 1915), 257–59.

42. Anthropologists today identify these people as Yao. See S. Robert Ramsey, *The Languages of China* (Princeton: Princeton University Press, 1987), 281.

43. [Margaret Moninger], *Isle of Palms* (1919; reprint, New York: Garland Publishing, 1980), 111–12; George and Clara P. Byers, Applications/Personal Reports, BFM.

44. Michael H. Hunt, "New Insights But No New Vistas: Recent Work on Nineteenth-Century American–East Asian Relations," in *New Frontiers in American–East Asian Relations,* edited by Warren I. Cohen (New York: Columbia University Press, 1983), 27.

45. For a discussion of how other women influenced American foreign policy see Edward P. Crapol, ed., *Women and American Foreign Policy: Lobbyists, Critics, and Insiders,* 2nd ed. (Wilmington, Del.: Scholarly Resources, 1992).

Chapter 2. The Immediate Aftermath of the Murder

1. Bristow to Jenkins, Kiungchow, 25 June 1924, NA.

2. Bristow to Jenkins, Kiungchow, 6 October 1924, NA.

3. Gilbert Rozman, ed., *The Modernization of China* (New York: Free Press, 1981), 236.

4. Warren I. Cohen, *Empire Without Tears: American Foreign Relations, 1921–1933* (Philadelphia: Temple University Press, 1987), 79.

5. Warren I. Cohen, *America's Response to China: An Interpretative History of Sino-American Relations,* 2nd ed. (New York: John Wiley & Sons, 1980), 110.

6. The incident involved Charles Coltman, an American businessman, who was shot to death by Chinese soldiers when they stopped the car in which he and Minister Jacob Gould Schurman were riding. The Chinese were slow to respond, but eventually paid a $25,000 indemnity, and the Americans later decided Coltman was breaking Chinese laws and had used Schurman to try to evade Chinese authorities. Thomas Buckley, "John Van Antwerp MacMurray: The Diplomacy of an American Mandarin," in *Diplomats in Crisis: United States–Chinese–Japanese Relations, 1919–1941,* edited by Richard Dean Burns and Edward M. Bennett, 27–48 (Santa Barbara, Calif.: ABC-Clio, 1974), 33–34.

7. Rawlinson edited the *CR* from 1913 to 1937 and has been termed one of the "opinion makers" of American public opinion regarding China. See Warren I. Cohen, *The Chinese Connection: Roger S. Greene, Thomas W. Lamont, George E. Sokolsky, and American–East Asian Relations* (New York: Columbia University Press, 1978), 300.

8. See Jessie G. Lutz, *Chinese Politics and Christian Missions: The Anti-Christian Movements of 1920–1928* (Notre Dame, Ind.: Cross Cultural Publications, 1988), as well as her earlier work, *China and the Christian Colleges, 1850–1950* (Ithaca: Cornell University Press, 1971); and Yip Ka-che, *Religion, Nationalism and Chinese Students: The Anti-Christian Movement of 1922–1927* (Bellingham, Wash.: Western Washington University Press, 1980).

9. Bristow to Jenkins, Kiungchow, 26 June 1924, NA. (Bristow is misidentified as M. M. Bristow in the typed record of this communication.)

10. Laurence Byers, telephone conversation with author, 5 October 1985.

11. Of the struggle for control in China, the American diplomat MacMurray reportedly said, "We have no favorites in the present dog fight in China; they all look alike to us." However, he did hope that someone would emerge victorious. Quoted in Akira Iriye, *After Imperialism: The Search for a New Order in the Far East, 1921–1931* (Cambridge: Harvard University Press, 1965), 28.

12. Moninger to Daddy and Mother, Kachek, 30 December 1923, MP.

13. George D. Byers to Frank H. Magill, Kachek, 5 March 1924; George D. Byers to Katherine Schaeffer, Kachek, 26 May 1924, BFM.

14. "Gleanings: Kidnapping Christians," *CR* 54 (1923): 563–64.

15. Byers to Scott, Aboard SS *President Pierce,* 10 August 1924, BFM. At the time Mrs. Byers made the statement to her husband, she knew her family would be alone at the mission compound when the others left for vacations.

16. *New York Times,* 29 May 1924; Daniel Ray, Interview with author, Sussex, N.J., 21 October 1992; telephone interview with author, 1 December 1995.

17. Tappan to Scott, Kachek, 4 July 1924; and edited version of Tappan's letter,

"Regarding the late Rev. George D. Byers of Hainan," n.d., BFM. Most accounts mention only three kidnappers.

18. Scott, "The Death of the Rev. George Douglas Byers of Hainan," New York, 30 June 1924, BFM.

19. Byers, Statement to Bristow, H.B.M. Consul, dated 9 July, sworn to 17 July 1924, Kiungchow, NA. Despite her reference here and later to "guns" there is no evidence as to how many weapons were involved.

20. Byers to Scott, Aboard SS *President Pierce,* 10 August 1924, BFM.

21. Scott to Relatives and Friends of the late Rev. George D. Byers, New York, 5 August 1924, BFM. A Chinese friend reported these details to Miss Moninger who in turn transmitted the account to the BFM.

22. Tappan to Scott, Kachek, 4 July 1924, BFM.

23. Byers to Scott, Aboard SS *President Pierce,* 10 August 1924, BFM.

24. Byers, Statement, NA. What the knocking was was never explained, but it was likely someone who had come to report that the telephone call had been made.

25. Moninger and Wilbur M. Campbell to Presbyterian China Council (PCC) and BFM, Kiungchow, 25 June 1924; Mabel L. (Mrs. Charles K.) Roys to Relatives and Friends of the Rev. George D. Byers, New York, 25 July 1924, BFM.

26. Ibid.

27. Byers, Statement, NA.

28. Byers to Scott, Aboard SS *President Pierce,* 10 August 1924, BFM.

29. Ibid.

30. Moninger to Daddy and Mother, Kiungchow, 30 June 1924, MP.

31. The missionaries referred to this individual as Lim Si-biao, which is a rendering of the Hainanese pronunciation of his name. The diplomatic papers refer to him as Lin Hsu-piao and Lin Shu-piao, which are Mandarin transliterations.

32. Bristow to Jenkins, Kiungchow, 25 June 1924, NA.

33. Ibid.

34. Ibid.

35. Ibid.

36. Byers to Scott, Aboard SS *President Pierce,* 10 August 1924, BFM.

37. Bristow to Jenkins, Kiungchow, 27 June 1924, NA. Mrs. Byers also detailed the finding of the ransom note in Byers to Scott, Aboard SS *President Pierce,* 10 August 1924, BFM.

38. Tappan to Scott, Kachek, 4 July 1924, BFM. The Rev. Tappan remained in Kachek to pack the Byers's belongings and arrange for the security of the mission compound.

39. Roys's memorandum, 30 June 1924, BFM. The Associated Press report was the only information the BFM had as to the date of the murder.

40. Schurman to Secretary of State, Peking, cable, 30 June 1924; BFM to Secretary of State, New York, telegram, 30 June 1924, both NA; Charles Evans Hughes to BFM, Washington, 1 July 1924, NA/BFM. The same news appeared in the *New York Times,* 1 July. For a discussion of Hughes's career see John Chalmers Vinson, "Charles Evans Hughes, 1921–1925" in *An Uncertain Tradition: American Secretaries of State in the Twentieth Century,* edited by Norman A. Graebner, (New York: McGraw Hill, 1961), 27–128.

41. Jenkins to Schurman, Canton, 1 July 1924, NA.

42. Moninger to Mother, Hoihow Harbor, 6 July 1924, MP. (Moninger had em-

barked for Hong Kong and her vacation at the time of this letter.) Nathaniel Bercovitz was returning from Hong Kong where he had been vacationing with his family.

43. Ibid.

44. Jenkins to [Schurman?], Canton, 7 July 1924, NA. The recipient of the cable is not noted, but since Jenkins refers to his 29 June and 1 July communications, both of which were to Schurman, one can surmise this cable was also to him.

45. Edward Bell to Secretary of State, Peking, 10 July 1924, NA.

46. BFM to the Missions in China, New York, 7 July 1924; Roys to Schaeffer, New York, 7 July 1924, BFM.

47. Willis C. Hawley to Hughes, Washington, 24 July 1924; Joseph C. Grew to Hawley, Washington, 31 July 1924, NA. Grew kept Hawley up to date on the case, reporting more developments in Grew to Hawley, Washington, 14 August 1924, NA. Later in his career Grew was ambassador to Japan at the time of Pearl Harbor. He probably met some of the Hainan missionaries when they were repatriated together on the SS *Conte Verde* and then the SS *Gripsholm* in the summer of 1942. For a discussion of his career see Edward M. Bennett, "Joseph C. Grew: The Diplomacy of Pacification," in *Diplomats in Crisis,* edited by Burns and Bennett, 65–89.

48. Moninger to the PCC and BFM, Hong Kong, 10 July 1924, BFM.

49. Jenkins to Schurman, Canton, 26 July 1924, NA. It is impossible to know exactly where the Rev. Byers was when he was attacked. The torn-up ground mentioned by Miss Moninger to the BFM was clearly inside the compound, suggesting that was the place of the attack. The official account of Mrs. Byers, given just days after the murder, states he was shot before she and Robert arrived on the scene, although they were clearly in mortal danger once they arrived at his side. See Byers, Statement, NA.

50. Byers to Scott, Aboard SS *President Pierce,* 10 August 1924, BFM.

51. Moninger to Mother, Kiungchow, 11 January 1925, MP.

52. Jenkins to Schurman, Canton, 26 July 1924, NA.

53. Minutes of the Executive Committee of the Hainan Mission of the Presbyterian Church, USA, Kiungchow, Hainan Island, S. China, 29 July 1924, Hoihow, NA/BFM. Members of the executive committee were McCandliss and Clarence G. Salsbury, both M.D.s, and the Revs. John Steiner and Campbell (chairman). The river near Kachek was not large so any gunboat sent there would, of necessity, have been too small to constitute much of a threat to anyone, and a gunboat on the coast nearest Kachek would have been quite some distance from the town.

54. Ibid. The minutes erroneously refer to Colonel Ho Chia-yu as a general.

55. Byers to Scott, at sea, 10 August 1924, BFM. In a second letter, Mrs. Byers informed Scott that her husband had had a $1000 life insurance policy. Byers to Scott, Aboard SS *President Pierce,* 10 August 1924, BFM.

56. Bristow to Jenkins, Kiungchow, 1 August 1924, NA.

57. Ibid. Ch'en Yun-liang's name sometimes appears in the documents as Chan Zun-liang.

58. Schaeffer to Arthur J. Brown, Somers, Wisc., 27 July 1924; Scott to Schaeffer, New York, 5 August 1924, BFM.

59. Byers to Scott, at sea, 10 August 1924, BFM. The Dr. Peter referred to was likely Dr. William W. Peter who was a member of the National Christian Council (NCC). Mrs. Byers wrote that it was hard for her to request the indemnity, but the

consul [council?] and Dr. Peter assured her she was asking "for a lifetime for less than passed over the gaming tables every night in Shanghai alone." Mrs. Byers apparently substituted consul for council, meaning PCC, in this letter as Chamberlain was not in Shanghai and there is no evidence that she had seen any other consular officials. She also told Scott that she had deleted some sentences before she sent the letter to the consul. These sentences stated that she would turn the $50,000 over to the BFM to hold in trust for her, but wanted $3000 per annum to live on, until her children were grown, at which time their part of the allowance would cease. She also noted in the 30 July letter that the executive committee of the Hainan mission recommended $20,000 to be raised locally, but wrote how it was raised was "immaterial to me," an opinion with which the men advising her disagreed, and which she deleted from the letter to the American consul in Canton.

60. Byers, with Tappan concurring, to American consul general, Canton, 30 July 1924, Shanghai, BFM/NA.

61. Tappan to Scott, Kachek, 4 July 1924, BFM. A handwritten note on this letter, probably by someone at the BFM, indicated the Byers family's traveling companions and their arrival date. David Byers recalled that various newspapermen aboard the ship tried to interview his mother about the murder, but she was reluctant to discuss it. David Byers, telephone conversation with author, 28 October 2000.

62. Jenkins to Secretary of State, Canton, 5 August 1924; "Report of the Death of an American Citizen: George Douglas Byers," 5 August 1924; and Jenkins to Milton D. Purdy, Canton, 5 August 1924, NA.

Chapter 3. The Extraterritoriality Case

1. C. B. Chamberlain to Jenkins, Canton, 1 August 1924, NA.
2. Ibid.
3. Ibid.
4. Ibid.
5. Ibid.
6. Jenkins to Schurman, Canton, 2 August 1924, NA.
7. Ibid.
8. Ibid.
9. Ibid.
10. Ibid.
11. Ibid. Jenkins followed this communication to Peking four days later with the resolutions of the Hainan mission and the 1 August letter from Bristow. Jenkins to Schurman, Canton, 6 August 1924, NA.
12. William J. Leverett to Scott, Clifton Spring, N.Y., 7 August 1924, BFM.
13. Bercovitz to Scott, [Kiungchow], 19 August 1924; Bercovitz sent the PCC a similar letter, Bercovitz to Charles Patton, [Kiungchow], 6 September 1924, BFM.
14. Bercovitz to BFM, Kiungchow, 25 August 1924, BFM.
15. Ibid.
16. Ibid.
17. Bercovitz to American Consul General, Canton; Kiungchow, 1 September 1924, BFM.
18. Ibid.

19. Ibid.
20. Jenkins to [Schurman], Canton, 27 August 1924, NA.
21. Bell to V. K. Wellington Koo, Peking, 3 September 1924, NA. For a discussion of Koo's career see Pao-chin Chu, "V. K. Wellington Koo: The Diplomacy of Nationalism," in *Diplomats in Crisis,* 125–51.
22. Jenkins to [Schurman], Canton, 6 September 1924; Bell to Jenkins, Peking, 7 September 1924, NA.
23. Bell to Secretary of State, Peking, 9 September 1924; Bell, Memorandum, Peking, 10 September 1924, NA.
24. Jenkins to Bell, Canton, 9 September 1924, NA.
25. Campbell, Chairman, Executive Committee, Hainan Mission to American Consul General, Canton; Hoihow, 19 September 1924, BFM. It is unclear whether some of the information in this letter was newly received or simply a repetition of the report Bercovitz had detailed the previous month.
26. Ibid.
27. Ibid.
28. Jenkins to Bell, Canton, 23 September 1924, NA. Bristow's personal note to Jenkins which is contained in the official letter to Bell was dated 16 September.
29. Bell to Jenkins, Peking, 23 September 1924, NA. The Rev. C. H. Fenn accompanied Tappan on his visit to the legation, J. Walter Lowrie to American Minister, Peking; Shanghai, 10 October 1924, BFM.
30. Wilbur J. Carr to James M. Byers, Washington, 26 September 1924, NA.
31. [Bell] to Koo, Peking, 4 October 1924; Koo to Bell, Peking, 9 October 1924, NA.
32. Bristow to Administrator, Hainan; Kiungchow, 3 October 1924, NA.
33. Bristow to Jenkins, Kiungchow, 6 October 1924, NA.
34. Moninger to Mother, Shanghai, 19 October 1924, MP.
35. Ibid. For a biography of Moninger see Kathleen L. Lodwick, *Educating the Women of Hainan: The Career of Margaret Moninger in China, 1915–1942* (Lexington: University Press of Kentucky, 1995).
36. Lowrie to American Minister, Peking; Shanghai, 10 October 1924, BFM.
37. The PCC's cable was received in New York on 11 October and telegraphed to Washington, Lowrie to Inculcate [BFM], [Shanghai], 11 October 1924, BFM; Arthur J. Brown to Secretary of State, telegram, New York, 11 October 1924, BFM/NA; J. Butler Wright to Brown, [Washington], 16 October 1924, BFM/NA.
38. "Advance Copy, PCC Minutes," [Shanghai], October 1924, BFM.
39. Jenkins to Bell, Canton, 14 October 1924, NA.
40. Arthur J. Brown to Schurman, New York, 11 October 1924; Schurman to Brown, Washington, 16 October 1924, BFM.
41. BFM Minutes, 20 October 1924, BFM; Ernest R. Ackerman to State Department, Washington, 20 October 1924, NA.
42. Lowrie to Scott, Shanghai, 25 October 1924; Lowrie to Inculcate [BFM], Shanghai, 27 October 1924, BFM.
43. Ferdinand Mayer to Secretary of State, Peking, 28 October 1924, NA.
44. Scott to Roys, New York, 28 October 1924, with handwritten reply of Roys, Pittsburgh, 29 October 1924, BFM.
45. Scott to Secretary of State, New York, 29 October 1924, BFM/NA.
46. Grew to Ackerman, Washington, 1 November 1924; Grew to Legation, cable,

Washington, 1 November 1924, NA; Grew to Scott, telegram, Washington, 1 November 1924, BFM/NA.

47. Scott to Department of State, New York, 3 November 1924, BFM/NA. [BFM] to Link, Shanghai [PCC], coded cable, New York, 3 November 1924, BFM.

48. Mayer to Secretary of State, Peking, 6 November 1924; Hughes to Legation, Peking; Washington, 13 November 1924, NA. Hughes also asked for an estimate of the expenses of the vice consul.

49. Campbell to Patton, [Kiungchow], 13 November 1924; PCC to American Legation, Peking, telegram, Shanghai, 22 November 1924, BFM.

50. Byers to Roys, telegram, La Mesa, Calif., 19 November 1924; Roys to Byers, New York, 20 November 1924, BFM.

51. Byers to Roys, San Diego, 24 November 1924, BFM. Mrs. Byers's reference to "public persons" probably refers to the Coltman/Schurman extraterritoriality case mentioned in chapter 1.

52. Ibid.

53. Ibid.

54. Byers to Selden P. Spencer, San Diego, 24 November 1924, BFM.

55. Mayer to Lowrie, Peking, 26 November 1924, BFM. Mayer also acknowledged the receipt of the PCC's letters of 11 October and 7 November.

56. PCC to James P. Davis, American Consul General, Shanghai; Shanghai, 26 November 1924, BFM.

57. Mayer to Secretary of State, Peking, 30 November 1924; Hughes to Legation, Peking; Washington, 3 December 1924, NA. The reply began, "Department approves your recommendation to postpone decision with regard to Hamilton's trip to Hainan until conference at Shanghai to which you refer." An initialed handwritten note asked if it could be shortened to "Your 462 November 30 1 p.m. Your recommendation approved." If that were too brief then "Postponement Hamilton's trip Hainan until Shanghai conference approved," because "every cent *possible* must be cut from our cable bills if we are to meet the real urgent need which China says she will have for an additional appropriation for cables." The department delayed the cable two days, apparently while trying to decide how to shorten it.

58. Lowrie to American Minister, Peking; [Shanghai], 3 December 1924, BFM.

59. Scott to Department of State, [New York], 3 December 1924, BFM/NA; Spencer to Secretary of State, Washington, 3 December 1924, NA.

60. Roys to Byers, [New York], 4 December 1924, BFM.

61. Hughes to Mayer, Washington, 6 December 1924; Mayer to Secretary of State, [Shanghai], 15 December 1924, NA.

62. Moninger to Mother, Kiungchow, 7 December 1924, MP.

63. Mayer to Jenkins, Peking, 10 December 1924, NA.

64. Hughes to American Consulate General, Shanghai; Washington, 15 December 1924, NA.

65. Byers to John B. Brown, San Diego, 13 December 1924, BFM; Brown to Hayden, Phoenix, 18 December 1924; Hayden to Hughes, Washington, 23 December 1924, NA. Hughes replied to the congressman giving the actions of the department, Hughes to Hayden, Washington, 7 January 1925, NA.

66. Hughes to Spencer, Washington, 15 December 1924; Hughes to Ackerman, Washington, 15 December 1924, NA.

67. MacMurray to Scott, Washington, 15 December 1924, BFM/NA. Three days later Scott replied acknowledging the actions of the department, Scott to Secretary of State, New York, 18 December 1924, BFM/NA; BFM to Link, Shanghai [PCC]; [New York], 18 December 1924; Patton to Edwin S. Cunningham, [Shanghai], 19 December 1924, BFM.

68. Mrs. Byers is probably referring here to the entire forty years of the mission's existence when she mentions that German ships called frequently at Hoihow, as none had been there since the war, a fact she probably realized as she also mentioned that the German consulate had been closed since then. Byers to Swing, San Diego, 21 December 1924, BFM. The five Californians were Dr. and Mrs. Bercovitz, Caroline McCreery, and the Rev. and Mrs. Tappan. Representative Phil D. Swing wrote to the BFM asking how he could help and the status of the financial arrangements for Mrs. Byers. Mrs. Roys replied that the BFM would meet on 19 January to discuss the support of Mrs. Byers, Swing to BFM, Washington, 29 December 1924; Roys to Swing, [New York], 30 December 1924, BFM.

69. Byers to Roys, San Diego, 21 December 1924, BFM.

70. Cunningham to Patton, Shanghai, 22 December 1924, BFM.

71. Schurman to Hughes, Peking, 22 December 1924; Schurman to Secretary of State, Peking, 29 December 1924, NA.

72. Byers to Roys, telegram, La Mesa, Calif., 24 December 1924; Roys to Byers, telegram, New York, 26 December 1924, BFM.

73. Byers to Roys, San Diego, 31 December 1924, BFM.

Chapter 4. The Indemnity Is Collected

1. Jenkins to Hamilton, Canton, 3 January 1925, NA. Hamilton was allotted $300 gold for his expenses and permitted to take Mrs. Hamilton with him.

2. Moninger to Mother, Kiungchow, 4 January 1925, MP. When Consul Hamilton and his wife arrived on Hainan, Moninger discovered she knew Mrs. Hamilton, who had been a missionary and had first arrived in China on the same ship Moninger returned on from her furlough in 1923.

3. Hamilton to Jenkins, Hoihow, 13 January 1925, NA.

4. Moninger to Mother, Kiungchow, 4 January 1925, MP.

5. Hamilton to Jenkins, Canton, 12 May 1925, NA.

6. Campbell to Frank Kellogg, Kiungchow, 27 May 1925, NA; "Report of Visit by Dr. J. Walter Lowrie January to April 1925 to Hainan," Hoihow, 22 April 1925, BFM/NA.

7. Moninger to Mother, Kiungchow, 11 January 1925, MP.

8. Hamilton to Jenkins, Hoihow, 13 January 1925, NA.

9. Ibid.

10. "Report of Visit," BFM/NA.

11. Moninger to Mother, Kiungchow, 11 January 1925, MP.

12. F. P. Lockhart to Scott, Washington, 7 January 1925, BFM/NA; MacMurray to Ackerman, Washington, 7 January 1925; MacMurray to Hawley, Washington, 7 January 1925; Hughes to Carl Hayden, Washington, 7 January 1925, NA.

13. Los Angeles Presbyterial, "Resolution Concerning Hainan Situation," [5 January 1925], BFM. Another woman wanted to discuss the matter of a memorial fund

for Mrs. Byers's support, but Mrs. R. W. Cleland indicated they needed to consult the BFM on that matter, too.

14. Byers to Roys, Los Angeles, 9 January 1925, BFM. Dr. and Mrs. Stuart Seaton had joined the mission since Mrs. Byers had listed five Californians on the island.

15. Ibid.

16. Ibid.

17. Ibid.; Roys to Byers, [New York], 16 January 1925; Roys to Cleland, [New York], 19 January 1925, BFM.

18. William S. Abernathy to Speer, Washington, 8 January 1925; Scott to Abernathy, [New York], 10 January 1925, BFM. Abernathy, an American Baptist, was a frequent correspondent of Hughes, Charles Evans Hughes Papers, Manuscript Division, Library of Congress, Washington, D.C.

19. Moninger to Mother, Kiungchow, 18 January 1925, MP.

20. "Report of Visit," NA.

21. Hamilton to Jenkins, Canton, 12 May 1925, NA.

22. Hamilton to Jenkins, Hoihow, 13 January 1925, NA.

23. Schurman to Hughes, Peking, 23 January 1925; Hughes to Legation, Peking; Washington, 6 January 1925, NA.

24. Hughes to Legation, Peking; Washington, 27 January 1925, NA.

25. "Report of Visit," NA.

26. Hamilton to Jenkins, Hoihow, 26 January 1925, NA.

27. Ibid.

28. Jenkins to Schurman, Canton, 3 February 1925; Schurman to Secretary of State, Peking, 17 February 1925, NA. Jenkins indicated he had cabled Schurman on 2 February concerning the indemnity, but no copy of the cable appears in the records.

29. Hamilton to Jenkins, Canton, 12 May 1925, NA.

30. C. J. Spiker to Hughes, Swatow, 12 February 1925, enclosing Spiker to Ch'en Chiung-ming, Swatow, 12 February 1925, NA.

31. Moninger to Mother, Kiungchow, 25 January 1925; Moninger to Mother, Kiungchow, 8 February 1925, MP.

32. E. C. Lobenstine to Scott, Shanghai, 13 February 1925, BFM.

33. Ibid.

34. Lobenstine to Scott, Shanghai, 19 February 1925, BFM.

35. Scott to Lobenstine, [New York], 17 March 1925; China Missions Letter, Number 85, 17 March 1925, BFM.

36. Moninger to Mother, Kiungchow, 15 February 1925, MP.

37. Hamilton to Jenkins, Canton, 12 May 1925, NA.

38. Schurman to Hughes, Peking, 25 February 1925, NA.

39. Lowrie to Patton, Pakhoi, 20 February 1925; Patton to Scott, Shanghai, 2 March 1925, BFM.

40. "Report of Visit," NA.

41. Ibid.

42. Schurman to Secretary of State, Peking, 1 March 1925, NA. Schurman seems to be a bit off in his calculation of $45,000 silver.

43. Schurman to Secretary of State, Peking, 3 March 1925, NA.

44. Hughes to Byers, Washington, 3 March 1925, NA.

45. Schurman to Secretary of State, Peking, 4 March 1925, NA.

46. Byers to Hughes, San Diego, 4 March 1925, NA. The full text of Hughes's telegram to Mrs. Byers was "Chinese local authorities Hainan offer twenty thousand dollars (silver) in settlement of your claim both consul and legation recommended that in view of local political conditions consul should be authorized to compromise on best possible basis the above stated amount constituting the minimum if payment is promptly made would you be willing to accept settlement on these terms prompt reply by telegraph essential. Signed Charles E. Hughes secretary of state" quoted in Byers to Roys, telegram, San Diego, 4 March 1925, BFM.

47. Roys to Secretary of State, New York, 5 March 1925, NA; Roys to Byers, telegram, [New York], 5 March 1925, BFM.

48. Roys to Byers, New York, 6 March 1925, BFM.

49. Byers to Roys, telegram, San Diego, 6 March 1925, BFM; Byers to Hughes, San Diego, 6 March 1925, NA.

50. Roys to Byers, [New York], 7 March 1925, BFM.

51. Ibid.

52. Byers to Roys, San Diego, 7 March 1925, BFM.

53. Byers to Hughes [*sic*], San Diego, 6 March 1925, NA. The time of receipt was typed over but was either 3:04 or 4:04 a.m. 7 March 1925; Kellogg to Legation, Peking; Washington, 6 March 1925, NA.

54. Unsigned to Secretary of State, Peking, 7 March 1925 (this cable was probably from Schurman and was sent at 11 a.m. 7 March from Peking and arrived at the Department of State at 5:06 a.m. that same morning); Kellogg to Legation, Peking; Washington, 9 March 1925, NA.

55. Byers to Roys, San Diego, 17 March 1925, BFM.

56. Ibid.

57. Ibid.

58. Roys to Byers, New York, 23 March 1925, BFM.

59. Moninger to Mother, Kiungchow, 1 March 1925, MP.

60. Moninger to Mother, Kiungchow, 8 March 1925, MP.

61. Moninger to Mother, Kiungchow, 15 March 1925, MP. I have been unable to locate the unnamed Chinese newspaper Moninger referred to.

62. Moninger to Mother, Kiungchow, 22 March 1925, MP.

63. Ibid.

64. Moninger to Mother, Kiungchow, 12 April 1925, MP.

65. Teng Pen-yin to Hamilton, [Hoihow?], 27 March 1925, NA. The word "property" appears in the English typescript but "poverty" is probably intended as it appears in Hamilton's reply.

66. Hamilton to Teng, Hoihow, 3 April 1925; Schurman to Secretary of State, Peking, 4 April 1925, NA.

67. Moninger to Mother, Kiungchow, 5 April 1925, MP. Moninger's reference to Hamilton sticking to the general "like a burr to a cow's tail" appears in this letter.

68. Jenkins to Schurman, Canton, 21 April 1925, NA.

69. Mayer to Secretary of State, Peking, 22 April 1925; Kellogg to Legation, Peking; Washington, 24 April 1925, NA.

70. Byers to Secretary of State, San Diego, 20 April 1925, NA; Unidentified newspaper clippings, 7 May 1925, BFM; Leland Harrison to Byers, Washington, 8 May 1925, NA.

71. Moninger to Mother, Kiungchow, 26 April 1925, MP.

72. Moninger to Mother, Kiungchow, 3 May 1925, MP.
73. Jenkins to Hamilton, Canton, 28 April 1925, NA.
74. Hamilton to Jenkins, Canton, 12 May 1925, NA.
75. Ibid.
76. Ibid.
77. Ibid.
78. Ibid.
79. Ibid.
80. Ibid.
81. Ibid. Mayer expressed the thanks of the department to Admiral Thomas Washington on 4 June 1925, Mayer to Washington, Peking, 4 June 1925, NA; and transmitted Hamilton's report to Washington, Mayer to Secretary of State, Peking, 4 June 1925, NA.
82. Hamilton to Jenkins, Canton, 12 May 1925, NA.
83. Moninger to Mother, Kiungchow, 24 May 1925, MP.
84. Bercovitz to Scott, Kachek, 24 May 1925, BFM.
85. Campbell for the Executive Committee of the Hainan Mission to Kellogg, [Kiungchow], 27 May 1925, NA.
86. Byers to Secretary of State, San Diego, 18 May 1925, NA.
87. Mayer to Secretary of State, Peking, 18 May 1925, NA.
88. Grew to Byers, Washington, 10 June 1925; Byers to Secretary of State, San Diego, 11 June 1925, NA.
89. Harrison to Byers, Washington, 1 July 1925; Byers to Secretary of State, San Diego, 11 July 1925, NA.
90. Byers to Roys, San Diego, 18 July 1925; Schaeffer to Friend, Kachek, 22 June 1925; Roys to Byers, [New York], 24 July 1925, BFM.
91. Wright to Byers, Washington, 26 August 1925; Byers to Secretary of State, Claremont, Calif., 26 August 1925; Byers to Secretary of State, Claremont, Calif., 3 September 1925, NA.

Chapter 5. The BFM and Support for the Byers Family

1. Robert Byers who had accompanied his mother to the murder scene in response to his father's cry for help recalled that his mother and Mrs. Roys met sometime in the late 1930s or 1940s—long after the case was resolved. Robert Byers, Telephone interview with author, 22 February 1996. David Byers confirmed that his mother did indeed meet Mrs. Roys, but he, too, was unsure of the year. David Byers, Telephone interview with author, 28 October 2000.
2. Jenkins to Schurman, Canton, 2 August 1924, NA.
3. Russell Carter to Byers, New York, 10 July 1924, BFM.
4. Byers to Scott, at sea, 10 August 1924, BFM. She also reported that anti-foreign remarks had been heard in Kachek market after the arrival of Vice Consul Chamberlain, and by the Nodoa missionaries on their way out to Hoihow after the murder. Additionally, she reported students went past the Nodoa compound singing, "We'll kill Dr. Salsbury first and then the others." She attributed the remarks to Bolshevism among the students, but noted Mr. Byers did not work among students and "had no enemies among the Chinese that we know of." Mrs. Byers was

not in Kachek when Chamberlain arrived nor in Nodoa, and none of the other missionaries reported such statements, and they do not appear in any of the government records.

5. Bercovitz to Scott, [Kiungchow], 19 August 1924, BFM. Bercovitz sent the PCC a similar letter, Bercovitz to Patton, [Kiungchow], 6 September 1924, BFM.

6. Jenkins to Schurman, Canton, 19 August 1924, NA.

7. Roys to Byers, New York, 2 September 1924, BFM.

8. Ibid.

9. Scott to Byers, New York, 3 September 1924, BFM.

10. Roys to Mrs. Ina Rittenhouse, New York, 20 September 1924; Byers to Roys, [San Diego], 11 September 1924; Roys to Patton, New York, 13 September 1924, BFM.

11. Roys to Patton, New York, 13 September 1924, BFM.

12. Ibid.; Untitled note on BFM meeting, 17 September 1906, SP. The Lienchow case demonstrated just how difficult such cases could become. The United States planned to seek a $50,000 indemnity, but a clerical error stated the amount in taels rather than dollars when the request was transmitted to the viceroy in charge of Canton, effectively cutting the amount in half. (Of the $25,000 collected $10,000 went to the two wards of Eleanor Chesnut, M.D., $10,000 was paid to the family of Rev. John R. and Rebecca G. Peale, and $5000 went to the Machle family for the death of Mrs. Machle. No compensation was paid for the death of Amy Machle.) When these missionaries were murdered the BFM informed the Department of State it would seek no indemnity, only to be told they had no basis on which to request one. Arthur J. Brown replied the BFM could make a claim since they supported the missionaries, but declined to do so. There was also confusion over whether separate claims for the lives and properties lost were to be made. Concerning the issue, Minister H. H. Rockhill observed that indemnities seldom punished those who needed punishing and the viceroy requested the indemnity be remitted once it was paid as the people of Lienchow were so poor they might have to sell their children to pay it, while the mission boards were lavish in their support of missionaries. See *Numerical and Minor Files of the Department of State, 1906–1910,* NA. I am indebted to Douglas J. Machle for this information.

13. Roys to Patton, New York, 13 September 1924, BFM.

14. Campbell to Patton, [Kiungchow], 23 August 1924, BFM.

15. Roys to Patton, New York, 3 September 1924, BFM.

16. "Report of the Foreign Department presented to the Women's Committee," New York, 15 September 1924, BFM. For a discussion of the much-reported infamous sign concerning dogs and Chinese see Robert A. Bickers and Jeffrey Wasserstrom, "Shanghai's 'Dogs and Chinese Not Admitted' Sign: Legend, History and Contemporary Symbol," *China Quarterly* 142 (June 1995):444–66.

17. "Report of the Foreign Department," BFM.

18. Roys to Byers, New York, 16 September 1924, BFM.

19. Ibid.

20. Byers to Roys, San Diego, 9 October 1924, BFM. The BFM customarily retyped letters from Mrs. Byers, presumably to make carbon copies for various people and the files. Part of this letter was deleted in the retyping, probably inadvertently by the typist as the omitted part follows the words "China Council" and the copy takes up after another "China Council."

21. Ibid.
22. Ibid.
23. Ibid.
24. Ibid.
25. Ibid.
26. Ibid.
27. Ibid.; Mrs. Margaret Melrose who served at Nodoa always carried a Colt .45 when she was itinerating and demonstrated she could use it before retiring for the night in a Chinese inn, Lodwick, *Educating the Women of Hainan*, 41.
28. Byers to Roys, San Diego, 9 October 1924, BFM.
29. Ibid.
30. Roys to Byers, New York, 24 October 1924; "Foreign Department Committee: Recommendations on the Byers Case," handwritten and typewritten versions, n.d., BFM. The note appears to have been written by Mrs. Roys.
31. William D. Murray to Speer, New York, 6 November 1924; Roys to Murray, New York, 10 November 1924; Murray to James M. Speers, New York, 11 November 1924; Speers to Murray, New York, 12 November 1924; Speers to Scott, New York, 12 November 1924, BFM.
32. Byers to Roys, telegram, La Mesa, Calif., 14 November 1924; Roys to Byers, telegram, New York, 15 November 1924, BFM.
33. Roys to Byers, New York, 15 November 1924, BFM.
34. W. Reginald Wheeler to Scott, [New York?], 17 November 1924; Roys to Byers, telegram, New York, 17 November 1924, BFM.
35. Roys to Murray, New York, 18 November 1924, BFM.
36. Roys to Byers, New York, 18 November 1924, BFM.
37. Ibid.
38. Rittenhouse to Roys, San Diego, 19 November 1924, BFM.
39. Ibid.
40. Byers to Roys, San Diego, 12 December 1924, BFM.
41. Ibid.
42. "Mrs. Byers Children's Allowances," n.d., BFM.
43. Byers to Roys, telegram, La Mesa, Calif., 23 December 1924; Roys to Byers, telegram, New York, 26 December 1924, BFM.
44. Byers to Roys, San Diego, 21 December 1924, BFM.
45. Roys to J. C. R. Ewing, New York, 31 December 1924, BFM.
46. Ewing to Roys, Princeton, N.J., 1 January 1925; Roys to Ewing, [New York], 2 January 1925; Roys to Jean Mackenzie, [New York], 3 January 1925; "Minute on Mrs. George D. Byers," 5 January 1925; Roys to Charles R. Erdman, [New York], 9 January 1925, BFM.
47. Roys to Erdman, [New York], 9 January 1925; Erdman to Roys, Princeton, N.J., 14 January 1925, BFM.
48. [Roys], "Concerning Indemnity," 9 January 1925, BFM. The LMS compound at Tsaoshi which was in Hupeh was incorrectly identified here as being in Hainan. The document was sent with Ewing's approval to BFM members, Roys to Members of the BFM, [New York], 14 January 1925, BFM.
49. Lillian Kelly to Roys, Los Angeles, 10 January 1925; Roys to Byers, [New York], 16 January 1925; Roys to Kelly, [New York], 16 January 1925, BFM.
50. Lucy Lepper to Roys, New York, 19 January 1925; "Minute," 19 January 1925;

Roys to Byers, telegram, [New York], 19 January 1925; [Roys] to Erdman, [New York], 20 January 1925; Byers to Roys, telegram, La Mesa, Calif., 21 January 1925; Roys to Swing, [New York], 23 January 1925, BFM.

51. Roys to Byers, [New York], 24 January 1925, BFM.

52. Ibid.

53. Byers to Roys, [San Diego], 26 January 1925, BFM.

54. Byers to Roys, San Diego, 1 February 1925, BFM.

55. Roys to Byers, [New York], 25 February 1925; Orville Reed to Roys, [New York], 26 February 1925; Roys to Byers, [New York], 28 February 1925; Rebecca A. Spalding to Roys, New York, 11 March 1925, BFM.

56. Hatch to Robert E. Speer, New York, 13 November 1925, SP.

57. Hatch [?], "Some Tentative Considerations Regarding Indemnities," n.d., SP.

58. Ibid.

59. Ibid.

60. Ibid.

61. Ibid.

62. Speer to Hatch, [New York?], 22 March 1926, SP.

63. Ibid.

64. Ibid.

65. Ibid.

66. Scott [?] to Speer and Roys, [New York?], 10 June 1927, SP.

67. Byers to Roys, Claremont, Calif., 2 March 1926; Roys to Schultz, Lepper, and Hodge, [New York], 9 March 1926, BFM. The actual wording of the memo to Miss Lepper differs slightly, but the quoted material appears in all three memos.

68. Byers to Roys, Pomona, Calif., 7 June 1927; Roys to Byers, [New York], 15 June 1927, BFM.

69. Byers to Roys, Pomona, Calif., 11 July 1927; Roys, "Mrs. George Byers, Salary Allowance," memo, [New York], 19 July 1927; Roys to Byers, [New York], 20 July 1927; Lucy Lepper Shaw to Speer, New York, 22 July 1927; Byers to Roys, Pomona, Calif., 10 October 1927, BFM.

Chapter 6. Conclusion

1. *Hainan NewsLetter* (Summer 1926):17–18; "From the 'Hainan Newsletter,'" *CR* 57 (1926):454.

2. Moninger to Daddy, Kachek, 17 March 1935, MP. The Rev. and Mrs. Arthur French had joined the mission in 1930 and served at Kachek.

References Cited

Archival Collections

Hughes, Charles Evans. Papers. Manuscripts Division, Library of Congress, Washington, D.C.

Moninger, Margaret. Papers. RG39. Presbyterian Historical Society, Philadelphia.

National Archives, "George D. Byers" and "Walter Coveyou." File 393.1123, RG59. *Papers Relating to the Foreign Relations of the United States, China.* Washington, D.C.

National Archives, *Numerical and Minor Files of the Department of State, 1906–1910.* File 167. Washington, D.C. Microfilm.

National Archives, United States Consulate, Canton. *Despatches from U.S. Consuls in Canton, 1790–1906.* Washington, D.C., 1947. Microfilm.

National Archives, United States Embassy, China. *Despatches from United States Ministers to China, 1843–1906.* Washington, D.C., 1946–1958. Microfilm.

Presbyterian Church, (USA), Board of Foreign Missions. RG82. Presbyterian Historical Society, Philadelphia.

Speer, Robert E. Papers. Princeton Theological Seminary, Princeton, N.J.

United Kingdom, Public Record Office, Foreign Office, "China: Consular Papers."

Periodicals

Chinese Recorder, 1900–1927.

Hainan NewsLetter, 1924, 1926.

New York Times, 1924–1925.

Books, Articles, and Dissertations

American Chamber of Commerce of Tientsin. *Memorandum of the American Chamber of Commerce of Tientsin Relative to Extraterritoriality in China.* Tientsin: n.pub., 1925.

American Presbyterian Mission, Hainan, Thirty-first Annual Meeting, Kachek, 1923, *Minutes,* Shanghai: Presbyterian Mission Press, 1923.

"Bandit Record Since the Lincheng Outrage." *The China Weekly Review* 2 (16 February 1924), 412.

Bennett, Edward M. "Joseph C. Grew: The Diplomacy of Pacification." In *Diplomats in Crisis: United States-Chinese-Japanese Relations, 1919–1941,* edited by Richard Dean Burns and Edward M. Bennett, 65–89. Santa Barbara, Calif.: ABC-Clio, 1974.

Bevans, Charles I., comp. *Treaties and Other International Agreements of the United States of America, 1776–1949.* Vol. 6, "China." Washington, D.C.: Department of State, 1968–1976.

Bickers, Robert A., and Jeffrey Wasserstrom. "Shanghai's 'Dogs and Chinese Not Admitted' Sign: Legend, History and Contemporary Symbol." *China Quarterly* 142(June 1995):444–66.

Billingsley, Phil. *Bandits in Republican China.* Stanford: Stanford University Press, 1988.

Borchard, Edwin M. *The Diplomatic Protection of Citizens Abroad, or The Law of International Claims.* New York: Banks Law Publishing, 1925.

Broomhall, Marshall. *The Jubilee Story of the China Inland Mission.* London: Morgan and Scott, 1915.

Buckley, Thomas. "John Van Antwerp MacMurray: The Diplomacy of an American Mandarin." In *Diplomats in Crisis: United States-Chinese-Japanese Relations, 1919–1941,* edited by Richard Dean Burns and Edward M. Bennett, 27–48. Santa Barbara, Calif.: ABC-Clio, 1974.

Caulfield, Caspar. *Only a Beginning: The Passionists in China, 1921–1931.* Union City, N.J.: Passionist Press, 1990.

Chan Lau Kit-ching. "The Lincheng Incident—A Case Study of British Policy in China Between the Washington Conference (1921–22) and the First Nationalist Revolution (1925–28)." *Journal of Oriental Studies* 10 (July 1972):72–86.

Chu Pao-chin. "V. K. Wellington Koo: The Diplomacy of Nationalism." In *Diplomats in Crisis: United States–Chinese–Japanese Relations, 1919–1941,* edited by Richard Dean Burns and Edward M. Bennett, 125–51. Santa Barbara, Calif.: ABC-Clio, 1974.

Coates, P. D. *The China Consuls: British Consular Officers 1843–1943.* Oxford: Oxford University Press, 1988.

Cohen, Warren I. *America's Response to China: An Interpretative History of Sino-American Relations,* 2nd ed. New York: John Wiley & Sons, 1980.

———. *The Chinese Connection: Roger S. Greene, Thomas W. Lamont, George E. Sokolsky, and American–East Asian Relations.* New York: Columbia University Press, 1978.

———. *Empire Without Tears: American Foreign Relations, 1921–1933.* Philadelphia: Temple University Press, 1987.

Crapol, Edward P., ed. *Women and American Foreign Policy: Lobbyists, Critics, and Insiders,* 2nd ed. Wilmington, Del.: Scholarly Resources, 1992.

Dennett, Tyler. "Extraterritoriality and Missionaries in China." *The Christian Century* 39(May 1923):625–26.

Fairbank, John K. *The Great Chinese Revolution, 1800–1985.* New York: Harper and Row, 1986.

Fairbank, John K., Edwin O. Reischauer, and Albert M. Craig. *East Asia: The Modern Transformation.* Boston: Houghton Mifflin, 1965.

Hertslet, Godfrey E. P. *Hertslet's China Treaties: Treaties etc. between Great Britain and*

China and between China and Foreign Powers . . . in Force on the 1st of January 1908, 3rd ed. vol. 1. London: His Majesty's Stationery Office, by Harrison and Sons, 1908.

Hinckley, Frank E. *American Consular Jurisdiction in the Orient.* Washington, D.C.: W. H. Lowdermilk, 1906.

Hunt, Michael H. "New Insights But No New Vistas: Recent Work on Nineteenth-Century American–East Asian Relations." In *New Frontiers in American–East Asian Relations,* edited by Warren I. Cohen, 17–43. New York: Columbia University Press, 1983.

Hyde, Charles Cheney. *International Law Chiefly as Interpreted and Applied by the United States.* 2 vols. Boston: Little, Brown, 1922.

Iriye, Akira. *After Imperialism: The Search for a New Order in the Far East, 1921–1931.* Cambridge: Harvard University Press, 1965.

Keeton, George W. *The Development of Extraterritoriality in China.* 2 vols. 1928. Reprint, New York: H. Fertig, 1969.

Latourette, Kenneth S. *A History of Christian Missions in China.* New York: Macmillan, 1929.

Lodwick, Kathleen L. *The CHINESE RECORDER Index: A Guide to Christian Missions in Asia, 1867–1941.* 2 vols. Wilmington, Del.: Scholarly Resources, 1986.

———. *Educating the Women of Hainan: The Career of Margaret Moninger in China, 1915–1942.* Lexington: University Press of Kentucky, 1995.

Lutz, Jessie G. *China and the Christian Colleges, 1850–1950.* Ithaca: Cornell University Press, 1971.

———. *Chinese Politics and Christian Missions: The Anti-Christian Movements of 1920–1928.* Notre Dame, Ind.: Cross Cultural Publications, 1988.

[Moninger, Margaret]. *Isle of Palms.* 1919. Reprint, New York: Garland Publishing, 1980.

Nozinski, Michael. *Outrage at Lincheng: China Enters the Twentieth Century.* Macomb, Ill.: Glenbridge Publishing, 1990.

Perry, Elizabeth J. *Rebels and Revolutionaries in North China, 1845–1945,* Stanford: Stanford University Press, 1980.

Ramsey, S. Robert. *The Languages of China.* Princeton: Princeton University Press, 1987.

Rozman, Gilbert, ed. *The Modernization of China.* New York: Free Press, 1981.

Spence, Jonathan. *In Search of Modern China.* New York: W. W. Norton, 1990.

Tappan, David S. "The Martyrdom of the Rev. George D. Byers of Hainan." *The Presbyterian Magazine* 30(October 1924):485–86.

Tyau, Min-chien T. Z. *The Legal Obligations Arising out of Treaty Relations Between China and Other States.* Ph.D. dissertation, University of London; reprint, Taipei: Ch'eng Wen Publications, 1966.

Varg, Paul. "The Missionary Response to the Nationalist Revolution." In *The Missionary Enterprise in China and America* edited by John K. Fairbank, 311–35. Cambridge: Harvard University Press, 1974.

Vinson, John Chalmers. "Charles Evans Hughes, 1921–1925." In *An Uncertain Tradi-*

tion: American Secretaries of State in the Twentieth Century, edited by Norman A. Graebner, 27–128. New York: McGraw-Hill, 1961.

Willoughby, Westel W. *Foreign Rights and Interests in China.* 2 vols. Baltimore: Johns Hopkins Press, 1927.

Yip Ka-che. *Religion, Nationalism and Chinese Students: The Anti-Christian Movement of 1922–1927.* Bellingham, Wash.: Western Washington University Press, 1980.

Oral Interviews

Byers, David. Telephone interview with author. 28 October 2000.

Byers, Laurence. Telephone interview with author. 5 October 1985.

Byers, Robert. Telephone interview with author. 22 February 1996; Interview with author. Des Moines, Wash., 29 March 1997.

Ray, Daniel. Interview with author. Sussex, N.J., 21 October 1992; Telephone interview with author, 1 December 1995.

Index

Numbers in italics refer to illustrations.

Anti-Christian activities, 31, 57–61, 66–67, 82, 84, 136, 146, 150, 156, 168, 170, 188–98n. 4, 190n. 48. *See also* Anti-foreign activities; "Blood of martyrs" argument; Boxer Indemnity/Uprising; Brigandage; Byers, George, murder of; Byers family, robbery of (1919); Extraterritoriality

Anti-foreign activities, 29–31, 35–36, 56, 62–64, 75, 81, 142, 145, 169. *See also* Anti-Christian activities; "Blood of martyrs" argument; Boxer Indemnity/Uprising; Brigandage; Extraterritoriality

Bell, Edward, 69, 85–86, 87, 88, 91

Bercovitz, Nathaniel, M.D., *49,* 59, 62, 63, 65, 67, 69, 70, 74, 82–85, 125, 127, 130, 134–35, 138, 145, 169, 180–81n. 42, 183n. 25, 185n. 68, 189n. 5

Billingsley, Phil, 37, 169

"Blood of martyrs" argument, 39, 40, 46, 48, 121–22, 140, 173

Board of Foreign Missions (BFM). *See* Presbyterian Church,(USA), Board of Foreign Missions (BFM)

Boxer Indemnity/Uprising, 39, 47, 76, 116, 140, 144, 150, 152, 166, 171, 177n. 21

Brigandage, 31, 37, 47, 58, 59, 60, 65–67, 70–71, 80, 82–85, 87–88, 90, 94, 96, 99, 104, 107–8, 110, 118, 127, 129–30, 133–36, 145, 168–70. *See also* Anti-Christian activities; Anti-foreign activities; Extraterritoriality

Bristow, H. H., 33, 56, 58, 65–67, 74–75, 80, 85, 88–89, 91, 94

Brown, Arthur J., 91–93, 153–54, 157, 189n. 12

Byers, Clara Laura Primm (Mrs. George D.), 29–34, 47, *49,* 51-*52,* 54–56, 58, 60–65, 69, 71, 74, 76–78, 80, 82, 88, 91–92, 95–96, 98–104, 106–7, 109–11, 116, 120–25, 129–31, 135–59, 161, 164–73, 180n. 37, 181nn. 49 and 55

Byers, George D., 39, *49*–51, 59, 60–62, 66, 70, 111, 137–39, 149, 156, 161, 169, 174, 175n. 3, 181n. 55

—murder of, 29–32, 35, 38, 40, 47, 54, 56–58, 60–66, 68–71, 75–77, 79–91, 99–100, 105, 108, 113, 118–19, 126–28, 131, 134, 142, 144, 148, 168, 170–73, 175–76n. 5, 181n. 49

Byers extraterritoriality case, 34, 35, 47, 48, 54, 56–58, 69–70, 79, 90, 92–94, 97, 101, 108–9, 112, 114, 116–17, 120, 126–27, 130, 133, 136, 140, 159, 161, 168, 170–71, 173

Byers family, 31–32, 39, 61, 67, 89, 159, 168, 182n. 61; children, 29–30, *49,* 58, 62–64, 69, 71, 76–77, 138, 142, 152–53, 156, 165, 166, 181n. 49, 182n. 61; robbery of (1919), 58–59, 146; support of, 32, 92, 99–100, 102, 106, 109, 111, 121–25, 135–67, 172–73, 181n. 55, 181–82n. 59, 185–86n. 13; supporters of, 70, 76, 77, 92, 94–97, 101–3, 105, 109–11, 124, 148–57, 165, 171–73, 181–82n. 59

Campbell, Wilbur, *49,* 51, 64, 141, 146, 181n. 53

Chamberlain, C. B., 34, 58, 67–71, 73–74, 78–82, 84–85, 87–90, 96, 102,

107, 118, 131–32, 135, 141, 144–45, 172, 181–82n. 59, 188–89n. 4
Ch'en Chiung-ming, 68, 73, 78, 80, 81, 112, 114, 121
Ch'en Feng-ch'i, 79, 80, 87, 108, 113, 132, 144, 172. *See also* Chinese military, on Hainan;—, in Kachek
Chinese Christians, 59–60, 67, 83, 85, 87, 96, 144–45, 155, 159, 169–71. *See also* Hainan mission, Chinese Christians at
Chinese ethnic groups, 51, 130, 178n. 42
Chinese government, 33, 40, 48, 59, 98, 126, 170
—at Canton, 59, 68, 73, 78, 80, 86, 111, 113
—on Hainan, 79, 87
—at Peking, 59, 73, 79, 86, 99, 101, 111–13, 123, 135; foreign office, 85–86, 89, 132. *See also* Chinese military, on Hainan;—, in Kachek
Chinese military, arrests and executions by, 32, 47, 71, 75, 79–81, 83, 87, 89, 91, 108, 129; on Hainan, 65, 67–71, 73, 78–85, 89, 91, 99–100, 103, 106–8, 113–14, 125–29, 131–33, 144, 169, 187n. 46; in Kachek, 63–65, 75, 87, 89, 96, 98, 113–14, 125–29, 131–34, 168. *See also* Chinese government; Hainan; individual names
Chinese Recorder (CR), 38, 41–47, 57, 60
Cohen, Warren I., 57
Coolidge, Calvin, 95, 97, 103, 105, 110, 120

Diplomats
—American, 32, 33–35, 38–41, 47, 54, 56–58, 65, 67, 69, 73, 78–115, 135–36, 189n. 12; attitude toward missionaries, 35–36, 38–41, 68, 71, 81–82, 88, 98, 131, 141, 145, 168, 170, 173; Canton consulate, 56, 67–69, 78–115, 118, 135–36, 169, 181–82n. 59; dealings with Chinese officials, 68, 71, 73, 78–82, 84–86, 89, 96, 100–101, 107–8, 111–15, 118–21, 125–33, 135, 144, 170; Peking legation, 56, 67–69, 123, 128, 141, 145, 169; Shanghai consulate, 56, 97, 101–2, 104; Swatow consulate, 56, 73, 81, 114
—British, 32, 33, 36, 40, 54, 64–65, 69–71, 80, 85–86, 89, 91–92, 95, 103, 110, 115, 118–19, 168, 176n. 7
—Chinese (*see* Peking government, foreign office)
—French, 56, 103, 113, 126. *See also* individual names; U.S. government, Department of State

Extraterritoriality, 33–48, 54–59, 97, 102, 159–64, 168, 173; cases, 40–41, 61, 120, 150, 152, 160, 179n. 6, 184n. 51, 189n. 12; Lienchow (1905), 40, 120, 140–41, 189n. 12; Lincheng Incident, 31, 120; missionaries' opinions on, 38–48, 115–117, 159–64, 168. *See also* Byers extraterritoriality case; Indemnities; Treaties, Sino-American.

Grew, Joseph, 70, 93–94, 135, 181n. 47
Gunboat diplomacy, 34–36, 58, 69–75, 78–82, 86–89, 92–136, 168–69. *See also* Gunboats; U.S. government, Navy
Gunboats, British, 98, 101, 103; French, 103; German, 103, 103n. 68. *See also* U.S. government, Navy

Hainan, *frontis,* 70–71, 80–82, 111–15. *See also* Chinese military, on Hainan; —, in Kachek
Hainan mission, 40, 62, 81–94, 97–100, 102–3, 135, 171, 173, 176n. 7; Chinese Christians at, 63, 85, 112, 174; executive committee, 34, 72–73, 82–83, 87, 90, 94–95, 117, 130, 137, 141–43, 145–46, 155–56, 181n. 53, 181–82n. 59; history, 48–51; Hoihow station, 39, 48, 51, 127, 188–89n. 4; Kachek station, 29, 32–34, 39, 48, 51, 59, 62, 65, 67, 84, 94, 97, 112–13, 117, 119, 127–28, 130, 133–34, 137, 146, 156, 170, 181n. 53, 188–89n. 4; Kiungchow station, 39, 48, 51, 127; meetings, *49,* 73–74, 107, 135; members, 33, 48–52, 61–67, 69–74, 77, 82–91, 94, 98–100, 102–3, 105–12, 117, 127,

130, 134, 146, 151, 156, 168–74, 181 n. 83, 185 n. 68, 188–89 n. 4, 190 n. 27, 191 n. 2; Nodoa station, 32–33, 39, 48, 51, 94, 112, 119, 127, 133, 146, 170, 188–89 n. 4, 190 n. 27; schools, 72, 82, 119, 127, 130, 188–89 n. 4. *See also* Hainan; missions/missionaries in China (non-Hainan); individual names
Hamilton, Maxwell M., 94, 97, 98, 100, 104, 106–8, 110–15, 117–20, 123, 125–33, 135–36, 144, 173, 184 n. 57, 188 n. 81
Ho Chia-yu, 74–75, 79, 85, 87, 100, 113–14, 119, 128, 131–32, 136
Hughes, Charles Evans, 68–69, 94, 97–104, 109–10, 112, 114, 118, 120–24
Hunt, Michael, 54

Indemnities, 32–35, 39–42, 44–48, 54–57, 100–102, 171, 179 n. 6; missionaries' opinions on 40, 45, 74, 94, 108, 115–16, 126–27, 134, 138, 140, 145, 148–50, 154–56, 159–64, 171–73; offered by General Teng, 119–25, 128; previous cases, 40, 100–101, 120, 140–41, 150, 152, 154–56, 171, 189 n. 12; sought/collected for Mrs. Byers, 40, 71–78, 91–92, 100–104, 106–7, 109, 110–14, 116, 118–30, 132, 134–36, 138–39, 141–48, 152, 153, 157–58, 161. *See also* Byers extraterritoriality case; Extraterritoriality

Japan/Japanese, 43, 47, 101, 160, 181 n. 47
Jenkins, Douglas, 56, 58, 65, 66, 68, 69, 71, 73–74, 76, 78, 80, 81, 85–89, 91–92, 98, 106–7, 114, 120, 128–31, 135, 138–39, 181 n. 44, 186 n. 28

Kidnappings, 29–32, 41, 60–61, 66, 83–84, 107, 130, 168

Lin Shu-piao, 65–68, 71, 73–75, 79–81, 84, 87, 89, 94, 99, 113, 119, 126–27, 129, 130–31, 133, 136, 169–71, 173
Lowrie, J. Walter, 91–93, 97, 98, 107, 108, 112–13, 115, 117–19, 125, 127–28, 130, 133, 161

McCandliss, (Dr. and Mrs.) H. M., 51, 64, 87, 90, 115, 126, 169, 176 n. 7, 181 n. 53
MacMurray, John Van Antwerp, 57, 92, 102, 109, 179 n. 11
May Fourth Movement. *See* Nationalism, Chinese
Mayer, Ferdinand, 92, 94, 97–100, 129, 135, 188 n. 81
McCreery, Caroline, *49*, 62, 67, 74, 134, 185 n. 68
Melrose, Margaret, *49*, 51, 82, 112, 190 n. 27
Missions/missionaries in China (excluding Hainan), 35–36, 40–41, 40–48, 51, 61, 70, 72–73, 90–91, 120, 140–41, 150, 155–56, 183 n. 29, 190 n. 48. *See also* Extraterritoriality, missionaries' opinions on; Hainan mission; Indemnities, missionaries' opinions on; National Christian Council (NCC)
Moninger, Margaret, *49*, 59, 60, 62–65, 67, 69–72, 74–75, 90, 100, 106, 108, 111–12, 115, 117, 125–28, 130, 133–34, 169, 174, 185 n. 2

National Christian Council (NCC), 44, 56, 57, 115–17, 181–82 n. 59. *See also* Hainan mission, missions/missionaries in China (excluding Hainan)
Nationalism, Chinese, 40, 57, 71–72, 115–16, 169, 170
1911 Revolution, 37, 59, 170

Opium Wars, 35–36. *See also* Treaties, Sino-American

Presbyterian Church, (USA), 54; attitudes about indemnities, 32, 34, 48, 73, 91, 94, 117, 119, 121–25, 137–50, 154–64, 167, 171–73; Board of Foreign Missions, 32, 34, 40, 48, 54–56, 60, 64, 67–68, 70, 73–78, 82, 89–100, 102–9, 111, 115–25, 129, 136–67, 171–73, 189 n. 12; Board of Ministerial Relief, 123, 137, 142–43, 148, 150, 152–53, 159; China Council (PCC), 34, 56, 64, 70, 72–73, 87, 89–95, 97–98, 102, 104, 107, 112, 116, 141–42, 146–47, 149–51, 155–56, 161, 181–82n. 59; Foreign Committee/Department, 137, 142, 154, 157; Home Department, 154; policy toward widows, 154–57, 164, 166, 172; relations with Department of State, 91, 98, 111, 116–17, 121–23, 136, 147–50, 152, 164, 172, 189n. 12; Sage Legacy Committee, 154, 159, 165; Women's Board/Committee, 142, 157; Women's Missionary Society of the Presbytery of Los Angeles, 109, 111, 185–86n. 13. *See also* Hainan mission; individual names

Ransoms, 29, 61, 66–68, 99, 131, 169, 174
Religious liberty, 45–46, 162–64
Rewards, 73, 79–80, 128, 131
Rittenhouse, Ina (Mrs.), 77, 124, 150–52
Roman Catholics, 46–47, 51, 169, 178n. 40
Roys, Mabel L., 33, *53*-55, 70, 92–93, 95, 96, 99, 101, 103–4, 109, 111, 121–25, 136–37, 139–43, 147–59, 164–67, 171–73

Schaeffer, Katherine, *49*, 51, 60, 62, 66, 70, 75–76, 108, 131, 134, 136
Schurman, Jacob Gould, 57, 68–69, 71, 73, 85, 92, 98, 101, 102, 104–6, 112, 114, 118–21, 123, 128–29, 138, 141, 179n. 6, 181n. 44, 184n. 51, 186n. 28
Scott, George T., 76, 92–93, 96, 98–99, 102, 111, 117, 123, 139, 148–49, 181n. 55, 181–82n. 55
Speer, Robert E., 148, 153–54, 157, 159, 161–64, 166
Steiner, John, *49*, 64, 67, 130, 181n. 53

Tappan, David S., *49*, 51, 61–62, 64, 76, 82, 88–90, 95, 125, 127, 130, 145–46, 169, 172, 175n. 3, 180n. 38, 185n. 68
Teng Pen-yin, 78, 80, 100, 108, 111–14, 118–21, 123, 125–33, 135- 36, 144, 170, 172
Thomas, (Rev. and Mrs.) David, *49*, 62, 125, 128, 130, 134, 174
Treaties, Sino-American, (1858) 36, 47–48, 161–62, 176n. 12; (1903), 161–62. *See also* Opium Wars

U.S. government, 32, 39–40, 54, 57, 77–78, 82, 89–91, 107, 116–17, 119, 122, 140, 171
—Congress, members of, 70, 92–93, 95–98, 101–3, 109–10, 152, 157–58, 181n. 47, 185n. 68
—Department of State, 67–68, 70, 91, 93–111, 120–21, 123, 128–29, 135–36, 148, 152, 155, 158, 170–71; policy on indemnities, 34, 40, 48, 68, 106–7, 112, 114, 138–39, 152–54, 161, 173
—Navy, 56, 67–69, 81, 87–88, 94, 97–98, 101, 104–7, 111, 114–15, 118, 125–29, 133. *See also* Diplomats: American; Gunboat diplomacy; Gunboats; individual names